Library of
Davidson College

SELEUKOS NIKATOR

Constructing a Hellenistic Kingdom

John D. Grainger

London and New York

First published 1990
by Routledge
11 New Fetter Lane, London EC4P 4EE

Simultaneously published in the USA and Canada
by Routledge
a division of Routledge, Chapman and Hall, Inc.
29 West 35th Steet, New York, NY 10001

© 1990 John D. Grainger

Typeset in 10/12pt Palatino by
Ponting–Green Publishing Services, London
Printed in Great Britain by T J Press (Padstow) Ltd, Padstow, Cornwall

All rights reserved. No part of this book may be reprinted or reproduced or utilized in any form or by any electronic, mechanical, or other means, now known or hereafter invented, including photocopying and recording, or in any information storage or retrieval system, without permission in writing from the publishers.

British Library Cataloguing in Publication Data
Grainger, John D.
Seleukos Nikator : constructing a Hellenistic kingdom.
I. Title
938'.107'0924
ISBN 0–415–04701–3

Library of Congress Cataloging in Publication Data
Grainger, John D.
Seleukos Nikator : constructing a hellenistic kingdom / John D. Grainger.
p. cm.
Includes bibliographical references.
1. Seleucus I, Nicator, d. 281 B.C. 2. Syria–History–333 B.C.–634 A.D. 3. Seleucids. 4. Syria–Kings and rulers–Biography.
I. Title.
DS96.2.G73   1990
939'.43'0099–dc20   89-10892
ISBN 0–415–04701–3

CONTENTS

1	CHILD AND SOLDIER	1
2	COMMANDER AND BETRAYER	9
3	SATRAP AND FUGITIVE	24
4	ADMIRAL AND SATRAP	52
5	GENERAL AND VICTOR	76
6	CONQUEROR AND KING	95
7	VICTOR AND ORGANIZER	114
8	DIPLOMAT AND RULER	139
9	DIPLOMACY AND DEFENCE	155
10	VICTOR AND VICTIM	173
11	RECONQUEROR	192
12	SAVIOUR	211
	Appendix	218
	Abbreviations	220
	Notes	223
	Bibliography	241
	Genealogies	251
	Maps	252
	Index	257

1

CHILD AND SOLDIER

Seleukos, later called Nikator, 'the Victorious', was born a Macedonian, an almost exact contemporary of Alexander the Great. That much is certain, but attaining any further precision is difficult. Certainty about his date of birth, where he grew up, the status of his parents, and the names of any brothers and sisters, is impossible. It is a fitting introduction to an extraordinary career, whose sources are more than usually awkward.

These details of dates and places and parentage are not really important, but the information we do have is worth setting out because it will set the scene for later problems. First, Seleukos' date of birth. He could have been born in 358 B.C., if Justin was right in saying he was 77 in the year of the battle of Korupedion; but Appian says he was 73, which would put his birth in 354. Eusebius improves the picture by giving his age as 75, which would have put his birth in 356, and this in turn would have made him a precise contemporary of Alexander's [1].

This last solution is too obvious. It is typical of an interpretation of the story of Seleukos which sees him as an alternative Alexander, with echoes of the career of Alexander at every turn. It is an aspect which must be heeded all the time, for biographical propaganda was a political weapon much deployed in later years. All this has effectively concealed the exact year of Seleukos' birth, for none of the authorities is any better than a distant and very much secondary source. Not that it matters much, though precision would be pleasant to have; it is, in fact, likely enough that Seleukos himself did not know the year of his birth. At this distance the problem is now insoluble. The nearest we can get is the mid-350s.

Seleukos' father was Antiochos, who became a commander in the army of King Philip II. So says the historian Justin, whose account was most likely based on one by Hieronymos of Kardia, a contemporary of Alexander's [2]. The father's name seems secure, since Seleukos named his eldest son Antiochos, but the status of the father is not so certain. There is no guarantee that the truth has been preserved by Justin. A more general consideration provides some support, however, for Seleukos was taken into the corps of Royal Pages by King Philip, in his teens, between 345 and 340. This body was composed only of the sons of high-born or otherwise eminent men of Macedonia [3]. Those pages who came from the highland cantons of Lynkestis, Orestis, and Tymphaia were the sons of princes, like Perdikkas of the royal house of Orestis. It is thus a safe claim that Seleukos' father was noble or eminent. No Macedonian of Philip's reign could avoid military service, and no eminent Macedonian could be anything other than an officer, but just how high Antiochos rose we do not know. Justin's word for his rank is *dux*, which is certainly 'commander', but he does not appear in any other source and is not recorded in any activity in Philip's reign. His son's entry into the corps of Royal Pages and Seleukos' officer status from the start of his later career show that the father was a high officer.

Seleukos' mother was called Laodike, but her name is the sum total of our knowledge of her. Seleukos gave her name, and his father's, to cities which he founded in his days of power [4]. A story is recorded of her, however, which is manifestly not true but whose existence is a clue to understanding later events. It is said that when Seleukos was about to go off to the wars with Alexander his mother revealed to him that she had dreamt that she had conceived him by Apollo, who had 'rewarded' her by leaving a ring engraved with an anchor. Sure enough, the morning after the dream a ring engraved with an anchor was found in the lady's bed. The anchor mark appeared as a birthmark on Seleukos' thigh, which birthmark is also said to have been borne by his sons and grandsons [5].

This is another of the Alexander-echoes. The story is in fact an adaptation of that told by Olympias to Alexander. In her case the god was Zeus Ammon, and the object in the bed was a snake – far more dramatic, of course, though hardly more believable [6]. Neither story was true, obviously, if for no other reason than that the suggestion of uncertainty as to paternity was one which no well-born Macedonian lady would boast about (Olympias was somewhat different, of course). The stories are clear inventions, and the main interest lies in seeing why they were worth inventing, repeating, and publicizing. The story was part of the propaganda surrounding the rise of Seleukos to kingship, designed to emphasize Seleukos' claim to be regarded as Alexander's true heir. Its general similarity to the well-known Olympias story makes it quite certain that it was a later invention.

In fact we can locate the origin and even the author of the story. It was invented by Seleukos himself. It is said to have been related to him in private by his mother before he left home. It is a transparent attempt to endow Seleukos with divine origins, and the citation of the birthmark as evidence is conclusive that he originated the story. By combining in one small anecdote a reflection of Alexander's glory, a claim to divine origin, an indication of a right to kingship, and a way of inspiring awe among his followers, the story is excellent propaganda. Such propaganda stories bestrew the historian's path all the time in studying Seleukos. They have to be watched for, identified, ignored as history, but they must be taken very seriously as propaganda [7].

One sister for Seleukos is recorded, by a very late source, Johannes Malalas, who recorded many details of this sort but who also made an enormous number of mistakes. Thus his details are unreliable. He reports that Seleukos had a sister called Didymeia, who in turn had two sons, Nikanor and Nikomedes [8]. There is no independent confirmation of this, but the sister's name given by Malalas is especially interesting. Those of the boys are about the most common of the day, but that of the sister is indicative. Seleukos set considerable store by the oracle of Apollo at Didyma, near Miletos, which features in a number of stories about him including the birth story. It is possible that here we have the traces of another propaganda story, a sister whose name was used to indicate a family preference for Apollo, and a family connection with Didyma which dated back to the Persian period. But the Didyma Oracle was inactive until Alexander's conquest [9], and an earlier Macedonian connection is, to say the least, unlikely. It is best to assume that Didymeia and her sons are later inventions.

There is one more possible relative. In the genealogical tables at the end of his book, Berve suggests that a man called Ptolemaios was Seleukos' uncle, a younger brother of Antiochos [10]. The grounds for this suggestion are that Ptolemaios' father was another Seleukos [11]. The argument is then that our Seleukos was named after his grandfather, who had two sons. This is by no means unlikely, but there is no ancient warrant for the assumption. The relationship of our Seleukos and Ptolemaios, son of Seleukos, is not suggested by any ancient source. The only connection remains the possible identity of Ptolemaios' father with Seleukos' unnamed grandfather. Like Didymeia, it is not enough.

The boy was born and grew up at Europos, according to Stephanos, who calls the place 'Oropos', though there was no Oropos in Macedon [12]. Malalas says he came from Pella, and is supported by implication by Pausanias [13], but this can be dismissed: it was Alexander's birthplace and thus was likely to be attributed to any prominent Macedonian. Even then, having removed this distraction, the problem is not solved, for there were two towns called Europos in Macedonia. One was in the north, under the Barmous mountains in the valley of the Astaios, an area called Almopia; the other was an old Macedonian town not far from the Axios, the river which flowed south from the inland Balkans. On the whole the second of these seems the more likely to be Seleukos' birthplace, since it was the more important of the two. The other would need to be distinguished from it in some way, so a reference purely to 'Europos' suggests the one by the Axios. To such expedients are we reduced [14].

Neither of these places is far enough from the northern frontier of Macedonia to be considered safe. If Seleukos really was born in 358, as Justin suggests, his home – if it was that by the Axios – had been threatened only the year before by a Paionian invasion from the north. The new Macedonian king, Philip, had scotched the invasion by a swift movement into Paionia when their old king Agis died. A few years later the Paionians were reckoned to be firmly under Philip's control. It is worth realizing that Seleukos grew up in a frontier

CHILD AND SOLDIER

atmosphere of uncertainty which will have developed into one of gratitude to Philip. Dealing so well with problems such as the Paionians is one of the reasons Philip was so well supported by the Macedonians [15].

The Europos which was by the Axios was in the heart of Macedonia, only a day's journey (20 kilometres) from Pella, the town which Philip developed as his new capital. Europos had rich agricultural land in the Macedonian plain and was on the main trade route through the kingdom and north to the inner Balkans. It was a moderately sized town, probably growing larger in the new peacefulness brought by Philip's success. It had its own internal government by magistrates, but this autonomy did not extend as far as a political independence. With fierce barbarians only a few kilometres to the north, independence was not a practical possibility. Greeks from Athens probably would not think of it as a *polis* but the Europans did and so would other Macedonians. The town invariably looked to the king for assistance and protection. It was an urban place nonetheless.

Seleukos grew up in a kingdom whose wealth was increasing as a result of the newly established peaceful conditions; in a town whose population was small and agricultural, which had a tradition of local government and an even stronger tradition of subordination to the kingdom; in a family where the father was often absent on the king's business, and in which the king's business was regarded as something which had a large claim on the family's time and energy. He was familiar from the cradle with a tradition of royal service which was highly militarized, for the very good reason that the king's main function, for a Macedonian, was to defend the borders of the kingdom and thus defend the people too. In such an enterprise whole-hearted commitment was expected, both as a soldier and as an administrator, and was given, since not to do so would condemn the community to invasion and poverty. All this was bred in the bone of the child, and he could no more think of avoiding such service than he would consider abandoning his family.

Seleukos grew up the son of a man serving Macedon's greatest king. During his childhood and youth successes were constant. Conquests, diplomatic victories, alliances, embassies of congratulation, all these came with repetitive frequency.

The ordinary Macedonian was no doubt sceptical of Philip at first. He was, after all, only the latest king of a family which had been demonstrating general incompetence and accident-proneness for over ten years. Yet Philip had organized the survival of the kingdom, defended it against attacks from all sides, strengthened and enriched and expanded it. The Macedonians will have been enthused and excited by their triumphs, which, after the débâcles of the 360s, they attributed, quite rightly, to Philip's military and diplomatic ability. When Seleukos was six (if he was born in 358) Thessaly was added to the kingdom. When he was ten Olynthos and the Chalkidike were conquered, to add to the various Greek cities which had been mopped up in the previous years – and the Chalkidian cities had at one time threatened to conquer the whole Macedonian kingdom. When he was twelve Philip made a triumphant peace with Athens. Yet it was not all plain sailing. Philip suffered his defeats, and his policy of repeatedly marrying local princesses from his conquests must have been regarded with a mixture of envy, amusement, and scorn by his people. Seleukos thus grew up in a political atmosphere of growing excitement, even euphoria, tempered by occasional setbacks, and leavened by Philip's combination of bluntness, devious diplomacy, military genius, and lust [16].

This was the man to whom Seleukos became a page. The Royal Pages were a select group of adolescent sons of important Macedonians. Some of them, from the recently autonomous mountain valleys, were quasi-hostages for their fathers' good behaviour. All of them were trained as future officers, diplomats, and governors of the Macedonian kingdom. They became competent fighters with all weapons, literate and well-read in Greek, up-to-date on the current international situation, and they got to know each other. All the later Macedonian kings and generals, satraps and diplomats went through this period of training, and the shared background in ways of thought and action which it gave them bound them together very powerfully for a time even after the kings they served had died.

Depending on his date of birth Seleukos would have been a page at some time between 344, the earliest date he could have been 14, and 336, the latest date he could have been 18. He was in attendance on King Philip, therefore – for even if

CHILD AND SOLDIER

he finished his page-hood in 340, he would continue at the court and in the army – during the final conquest of Greece, the formation of the League of Corinth, the preparation and despatch of the first expedition against the Persian king, and the assassination of Philip.

He was, then, a part of the army of the new king, Alexander, his contemporary, though while the 20-year-old Alexander was the commanding general, the (approximately) 20-year-old Seleukos was a junior officer. The army was effectively Philip's still, under Philip's officers, but with a new commander. It took several years for Alexander to establish his full authority, and even as late as 330, when he had Parmenio and his family killed, Alexander was still uncertain of his power [17].

So the young men who had been Philip's Royal Pages were his own and his son's junior officers. They did not emerge into prominence and to positions of command and authority until the eastern campaigns in Baktria and India. Erigyios, Krateros, and Hephaistion were among the first to be given independent commands, but by the time the army reached India others had also emerged. It was then that Seleukos was appointed to command a formation called the Royal Hypaspists, the cream of the Macedonian infantry, distinguished from the rest by a different name, and, to the very end and beyond, by their total loyalty to the king [18]. By this appointment Alexander singled out Seleukos as one of the men who would be his personal instruments for ruling his empire. Seleukos is referred to also as an *hetairos*, a Friend. Under the Hellenistic kings, if it was not so already, this became a distinct rank, bestowed on men close about the king, a formalization of the camaraderie of the former pages. In the eight years of Alexander's wars (334–326) Seleukos had risen from a junior officer to high command. It was a remarkable progress, and a tribute both to Alexander's eye for talent and the training imparted to Philip's pages.

The harvest of Seleukos' personal history has been meagre so far: there is certainty about Seleukos' parents' names and about his higher education, but uncertainty about everything else. On the other hand a good deal of contextual information is available. This is normal. Personal information is at a premium in the ancient world, so Seleukos is by no means unusual in this. The temptation to fill up with background and contextual information has to be resisted.

Yet there is also a different dimension. The story told of Seleukos' birth is only one of a dozen or so such stories told about him at various stages of his career. Some of these stories are as absolutely unbelievable as Laodike's birth story, others come somewhat closer to a possible reality. Yet none of them can be accepted as true, all of them must be disbelieved. At the same time, however, they can be put to use: they do provide information. The fact that the story of Seleukos' birth is so deliberately similar to that told of Alexander's is a clear indication that it was felt necessary to echo the Alexander-story as a means of boosting Seleukos' prestige. It can therefore only date from a time when Seleukos' social and political position had reached that which approximated to Alexander's – when he was a ruler, in other words. These stories can thus be used to illuminate the aspirations and policies of Seleukos; it may also be that they were invented, or adapted, to denigrate him. Both types have to be watched for; both will be useful.

The approach here will be to disbelieve those stories which common sense insists are nonsense, but to use them at the appropriate point to illustrate or reveal details which might otherwise be hidden. Suspicion falls on many incidents which are faithfully retailed by the ancient historians. What is lost in picturesqueness will be gained, hopefully, in political clarity.

2

COMMANDER AND BETRAYER (326–320)

Seleukos' appointment as commander of the Royal Hypaspists made him one of the more important officers of the army and put him close to Alexander. Yet it is not possible to quantify or qualify 'important' in this context. E.R. Bevan claimed, without discussion, that Seleukos' appointment meant that he became 'one of the staff' of the army [1] but this cannot be substantiated. For the fact is that, apart from several occasions in the Punjab, Seleukos is not mentioned by any of our extant sources until the day of Alexander's mass wedding at Susa in 324, two years later. Nevertheless, this does not mean that nothing of Seleukos' career can be discovered.

Seleukos' appointment took place shortly before the battle of the Hydaspes, the great fight against the Paurava Raja, who was called Poros by the Greeks. In that battle the Hypaspists, commanded presumably by Seleukos, held the right of the phalanx line and took part in the terrible fight with the war elephants and the Indian infantry. Casualties among the Macedonian infantry were very heavy. It was a ferocious introduction for the army and for Seleukos to the fighting qualities of the trained Indian war elephant and the Indian soldiers [2].

There is, however, nothing to indicate that Seleukos was anything more than a regimental commander at this point. He took no part in the planning – it was Alexander's masterpiece among his battles, and all his own work – nor was Seleukos employed in an independent role during the preliminary manoeuvres, as Krateros was. Nor, afterwards, does Seleukos appear in any independent command, though Krateros, Hephaistion, Peithon, and Leonnatos are all recorded as commanding sizeable detachments. Before the battle he is recorded as being with Alexander, Perdikkas, Ptolemy, and Lysimachos crossing the river in a boat with some of the Hypaspists [3]. The use made of the story later, to point to the coincidence of talent and the collection of present and future rulers in one boat, renders the story itself somewhat suspect. It might be regarded as one of the propaganda tales later put about in such quantity. Yet it is a story which does not emphasize any particular future ruler, while the rest always single out one man, having been constructed for that very purpose; this rather suggests that this is a true story, not merely propaganda.

This collection of exalted personages in the one boat should not blind us to the fact that they were by no means men of equal rank and importance at the time, or to the evident but usually ignored fact that Seleukos was the most junior of the officers. His presence is, in fact, to be explained by the presence of the Hypaspists. That is to say, Seleukos was actually no more than the commander of the bodyguard in attendance on Alexander.

There is no mention of Seleukos for two more years and this is rather strange. Even though he was no more than a regimental commander, the regiment he commanded, the Hypaspists, was virtually the only one which stayed with Alexander continuously from the battle at the Hydaspes to the final weary return to Babylon. They were in Alexander's own detachment when he moved down the Indus [4], and at the fight at the Malli towns [5]; they were the only major Macedonian infantry unit with the king in and through the Gedrosian desert [6].

Yet Seleukos, the commander, is not mentioned in any of the accounts, though he was surely present. It is possible that Seleukos was no longer in command of the Hypaspists, but if so he was their commander before his name disappears, and afterwards; if he was not we do not know who was, nor do we know what Seleukos was doing. The easiest explanation is that Seleukos was in command all along, but that our sources have no eyes for anyone but Alexander. The narrative of the sufferings of the army in the Gedrosian desert is little more than a conventional desert disaster story, helmet of water, flash floods, miraculous pools of water (found, of course, by the king) and all. It is a good piece of journalese, purple patches well to the fore, but essentially a rhetorical exercise [7].

There is no place in the story for Hephaistion the second-in-command, or for a regimental commander such as Seleukos [8].

It can be cautiously accepted that Seleukos was the commander of the Royal Hypaspists from the arrival of the army in India to the end of Alexander's life. This was a post of some delicacy, particularly in the tense atmosphere in the army after the dreadful battle with the elephants. The combination of the monsoon, fear of the elephants, deceit by Alexander, homesickness, and sheer weariness produced a glum strike by the soldiers. Alexander tried to break the strike by winning over the officers. Seleukos must have been there, one of those who sat in silence until old Koenos spoke up for going home. He must have been at the second meeting, where no-one at all spoke. He may have been one of the group to whom Alexander, after his three-day sulk at being defied, made it known that the omens of the sacrifice were unfavourable and so he would turn back [9].

That Seleukos in this fraught situation did not do anything that might bring down the wrath of Alexander on his head is not really surprising. Koenos earned Alexander's enmity by his outspokenness, but Seleukos was merely one of those who kept his mouth shut, not a glorious reaction, but intelligent in the circumstances. From then on, however, Alexander will have required his commander of the Hypaspists to be well and truly on top of the job. The regiment was constantly under his eye and constantly being used by him. Whereas in the Indus valley campaign the army as a whole was reluctant to massacre yet more Indians, the Hypaspists do not seem to have been in any way reluctant to do as Alexander bade them. Since Seleukos presumably held on to his command all down the Indus and through the Gedrosian desert, the assumption must be that he performed his duties at least to the king's satisfaction. Seleukos was thus partly responsible both for the Indian massacres and for holding the army together in the Gedrosian disaster, where a breakdown of discipline would have meant the deaths of even more men.

When the army approached the damp richness of Babylonia again, Seleukos reaped his reward. In the mass marriage at Susa, one of Alexander's most bizarre performances, Seleukos was married to Apama, daughter of Spitamenes. Spitamenes had been the most effective Persian opponent Alexander had faced, keeping the Macedonian army pinned down in Baktria for at least two years. Alexander must have been very sure of Seleukos' loyalty to have arranged that particular marriage for him [10]. All the more so since Alexander himself had been displaying alarming signs of paranoia. As it turned out, the marriage of Seleukos and Apama is reputed to be the only one of those performed at Susa which lasted, though in fact we do not know the details of most of the others. No doubt most of the male participants regarded the affair as either a joke or an imposition, in which Alexander had to be humoured and obeyed.

That the marriage lasted, and that Apama became the mother of Seleukos' eldest son, Antiochos, and saw her name given to several cities, suggests affection, at least on Seleukos' part. Later this Persian marriage stood him in good stead politically, but that fruit was a long time in ripening. Not until after 312 was it politically useful for Seleukos to be married to a Persian princess. It would have been, on the other hand, quite acceptable, politically, to repudiate Apama after Alexander's death, as most of the other wives were repudiated. That the marriage was maintained when it was in a sense disadvantageous for Seleukos is a strong indication that Seleukos' affections were engaged. Apama must have been a remarkable lady. Their son Antiochos was born within the next year or two for he was old enough in 301 to command half his father's army. Malalas produces two daughters as well but there is no other evidence of their existence and they are probably a product of Malalas' confusion [11].

The Hypaspists were no doubt in attendance on Alexander all through his final year. There is one occasion on which their loyalty was tested and proved, and when Seleukos will have been present. Alexander's initial weeding-out of old, lame, and time-expired Macedonians, when they all reached Babylonia again, produced an ugly scene. The men shouted catcalls, the king lost his temper. He strode into the crowd with those Hypaspists who were near him at the time, some of them officers, and picked out thirteen ringleaders for arrest and immediate execution. It is clear that Alexander was prepared for some sort of trouble at the meeting; it would have been very odd indeed if he was not supported by his senior officers in full; since it was Seleukos's regiment which was on duty,

Seluekos will therefore have been present, and he will not have endeared himself to the soldiers by acting as Alexander's enforcer on this occasion [12].

There are two stories told in which Seleukos features during this time spent in Babylon, but in neither case can the story be accepted as historical truth. In the first Alexander was piloting his ship along the Euphrates when the fillet around his head, the emblem of royalty, blew off and was caught in some reeds on the bank. Seleukos is said to have jumped into the river, swum across to the bank, rescued the fillet and, in order to keep it dry and clean, to have put it on his own head for the swim back. In another version, the story has an ordinary seaman as the rescuer. He is reported to have either been rewarded for his deed and then punished for wearing the fillet, or to have been executed for his presumption [13].

In its very basic form – simply that a sailor rescued the fillet – the story might well be true. At least the sailor-version carries a certain conviction, for 'senior officers do not jump in rivers to rescue pieces of cloth; they send ordinary sailors to do the job' [14]. However, the versions vary sufficiently for the whole story to be rendered doubtful, and it is the elaborations which are difficult to believe. The simultaneous reward-and-punishment is quite possible, for Alexander had wholly lost his sense of proportion and his sense of humour (if he ever had one) by this time. A further improvement on the story has the riverbank reeds growing at the foot of the gravemounds of the old Assyrian kings. But Assyrian kings were buried in Assyria, not in Babylonia. The story has clearly been 'improved' to become an omen of Alexander's death and the transfer of kingship from the Macedonian conqueror to a local king. The insertion of Seleukos is the final stage of the embellishment and clearly dates that version of the story, and possibly the whole of it in all its parts, to the time when Seleukos ruled in Babylon, and probably, since the kingship is involved, after 312 or even after 304. It may be that these improvements are Seleukos' own work: he was certainly capable of such invention; it may also be the work of Babylonians anxious to ingratiate themselves. As it stands, the story is almost entirely a propaganda exercise, designed to demonstrate Seleukos' predestined rise to the kingship. It can be dismissed as history, and, as an incident in Seleukos' life, it is just as unacceptable.

The other story in which Seleukos appears purports to take place as Alexander lay dying in Babylon. Seven Macedonian officers, it is said, including Seleukos, spent an all-night vigil in the temple of Sarapis. They enquired of the god if Alexander should be brought to the temple for a cure, but the god replied in an oracle that Alexander should stay where he was. The next night Alexander died. By a curious twist, this is interpreted in favour of the god [15].

This story has been widely accepted as true, either literally or with adaptations [16]. It is, in fact, another propaganda invention. The source quoted by Arrian, the 'royal journals', is probably a later compilation, perhaps even a forgery [17]. The discussion of these two matters is complex and made worse than need be by beginning with the problem of the 'journals'. Here the main issue is the vigil in the temple, and there are so many problems with the story that it is best to assume that it is an invention.

First, the god to whom the men are said to have appealed, Sarapis, did not have a temple in Babylon in 323 or later; in fact, the god did not even exist for several more years [18]. The men themselves could not have met as a group in Babylon in 323, for one of them at least (Kleomenes) is known to have been elsewhere. The story, as we have it, is a propaganda story of the wars between Antigonos and the others some years later (and it will be discussed in more detail in Chapter 4). It may be that the core of the story – the visit of some prominent men to a temple to plead for Alexander's life – actually happened. We do not know. If it is based on a true event, then Seleukos may have been involved. It is the sort of thing a group of men in the second rank might do; those in the first rank were too busy staying close to the source of power, the dying Alexander, to consider crossing the river and spending the night away from the camp.

Next morning Alexander was dead. Every officer was cut adrift and only some of them would survive. Seleukos had by this time been commander of the Royal Hypaspists for just about three years. He had shown himself a competent soldier, otherwise he would never have reached that position, nor kept it. He had shown, if he was present at the 'mutiny' at Opis, that he would carry out any order Alexander gave him, even arresting and executing his old comrades. He was a high officer of proven loyalty, perhaps of somewhat limited initiative, and maybe not too popular with the general run of soldiers. By the time of Alexander's death, Seleukos was in his early thirties, married, perhaps with a son, but he had not notably distinguished himself. This position, in the second rank of high officers, was one he was to maintain, virtually unchanged, for several more years.

Alexander's death inevitably caused a crisis. His irresponsibility in neglecting to provide an heir, his self-indulgence in conquest and victory, even his tactical methods of appealing to the soldiers in a series of political meetings, had all resulted in making him indispensable. So when he died young and without an heir, there was inevitably a great deal of confusion among his soldiers and administrators.

Philip's institution of the Royal Pages had provided a supply of highly competent men who became commanders of the detached military units, governors of the provinces of the empire, and administrators at the centre. It was Philip's men such as Antipatros, Antigonos, and Menes who had held together the essential western base from which Alexander had mounted his eastern campaigns. Antipatros, Antigonos, and Alexander had at one time all been fighting simultaneously, in Greece, in Asia Minor, and in Baktria respectively. These great multiple campaigns of the year 331 were all victorious and ensured that the conquests continued. But these were Philip's men. The greatest of them was Parmenio, and after his killing in 330, Alexander had begun the process of promoting his own contemporaries into positions of authority.

In the eastern campaigns he had begun by entrusting armies to his contemporaries, at first, during the Baktrian war, without much success; then, in India and under his close supervision, with greater success. Finally he had picked out Krateros, Hephaistion, and Nearchos for independent commands, and each had successfully brought part of the army back to the west from India. Meanwhile Alexander's own section of the army suffered badly in the desert. Of these men, Nearchos was a Cretan, the other two were Macedonians; similarly Alexander's administrators and governors were a mixed lot. Some of them were rather too successful, like Kleomenes in Egypt who had eliminated his rivals and colleagues and made himself immensely rich. Others had been trusted too much, like Alexander's boyhood friend Harpalos, who had been made treasurer, and had run off with part of the public treasury. Yet others had been actively disloyal, or so it seemed, like the satraps near Alexander's route from India, who had failed to send him help in his extremity [19].

Even so the programme of education and training under Philip had been successful enough to produce a good reservoir of Macedonian talent, especially when supplemented by Persians and Greeks. Alexander's death at an inopportune moment meant that this set of ambitious, trained, and able men were set loose without a guide and without a focus of loyalty. They had been trained for ambition and for command, but this had been tempered and limited by their loyalty to the king. This had been the essential purpose of the institution of the Royal Pages. Without a king to work for, however, they now worked for themselves. Not at first, and not, perhaps, always; but Philip Arrhidaios was no substitute for Alexander, and as the memory of Alexander faded, as events crowded in, and as their Macedonian homeland became ever more distant and less accessible, their self-interest and ambition inevitably triumphed [20].

Alexander had singled out Perdikkas by giving him his ring; he had also confused matters by dying without a legitimate heir, yet at the same time leaving several possible successors. His wife Roxane was pregnant, his wife Parysatis was pregnant, his bastard son Herakles was unacknowledged, and he had a half-wit half-brother, Arrhidaios. Too much and too little. Disputes developed within days. Parysatis was killed, a victim of Roxane's jealousy. Perdikkas survived in authority, but only as regent for Arrhidaios who was proclaimed as King Philip III along with Roxane's unborn child, if it was male. In the process of survival, however, Perdikkas' authority was damaged [21].

In particular Perdikkas resorted to the practice which Alexander had lately used, of appealing to an assembly of soldiers for the authority to do something. He had not wished to do this, nor had the other Macedonian notables, but one of the phalanx-commanders, Meleagros, roused the troops to proclaim Arrhidaios, and Perdikkas had then had to accept both Arrhidaios and the troops' power – though Meleagros was soon murdered along with the other ringleaders. The Macedonian leaders closed ranks against Meleagros in the end, but the lesson of his temporary success was not lost on them.

Seleukos is named by Arrian, in Photios' summary of his account of these events, as one of the leaders who supported Perdikkas in the struggle for power following the death of Alexander. The others named in the same breath are a formidable group of powerful men – Leonnatos, Ptolemy, Lysimachos, Aristonous, Peithon, and Eumenes [22]. Of them, only Aristonous failed to distinguish himself in the succeeding years. These were the great men of the empire, together with Antipatros in Macedonia and Krateros in Kilikia. The group is a very different set of men from those who were named in the story of the temple vigil, which has been supposed to have taken place only a few days before. If Seleukos was of this rank, he was now one of the great lords of the empire, and he had risen since Alexander's death.

Investigation rather undermines this list, however. The source is a summary by Photios of a summary by Arrian of an original account by Hieronymos of Kardia. Hieronymus was a fellow-citizen of Eumenes, who had been Alexander's secretary and was a major participant in these affairs at Babylon. Hieronymos himself was probably present in the camp at the time, and he certainly had the opportunity to find out what was going on, either in person or later. This is not to say that he told the truth, or that he was unbiased, or that he knew all that happened, or told all that he knew. One might expect, for example, that he would favour Eumenes, and this is the obvious reason for Eumenes' good repute in the sources and his most unlikely prominence in affairs. Hieronymos also pursued a feud with the tyrant of his home city, and he certainly allowed this to distort his account of events. His animosities and loyalties were clearly of more importance to Hieronymos than merely telling the truth.

Later, Seleukos was himself opposed to Eumenes, being for a time on the side of Antigonos in the campaign which ended in Eumenes' death. Hence Hieronymos cannot be accepted as a reliable source for the opinions or even the actions of Seleukos. Perdikkas on the other hand was constantly friendly with Eumenes, though he and his supporters were later condemned as outlaws. By that time Seleukos had changed sides. There is enough confusion here to indicate that it is not safe to accept Hieronymos' account without some further confirmation [23]. Hence everything which appeared to be based on Hieronymos has to be regarded as suspect. And this includes the suggestion that Seleukos had been advanced in importance.

The settlement of affairs which followed the 'mutiny' led by Meleagros resulted in a distribution of offices among those who had been on the winning side. Perdikkas had only a limited influence over this process. The most powerful men took their pick of offices, and the second rank then received their rewards from Perdikkas. The distribution produced a situation where the most powerful men were scattered to fairly distant satrapies – Ptolemy to Egypt is the best example, but Peithon in Media is another, as are Krateros, Antipatros, and Antigonos. Perdikkas' position at the geographical centre of the empire was bolstered by his possession of the royal court and by the effective absence of powerful men nearby. Laomedon in Syria, Archon in Babylon, and Eumenes in (unconquered) Kappadokia were not men who could compete with Perdikkas in power, potential, or charisma. Seleukos was one of those who could. He was given an office close to Perdikkas, hipparch of the Companion Cavalry. Since in this post he does not seem to have had any truly independent authority, Seleukos must be relegated again to the second rank of officers.

There is, however, a certain confusion about the office he was given. It is described as having been held previously by Hephaistion and then by Perdikkas himself [24]. This has led to its being described as the chiliarchy [25], an office which Alexander found that he needed as his court expanded and the work he had to do grew, for it was the chiliarch who had become the controller of affairs in the court, an office similar to the later Islamic vizirate, the filter through which matters had to pass on the way to the king. Its purpose was to eliminate much of the minor detail which could easily fill up the king's day. In Macedon this detail had been manageable, and Philip had not needed a chiliarch; but for the lord of Asia, the detail threatened to become overwhelming. It was an office which Alexander took over from the Persians, but it is not a sign of Iranization, merely an inevitable result of his increased work load. It was, however, an office of great potential power, and Alexander had hesitated to fill it after Hephaistion's death, perhaps simply because, in his mood of tense suspicion, he did not trust anyone sufficiently, perhaps also because his own administrative methods were slack and careless.

It was this office in which Perdikkas was confirmed after the disturbances at Babylon which followed Alexander's death. Even more than Alexander, Philip Arrhidaios would need a chiliarch, which is why Perdikkas' office is usually referred to as a regency, and this is a good example of the way the chiliarchy could easily expand its authority. It was protean in effect, filling all the space available to it. With a strong king, or a ruthless and vigorous one like Alexander, it was controllable. With a weak nonentity on the throne, the chiliarch seemed like a ruler, not an official. Hence Perdikkas is sometimes given the modern title 'regent' when he was, in fact, merely chiliarch.

Hence, since Perdikkas was chiliarch, Seleukos could not be. But Perdikkas now looked like a ruler, in effect *was* the ruler of the empire, since the kings were ineffectual. The great burden of administration which would fall on the chiliarch now included both his own and the king's duties, and so his second-in-command effectively became the chiliarch's chiliarch. This was the post which Seleukos held, under the title hipparch of the Companion Cavalry. But his effective office would last only so long as there was an effective administration at the centre of the empire. As that central administration faded away over the next few years, so the office of chiliarch faded away with it; there is no record of any holder of the office after Perdikkas.

Seleukos' position was thus one of subordination to Perdikkas, but he was still, at least, at the centre of power. His position was in the gift of Perdikkas, who in this was following Alexander's example. Given that Seleukos had been a constant and loyal subordinate to Alexander, and given that he had never had a shred of independent authority, and given that his presumed actions in support of Alexander may well have made him unpopular with the infantry, it seems reasonable to assume that Seleukos lacked any real personal authority. His appointment to the command of the Companion Cavalry, when his earlier experience had always been with the infantry, also implies that Perdikkas felt he could shift Seleukos around with impunity. Seleukos, therefore, was seen by Perdikkas as being competent both as a commander and as an administrator, but with no independent political base, and in this he was in the same position as Eumenes. Both were beholden to Perdikkas and without him neither had access to any real power independently of their offices.

This estimate of his position does not imply a lack of ambition or ability on Seleukos' part. He could scarcely complain that his career was stagnating, having risen from an ordinary officer in 326 to second in the empire in 323. Whether Perdikkas trusted Seleukos we do not know. It is perhaps unlikely; there was nothing to suggest that he should trust anyone. He could count on Seleukos' gratitude to a very limited extent, but not for long, for gratitude is the most evanescent of political qualities.

Whatever Perdikkas' motives and policies were, it soon became clear that the attempt to defuse the political situation at Babylon by appointing the great men to distant posts (if that was what it was) produced as much disturbance as keeping them together in one place would have done. Peithon in Media had been given the task of destroying a rebellion of Greek mercenaries, left in Baktria by Alexander as colonists. He tried to enlist them to his own service, but his Macedonian troops massacred the Greeks for the sake of their loot. This in fact was Perdikkas' doing, for he had promised the loot to the Macedonians before they set off. He presumably knew that Peithon's ambition had already outrun his gratitude. There was certainly no trust involved here [26].

Seleukos' position in the central government of the empire makes it certain that he will have taken part in the campaign which Perdikkas waged on behalf of Eumenes to install the latter in his Kappadokian satrapy. More, since the army which Ariarathes of Kappadokia had collected was largely cavalry, Seleukos' command as hipparch was crucial to the success of the campaign. Two battles were needed before Ariarathes was defeated and captured and it may be presumed that Seleukos commanded the cavalry in these battles. To his experience as a regimental commander was thus added experience in command of half an army [27].

The court could then move on to Sardis. It was at Sardis that Perdikkas began to make mistakes. He had contracted a marriage alliance with Antipatros, agreeing to marry his daughter Nikaia. But Olympias thrust forward her daughter Kleopatra, sister of the dead Alexander. Perdikkas wavered, no doubt tempted not just by Kleopatra, but by the throne itself. Then there appeared yet another daughter of Philip II, Adea, long betrothed to the half-wit Philip III Arrhidaios. She arrived at Sardis with her mother Kynnane, who was promptly murdered by Perdikkas' brother Alketas. Perdikkas' half-formed scheme collapsed. A soldiers' riot compelled him to accept the marriage of Adea, now calling herself Eurydike, with Philip Arrhidaios, to renounce any plan to marry Kleopatra, and persuaded him to cover his rear by marrying Nikaia after all [28].

He had come to Sardis in the first place to discipline the satrap of Phrygia, Antigonos, who had failed to turn out to help in the war against Ariarathes. Why Antigonos failed to help is unclear, though it is possible that Eumenes' successful installation in Kappadokia may have been seen by Antigonos as a threat to himself. He would then have much less reason for maintaining a large force under his own control, since the only major threat to Phrygia came from Kappadokia. Whatever the reason, Antigonos had compounded the felony by deserting his post and fleeing to Europe to take refuge with Antipatros and Krateros, who had at long last actually joined forces [29].

Meanwhile Ptolemy in Egypt had also done things to which Perdikkas took exception. He had been drawn into a war in Kyrene, where a group of Greek mercenaries who had survived the war in Greece had attempted to seize power. Of this move by Ptolemy, Perdikkas could hardly complain, though no doubt he would, claiming that Ptolemy had moved out of his satrapy without permission [30]. Then Ptolemy had presumed to defy Perdikkas over the issue of the burial place of Alexander. Perdikkas had altered the original plan and had told Arrhidaios, the builder of the catafalque (not the king, of course), to go to Macedonia with the body rather than to Egypt, as Alexander is said to have wished. Ptolemy persuaded Arrhidaios to hold to the original plan, and to assist him had gone to Damascus with a sufficient escort to overawe the smaller force Perdikkas had sent on the same mission [31]. The difference was not only between success and failure: Perdikkas, lord of the empire, clearly did have authority in Syria, Ptolemy, satrap of Egypt, clearly did not. Once again, Ptolemy had operated outside the circumscribed area of his authority. Perdikkas might ignore Kyrene, but he could not ignore Damascus. Perdikkas set the court and his army on the march towards Egypt to punish its satrap.

In Egypt, Perdikkas faced major difficulties in reaching Ptolemy. He seems to have decided that he had to get across the Damietta distributary of the Nile, and tried three times, each time with greater casualties. Ptolemy stayed behind the river, either because at first he was too weak to face Perdikkas' force, or because he was unwilling to be the one who initiated intra-Macedonian fighting. (This was not a scruple which hindered Antipatros and Krateros, who attacked Eumenes in Asia behind Perdikkas' back, but then their opponent was a Greek, whatever components were in his army.) Ptolemy defended his satrapy when attacked, but did not counterattack, and meanwhile he worked on the basic disaffection which had existed in Perdikkas' army from the affair of the succession in Babylon. Ptolemy ostentatiously gave honourable cremation to those killed in the abortive attempts to cross the river. Clandestinely he established contact with Perdikkas' immediate lieutenants. He set himself before them as a man wrongfully attacked in his own satrapy. One of those he approached was, at some time, Seleukos.

The leading man in Perdikkas' force whom Ptolemy contacted, however, was not Seleukos but Peithon, the satrap of Media, the man whose attempt to recruit the Greeks from Baktria had been foiled by Perdikkas. Ptolemy clearly knew his man. Other officers, a hundred according to one source, joined in Peithon's plot. Antigenes, the commander of the Argyraspides, an elite unit formed out of the original hypaspists, who had joined Perdikkas in Kilikia, led the way in assassinating the chiliarch in his own tent [32].

Only one source, Cornelius Nepos in his short biography of Eumenes, says Seleukos was one of the assassins [33]. But he also says that 'Antigonos' was the other. This can be emended to Antigenes, but it does not inspire much confidence in Nepos' accuracy. Yet objectively it must be acknowledged that Seleukos' participation is certain. He got a similar reward (if it was a reward) to that given Antigenes. He was not eliminated in the aftermath of Perdikkas' death, as others of Perdikkas' friends were. Thus Seleukos had clearly stepped across to join the plotters in time to be counted as one of them. The man who had been raised up by Perdikkas had betrayed him [34].

3
SATRAP AND FUGITIVE
(320–315)

The chief Macedonian now, as a result of the killing of Perdikkas, was Antipatros, who had advanced with Antigonos from Macedon to Kilikia, brushing Eumenes aside on the way. By a quite normal historical irony, the man who had done no fighting in the crisis emerged on top. This was partly due to others' forbearance, and partly to Antipatros' own priorities.

Ptolemy's response to the death of Perdikkas had been to emphasize reconciliation. His primary political objective at the time was to get rid of Perdikkas' army and the royal court which it was carrying with it. Whatever his original intentions with regard to Egypt, it seems clear enough by now that Ptolemy had reached the conclusion that the essential basis for power was no longer access to the royal court and the favour it bestowed, but the possession of a distinct territory. This did not necessarily imply the break-up of the empire into independent states, though this was to be the actual result of this prolonged crisis. It did require that Ptolemy and his forces should be the one and only source of political power in the Nile valley. Hence Perdikkas' army and its court had to be removed.

Probably by pre-arrangement, Ptolemy visited the camp of the royal army, addressed the troops and proposed that, as a temporary measure, Peithon and Arrhidaios be appointed joint *epimeletai* [1]. This term seems to suggest that the men were to be not so much administrators, more guardians of the two kings. It was a temporary arrangement because a more permanent answer to the problem demanded Antipatros' agreement. Once again, the passing over of Seleukos is very noticeable. Peithon was chosen presumably because he was the arch-conspirator. Arrhidaios was the commander of the catafalque of Alexander and was thus Ptolemy's nominee. But Seleukos had been Perdikkas' second-in-command for nearly three years, and that is where he stayed, for the moment. Ptolemy's actions had emphasized once more the role of the assembled soldiers as the legal ratifiers of settlements. This may be the explanation for Seleukos' non-preferment, since he is likely to have been unpopular still. Yet it is just as likely that Seleukos was not interested in such an ephemeral post. By this time, like Ptolemy, he was probably looking for a firmer political footing than the unstable royal court and army could provide.

Presumably Seleukos was retained as hipparch, and was no doubt busy with many duties as the army evacuated Egypt, since he would now be functioning as a chief of staff. Certainly neither Peithon nor Arrhidaios had any great reputation as administrators, while Seleukos had been running things for Perdikkas for two years. Once more it becomes clear that Seleukos had become a very skilled administrator and commander. Twice now, by Alexander and by Perdikkas, he had been retained for two or three years in sensitive and demanding posts. He was, we must conclude, notably competent in them. And he had learnt the hard way how to run an army, a court, and an empire.

The two anti-Perdikkan armies, that of the assassins and that of Antipatros, met in camp at Triparadisos in central Syria, a Persian hunting park large enough to be the site of a great military camp. The meeting did not go well [2]. The purge of the Perdikkans had not been thorough enough. Perdikkas' brother-in-law Attalos had been in command of the fleet, and after Perdikkas' death he had sailed off with that fleet to Tyre. There he had gained control of a treasure of 800 talents which was now badly needed to pay the wages of the soldiers in the great camp. Eurydike, Philip III's new wife (formerly Adea), began an intrigue to gain the now-vacant royal protectorship for herself. Antipatros, eighty years old and direct from Macedonia where he had spent the great years of the conquest, did not realize just how much the atmosphere of the old army of Alexander the Great was different from what he was used to. This army was now possibly somewhat ashamed at the events in Egypt, was short of cash and was being subjected to emotional appeals from Eurydike. Above all the army had become used to being consulted on major decisions, and Antipatros could not bring himself to do that.

Even before he arrived at Triparadisos, with his own army, Macedonians who had, many of them, now left Macedon for the first time, Antipatros had been pitchforked into the top position. Peithon and Arrhidaios resigned and an assembly of officers had at once acknowledged Antipatros' dominant prestige by making him *epimeletes*. This is the term used for Antipatros' office, as it had been for Peithon and Arrhidaios, but it was now qualified by being described as *autokratoros*, 'with full powers' [3]. This combination, 'guardian with full powers', is precisely the office which Perdikkas had held. Presumably 'chiliarch' was now unacceptable, especially to old hide-bound Antipatros, whose notions of government had not advanced beyond those of Philip II, his old master. (They had not had to, for he had been in Macedon all the time, where Philip's methods were still perfectly adequate.)

Antipatros' stiffness, and his inability to find the cash with which to pay the troops, nearly led to him being lynched at a meeting of the soldiers. He was saved by the intervention of Antigonos and Seleukos, a richly ironic juxtaposition [4]. They represented the leadership of the two armies which had met at Triparadisos, which suggests that these two were the men identified by the soldiers as being the men in charge. The rapid fading of Peithon and Arrhidaios is very striking. It also indicates very clearly just how important Antigonos and Seleukos had now become. Antipatros, once he had got over the shock of the event and had squashed Eurydike's attempts to acquire power, no doubt took due note of just who his competitors were. Antigonos had been as ignorant of the new army atmosphere as Antipatros, but he proved to be much more adaptable. It is also clear that Seleukos was a man capable of influencing the troops and of deflecting their riot. His passing over at the meeting at Memphis had not, after all, diminished his influence very much.

The problems sorted themselves out fairly quickly, especially once Eurydike was terrorized into silence and Attalos into flight. Antipatros was confirmed as the man in command. This was a disastrous decision for the empire as a whole. Antipatros had never shown any sign of interest in lands beyond Macedonia, and now he showed no sign of any ability to rise to the situation. In retrospect, it is now clear that the meeting of officers which took place after the soldiers' riot, at which the satrapies were redistributed, was the episode which marked the end of the united empire. Under Perdikkas there had been a serious attempt to run the whole as one state. Antipatros was unconcerned. He wanted to return to Macedon, and to have as little in the way of problems to deal with as possible.

Thus the easy way out was taken in dealing with Ptolemy, who was left strictly alone and confirmed in office as satrap of Egypt. He was not, as is often assumed, too strong to be shifted. Had Antipatros insisted, Ptolemy would have had to appear at Triparadisos. To Antipatros it was too much bother. He was more concerned with protecting his position in Macedon by installing friends and relations and clients in the nearby satrapies. Antigonos was returned to Phrygia and given Perdikkas' army with which to fight Eumenes. Just to show that the war against Eumenes really was a war of right against wrong, Antigonos was also given charge of the royal court. So the army of the ally of Eumenes now knew that it had really done the right thing in murdering Perdikkas. Antigonos was a brave man to take on such a task with such an instrument. His chiliarch was Kassandros, Antipatros' son, all too obviously appointed as commissar to ensure Antigonos' good conduct; he was also presumably Seleukos' replacement. To make certainty doubly sure, the rest of Asia Minor was packed with satraps of Antipatros' friends and clients: Arrhidaios, Klitor, Asandros, and Philoxenos, in Hellespontine Phrygia, Lydia, Karia, and Kilikia respectively, ringing Antigonos round in a great half circle.

In all this it is clear that the importance of the royal court was now minimal. So long as a vigorous unifier was in charge, such as Perdikkas had been, political advantage lay in being associated with it. But now authority lay with Antipatros and the court was given to Antigonos as a badge of authority. For Seleukos the court was therefore no longer a path to power and influence and he will have indicated a desire to move. In the circumstances he could have first choice of the satrapies. There were, of course, some constraints: Egypt, Phrygia, and Media were already spoken for by Ptolemy, Antigonos, and

Peithon. There was clearly no future in being close to Antipatros so Asia Minor as a whole was not to be considered. But Babylon was available. Seleukos could step sideways from second-in-command of the empire to being governor of the second richest satrapy with no loss of honour. The difference in influence between Seleukos and Antigenes, another conspirator and the actual murderer of Perdikkas, is shown in that Antigenes became satrap of Susiana, a thoroughly backwater satrapy, though he kept command of the Argyraspids, the 'Silver-Shields'.

Seleukos' appointment may have been made on the initiative of Seleukos himself, or of Antipatros. At the very least Seleukos had agreed to it. Given his influential role at Triparadisos, at the death of Perdikkas, and in the general imperial administration, one may say that Babylon was effectively Seleukos' own choice. At the same time, the general situation in which Seleukos found himself when he reached Babylon bears all the marks of another of Antipatros' balanced constructions. Just as Antigonos was to be boxed in by men whose loyalty was to Antipatros himself, so Seleukos was to be enmeshed in a surrounding network of other satraps who might be expected to hold him in check, with Antigenes in Susiana, Peukestas beyond in Persis, and Peithon in Media [5]. Before they became a problem, however, Seleukos had to establish himself in Babylon.

The Babylonian satrapy was the geographical centre of the Macedonian empire. It was, as well, one of its economic powerhouses, along with Egypt, Phoenicia, and Greece. On the other hand, it was not – and this was the most important thing in the short term – a serious military power base. So Seleukos would be able to build up strong economic resources, but his military power meanwhile would remain moderate. Further, such military power as he was likely to develop – for his economic power would enable him to hire mercenaries – would be held in check by the existence in nearby satrapies of other Macedonian lords with their own forces and resources, in particular by Peithon in Media and Peukestas in Persis. The whole arrangement, together with Antipatros' disinclination to bother about the east, was clearly aimed at securing a balance of local power and at preventing the rise of any one Macedonian above all the rest in the east. As usual with a

SATRAP AND FUGITIVE

political balance of this sort, it was very easily upset, and thus instead of a peaceful balance, it entailed constant conflict.

It was the late-concluded conflict which had made Babylonia available for assignment to a new satrap at Triparadisos. The satrap appointed after Alexander's death was a man called Archon of Pella, who is otherwise unknown [6]. His obscurity perhaps means that he was expected to be a mere functionary, so that Perdikkas as lord of the empire should have no local rival, but it may be that Archon was more important than that. Our sources are concerned overwhelmingly with Greece and the west; events east of Syria receive scant attention except when a matter vital to the fate of the west is involved. But this does not mean that people at the time had that perspective, and it is certain that Perdikkas did not regard Babylon as unimportant.

Archon had in some way fallen foul of Perdikkas during the dispute with Antipatros and Ptolemy. Presumably the intrigues between Ptolemy and Arrhidaios over the destination of the corpse of Alexander had not been hidden from the Babylonian satrap. (Nor, since the interception by troops from Egypt took place in Damascus, could the satrap of Syria, Laomedon of Mytilene, have been ignorant or uninvolved.) Once the hijacking of the catafalque had occurred, an intrigue between Ptolemy and Archon would have to be assumed, and Perdikkas sent a small force to eliminate Archon while he himself concentrated on attacking Egypt.

This small detached force was commanded by Dokimos, appointed by Perdikkas as satrap in Archon's place. Archon was to become revenue-collector under Dokimos. That, at least, was the published account, though it sounds more like a ploy to pin Archon down. In fact, as the forces assigned to Dokimos showed, Archon was to be removed altogether from power. The fate of Kleomenes in Egypt at Ptolemy's hands was warning enough. Archon resisted his demotion in arms. But he had been satrap for over two years, and had made himself disliked by the local Babylonian population, who were clearly not pleased at the prospect of him continuing as revenue-collector. Dokimos received significant armed assistance from Babylonian groups, and the conflict ended with Archon's defeat and death [7].

Thus, when Perdikkas was killed, not only his family

became targets for his enemies, but his more distant adherents as well. Eumenes in Asia Minor was the most prominent, but Dokimos in Babylon was also to be dealt with, and his satrapy was thrown into the pot as one which was available to reward the conspirators. That is to say, Seleukos would have to fight for his satrapy.

Of this fight, however, only one possible hint remains. A fragmentary Babylonian chronicle records that something was destroyed and then burnt. By implication that something was in or near the city of Babylon, and by implication also it was an important building; it would scarcely be worth mentioning otherwise. This took place in the fifth year of Philip III, which ran from March 320 to March 319, and after Antipatros' return to Macedon had taken place [8]. Since the Triparadisos meeting was in the summer of 320, Seleukos will have reached and possessed himself of Babylon during the late summer and autumn (say, August to November) of 320. The fighting appears to have been brief, but Dokimos escaped, to re-appear later.

The previous year had revealed some volatile stuff in this whole eastern region. Peithon in Media was very clearly playing for power on his own behalf. He had been quite consistent in this, first in his attempt to enlist the rebellious Greeks in Baktria, then in participating in the murder of Perdikkas, whose success against Ptolemy would ensure an automatic reduction in power for all independent-minded satraps. Now he was at it again. Soon after returning to Media, Peithon carried through a *coup* in the neighbouring satrapy of Parthia by killing the satrap (called either Philip or Philotas) and installing his own brother Eudamos in his place [9].

Then there was the developing problem of the conflict between Antigonus and Eumenes in the west. This had direct implications for Seleukos in Babylon because Eumenes had been a lieutenant of Perdikkas just as Dokimos had been, and Dokimos, together with other Perdikkans, had fled to Asia Minor after his expulsion from the Babylonian satrapy. For the present, during the period following the appointment of Antigonos to the command against Eumenes, the danger, like that of Peithon, remained distant. Both Antigonos and Eumenes wintered during 319–318 in Kappadokia, Antigonos having beaten Eumenes' army, and from the summer of 318 on, for a year, Eumenes was reduced to a few hundred men and a single fortress, which Antigonos kept under a slack siege [10]. It was always a characteristic of Antigonos to assume a task finished before it really was. An eternal optimist until the very moment of his death, he failed in 318–317, by culpable negligence, to eliminate Eumenes when he could have done so. But for Seleukos, as for everyone else involved (except Eumenes) the problem seemed to have been all but solved.

Seleukos' main problem in the two years after his arrival at Babylon was with Babylonia itself. The disturbances surrounding the downfall of Perdikkas had produced problems which would have troubled any ruler of Babylonia. The ominous signs were the rising of part of the Babylonian population against Archon when Dokimos arrived, and the power of the local Babylonian priesthood. This latter manifestation was not new, for the Babylonian priests had successfully exercised their powers on Alexander, extracting large sums from him for 'repairs' to temples, and presenting awkward conditions to be fulfilled by him in his plans for the land [11]. These conditions and demands had been successful with Alexander because of the king's superstitious nature, and it established the reputation of the priests; no doubt, it also gave them considerable self-confidence.

Thus Seleukos must cope with two local groups, who may not necessarily want the same thing or things, but whose cooperation might pose a considerable danger to his rule. Nor were these two the only groups in the land. One other group can be confidently named: the Greeks and/or Macedonians who were settled in the towns which had been established by Alexander. These settlers may or may not have had different interests from the active professional troops which were under Seleukos' immediate command, but the number of these professional troops was small, and, in the event of military trouble, Seleukos would be dependent on the reinforcements provided by the colonists.

There was thus combustible material in all this. Under the rule of the Persian kings, large estates in Babylonia had existed, some of them privately owned, some royal. The impression is that many of the private estates were granted by the kings and ultimately reverted to the king. What happened to the Persian owners of private estates at the time of the

Macedonian conquest and after is not known, but Seleukos will have had the royal land under his control as soon as he arrived, theoretically administering it for the two kings, though a subsequent quarrel with Antigonos suggests that little of the Babylonian revenues were ever forwarded to the royal court. The royal lands will have been the source of the land provided to the new cities of Alexander and these cities were probably fully established by the time Seleukos arrived. At least one of them retained the name Alexandria afterwards, which suggests that it was a reasonably firm foundation. A second lost that name, which may only be because there were two of them and so a different name became current in order to distinguish the two; or it may have failed, at least temporarily [12].

Alexander had shown notable respect for the religious powers of the priests of Babylon – or perhaps 'fear' is a better word. They had warned him not to enter the city, and for months he had stayed away [13]. Seleukos was not, perhaps, treated in the same way. After all, Alexander had died in the city, and this could be regarded as a sufficient demonstration of the power of the priests. Or perhaps Seleukos could not be bluffed so easily. He certainly is recorded as 'entering Babylon' on a day in the month of Marchesvan of the fourth year of King Philip, that is, in October or November 320 [14].

The next entry in the local chronicle which recorded Seleukos' arrival is highly significant. The chronicle is a document of the traditional Babylonian type, in cuneiform script in the old Akkadian language, on a tablet of clay. That is, it was the product of a temple, written by a priest, recording matters of importance to the priests. Hence the record of the arrival of the 'satrap of Akkad', that is, Seleukos. The next record is that the 'dust' of Esagila was removed, which is to say that the new satrap provided money for the priests of the great temple of Bel-Marduk in Babylon, known as Esagila, to clean the great enclosure [15]. Whether they actually used it in that way is perhaps only a possibility; it is quite likely that the cash reached their pockets directly. The significance is that, within a short time, Seleukos the satrap had won over, by the traditional form of subsidy – 'bribery' is surely too coarse a term for such holy men – one of the main sources of local power in Babylonia.

The priests were important because of the influence they

had in the rest of Babylonia. The cities of that land were by this time cities centred on a temple. The ones we know of in any real detail – Babylon and Uruk, and to some extent Larsa and Cutha – conform more or less to this pattern [16]. The temples had become the only native institution in Babylonia with any power under the Persians, and thus they had been both the targets of Persian reprisals and the objects of Persian conciliation. The Persian role as conquerors of Babylon had rendered them eternally disliked, a dislike which could be transmuted into an acceptance of the Greeks and Macedonians, conquerors of the Persians, by a skilful politician. Alexander had made the initial mistake of confirming a Persian in office as Babylonian satrap. The appointment of Archon by Perdikkas seems to have been ultimately just as unpopular a move, since the arrival of his successor was the signal for a rising. Dokimos did not have time to make much of a mark, but the arrival of Seleukos can only have produced reactions of weary contempt from Babylonians. He was the third satrap in less than a year. Such respect as the new conquerors had acquired by their defeat of the detested Persians was rapidly being dissipated.

It would appear that Seleukos saw the danger. This is to be laid to his credit, despite the undoubted fact that his options were very limited. He had the choice between Macedonian arrogance which would lead to the inevitably crushed rebellion, and, on the other hand, an intelligent appreciation of the situation leading to conciliation. He was assisted in choosing the latter alternative by the prospect of trouble from his Macedonian neighbours, by his lack of armed force, and by his own political sense. Hence his contribution to Esagila, so leaving the influential priests purring with satisfaction at their saucer of milk [17]. Yet it would be a mistake to see this as anything other than a matter of dire necessity. It went very much against the grain for any Macedonian lord to be anything but arrogant, especially after the great events of the last fifteen years. Seleukos will not have liked the suggestion of governing by conciliation, but he had the political intelligence to choose it. It is one of the reasons he was ultimately so successful, and one of the reasons for his eventual untimely death.

The conciliation of the Babylonians was achieved swiftly:

the contribution to Esagila was made before the Babylonian New Year in March of 319. Meanwhile Antigonos had squared up to Eumenes and then besieged him. Antipatros died in Macedon, having appointed Polyperchon as his successor as *epimeletes autokratoros*. Polyperchon soon became inextricably involved in conflicts in Greece, where Athens was in a ferment, and with Antipatros' son Kassandros, who appeared to believe that his paternity entitled him to power and authority. When it was not forthcoming instantly, he set about taking it. In the midst of all this, while Antigonos was carefully watching events in Greece, Eumenes escaped from the besieged castle at Nora. He moved south, collected a force in Kilikia and occupied northern Syria. Part of the force he now had consisted of the Argyraspides, Seleukos' old command, the former Hypaspists. In all ways, the conflict was moving towards Seleukos in Babylon [18].

As it happened, it was Peithon of Media who impinged first. His installation of his own brother Eudamos in the Parthian satrapy, and his all-too-obvious intention of establishing himself as lord of the east from his Median base, had alarmed all the other satraps in the area. Some of these men had been in office for years and at least two of them had been appointed by Alexander, back in 324: Peukestas the satrap of Persis, and Sibyrtios in Arachosia. Oxyartes in the Paropamisadai was grandfather to the child-king Alexander IV. Others had been shifted about in various of the grand reshuffles, but always in the east. Stasanor had moved from Aria to Baktria in 320, to be replaced in Aria by Stasandros, who came from the same town, Soli in Cyprus, and was presumably Stasanor's brother. In India the power was held by another Eudamos, who had done in India what Peithon was doing in Iran, for he had begun as supervisor of King Taxiles, and had ended, over the bodies of King Poros and the satrap Philip, as satrap of all India [19]. Eudamos' attention was concentrated on India, however, and his ambitions had not yet disturbed the satraps in Iran.

Peithon and Seleukos were to some extent intruders in this cosy Iranian world. These eastern satraps had been in undisturbed possession for several years. Peithon himself was in a way an old-established satrap, having been made satrap of Media in 323, but he had been away with Perdikkas in the west, and had not returned until after Triparadisos. What made Peithon really different – for his ambition only made him normal – was that he had more military muscle at his disposal than any of the others.

The strength of the individual satraps was relatively small when counted in numbers of troops; but in combination they were formidable. We do not know what Peithon's exact strength was, but the worried and threatened satraps combined to muster a force of well over 20,000 men to stop him [20]. This suggests that Peithon had a respectable force. The largest contingent of the allied satraps' force was from Peukestas, who brought up 3,000 heavy infantry, 10,000 archers and slingers, and 1,000 cavalry. This was clearly not enough for Peukestas to scotch Peithon by himself, so Peithon will have had more than that. The contingents of the other satraps were all less than 2,000 men each, except that from Karmania. Stasandros of Aria, along with his own force, brought up a contingent sent from Baktria, which was too sensitive a post for its satrap to leave, from which he dared not send many soldiers. Stasandros, even so, had only 2,500 men with him.

This force of 20,000 men was sufficient to do down Peithon. He was defeated with loss in a battle somewhere in Parthia, and retreated into his own satrapy of Media. From there he came down through the Zagros hills to visit Seleukos. He was not actually driven from Media, since that would have put the allied satraps themselves in the wrong, but they carefully kept their army together for the moment, presumably because of Peithon, but also because the war in the west was approaching.

Eumenes had occupied northern Syria with the intention of sailing to Greece to join Polyperchon. He had begun the construction of ships, but, before he was ready for sea, Antigonos approached with a superior force. This compelled Eumenes to withdraw eastwards, across the Euphrates. The satrap Amphimachos of Mesopotamia joined him readily enough; since he had only a few hundred troops, he had little choice. Eumenes moved further east, and then south, to winter in either Mesopotamia or northern Babylonia, in an area inhabited by transplanted Karian peasants.

Eumenes was followed by Antigonos, who took up his winter quarters to the north, in Mesopotamia. From the points of view of both Peithon and Seleukos, the situation was going from bad to worse. They were hemmed in by enemies. Eumenes was somewhere to the north of Babylon with an army over which he had only a precarious control. To *his* north was Antigonos, with a larger army, intent on destroying Eumenes. South-east of Seleukos was the army of the allied satraps, which had moved to Susiana after expelling Peithon from Parthia [21].

Susiana contained, at Susa, a major portion of the royal treasure, and by stationing themselves in Susiana, the allied satraps had accomplished several purposes. First, they had put Seleukos and Peithon between themselves and the two western armies. Second, they had put their own forces between the fighting and their own provinces. In particular their station in Susiana covered Persis, Peukestas' satrapy, from which half their army came, and from which reinforcements could most easily be brought. Third, they had the treasure to hand. Fourth, they had supplies to hand from someone else's satrapy. For the satrap of Susiana, Antigenes, the murderer of Perdikkas, was joint commander of the Argyraspides. These troops were in Kilikia when Eumenes persuaded them to join him. They had convoyed some of the royal treasure from Susa to Kyinda, this being one of the satrap's tasks imposed on him by Antipatros at Triparadisos [22]. The alliance was uncomfortable, partly because of the Macedonian troops' resentment of Eumenes as a Greek and as a Perdikkan. No doubt Antigenes' participation in the murder of Perdikkas, Eumenes' patron, also rankled. But to Eumenes, his attachment was useful, in that he could legitimately claim to be heading for Susiana to emplace its satrap. It seems that Antigenes had not spent more than the minimum of time in Susiana since his appointment, but, having taken the treasure to Kyinda he had not had the chance to return before becoming involved in the war between Antigonos and Eumenes [23].

Thus the absence of a satrap can be explained, as perhaps can the arrival in Susiana of the army of the eastern allied satraps. Also, within the citadel of Susa there was a garrison commanded by a man called Xenophilos, who seems to have tried to keep his distance from all these forces. He had presumably been appointed by Antigenes, and loyalty to him is a reasonable explanation of Xenophilos' behaviour.

Seleukos and Peithon therefore had a lot to discuss when

Peithon arrived at Babylon in the autumn or winter of 317. Peithon still had some military resources, though fewer than before his lost battle; Seleukos seems to have had much less. We have no figures, but the assumption must be that he had something of the same numbers of troops as the other satraps of the east, say; since Babylonia was rich, 2,000 or even 3,000 men. Eumenes had a force of about 15,000, to which he had added the 600 of Amphimachos of Mesopotamia; Antigonos had perhaps 25,000. Peithon and Seleukos were outclassed even if they united their forces. Nevertheless it was officially winter, even in Babylonia and Mesopotamia, and the pause thereby imposed on the movements of the armies provided a time for diplomacy, intrigue, and bribery.

Eumenes took his stand on his appointment by the *epimeletes* Polyperchon and Olympias, the mother of Alexander. His army was the 'army of the kings', and was apparently recognized as such by various parties, including the priests of Esagila [24]. This did not, in the eyes of Peithon and Seleukos, expunge the condemnation meted out to Eumenes at the conference at Triparadisos by the earlier *epimeletes* Antipatros, the assembled Macedonian nobles, and the Macedonian army. These two legalistic arguments were nicely balanced, each side appealing neatly to an authority it knew the other would never accept. Thus far propaganda.

Intrigue was more likely to produce results. The past association of Antigenes, Peithon, and Seleukos as co-assassins might provide a basis for joint action. There would be a certain symmetry in jointly ditching Eumenes as they had jointly dealt with Perdikkas. In addition there was the past association of Seleukos with the Hypaspists, from whom the Argyraspides were extracted, which he had commanded between 326 and 323. If this corps, perhaps no more than 3,000 strong, could be detached from Eumenes, the rest of his army might well break up, for it was the relationship between Eumenes and the Argyraspides which was the core of his force. It was for their benefit that Eumenes had developed the command-system of meeting in the presence of the ghost of Alexander in the royal tent, which permitted the snobbish Argyraspides to claim that they were not under the command of a mere Greek secretary [25]. But the very fact that they had been gulled into accepting this nonsensical arrangement prevented them from backing out of it. Whatever their feeling for Seleukos – and we have no firm evidence for either friendship or dislike – the royal tent stood in the way of any real contact.

Eumenes, reassured by the lack of response by Antigenes and the Argyraspides to Seleukos' blandishments, broke camp and marched towards Babylon. It appears that he knew that the allied eastern satraps had met in Susa and had declared their support for the kings' government. It was therefore safe for him to go to Susa; indeed, it was safer to go to Susa and join his new allies than to stay where he was, threatened by armies to north and south. Exactly when he moved is difficult to say. It seems that the river Tigris was unfordable, and the canals full of water, which suggests late spring. There is no comment on timing in Diodoros, whose source for all this is reckoned to be Hieronymos, who was present as a member of the expedition, and can thus be considered a primary source. In later years, when Antigonos broke up his winter quarters early, Diodoros regularly reports it; it may thus be assumed that Eumenes waited for full spring before setting off. Antigonos did not follow him at once, but first recruited more men, then marched to Susa, which he reached in June. By that time Eumenes had been there long enough to establish his authority, more or less, over the assembled satraps [26].

If Diodoros was the only source there would be an end to the discussion at that point. But the Babylonian cuneiform chronicle used before provides some awkward and enigmatic 'facts'. It records that 'the army of the king' was stationed at a place whose name began Du... in the month of Tishri, that is September/October of 317. Then, on the next line, and thus in or after Tishri, but before the New Year in March 316, three events are recorded: first, something occurred at the palace at Babylon; second, the 'officer of Akkad', and so not the satrap but one of his subordinates, did something; third, something was done by or to European troops of 'the king' [27]. All this suggests a considerable degree of military disputation, but no real fighting. The real problem is the reference to the palace at Babylon, for the interpretation must be that there was fighting at the palace itself, which can only mean that Eumenes was attacking the city. (Yet the chronicle regularly mixes events together with no regard for continuity, and it may here be reporting something very different.)

Diodoros describes a rather different situation. He reports that Eumenes brought his army to within 300 stades of the city (say, 35 miles), and camped before the Tigris, intending to cross the river. Peithon and Seleukos at once communicated this news to Antigonos, and tried to prevent Eumenes from getting across. Thus Seleukos had been compelled to declare himself. He brought out two triremes, ships built in Alexander's time, together with many more small craft. Eumenes needed to cross the river in order to get supplies. Diodoros says the land had been plundered of its food, which may be true, but it is likely that even if Eumenes had not moved early, he had moved before the harvest. (Foraging far and wide for food may be the explanation for the entries in the cuneiform chronicle which refer to the 'officer of Akkad' and the king's European troops.) At all events, Eumenes had to cross the river quickly, and Seleukos' ships were a major problem.

Or rather, perhaps they were meant only to seem to be a problem. Seleukos used his ships more as propaganda vehicles than as serious weapons. He brought them close to the embarkation point and appealed once more to Antigenes and the Argyraspides, again in vain. Seleukos, despite having triremes, made no attempts to seize or destroy the small boats which Eumenes' people had acquired. For Seleukos was playing a double game: pretending to be blocking Eumenes' advance, while actually encouraging it.

In fact Seleukos had little choice in the matter. Antigonos was too far off to have any effect on the situation except as a distant threat. If Eumenes camped in Babylonia for any length of time, his army would destroy the satrapy. So Seleukos' next move was to open the dike and threaten to flood Eumenes' camp. But it was, as he well knew, only a threat. The water enclosed the camp, but the men there had boats, 300 of them, sufficient to get most of the army across in one day. After a day's delay, presumably to plan and organize, this is what Eumenes did. Seleukos brought up his cavalry to watch, but of course, no-one blamed him for not interfering in the crossing, for he had so few troops.

What, one may ask, had happened to the two triremes? And

all the other triremes Alexander had built? What of Seleukos' own small boats? In combination with cavalry patrolling the bank, it would have been possible to make things very awkward indeed for Eumenes' troops. Two triremes, or more, patrolling the river would have upset so many small boats that the cavalry would have been no more than a mopping-up force. Eumenes could see full well what Seleukos was up to. He made the right gesture, commencing the excavation of a new course for the canal whose bank Seleukos had broken. Seleukos offered a truce; Eumenes accepted. Then Eumenes got his baggage across, ceased excavations, and marched off towards Susiana. Seleukos sent off more messengers to Antigonos, pretending that the allied satraps were advancing to join Eumenes, whereas the opposite was happening. And he still knew that Antigonos could not arrive in time [28].

For the news that Eumenes and the allied satraps were about to join forces stopped Antigonos in his tracks. And Seleukos will have known that this would happen. Antigonos' force was large enough to tackle Eumenes – that was inherent in the situation – but it could not face the combined forces of Eumenes and the allied satraps. Seleukos' lie about the allied satraps approaching was no doubt intended to stop Antigonos; it also gave Eumenes time to get clear; it also cleared Babylonia of all hostile armies, at least for the moment.

Antigonos had to call up reinforcements, either by recruiting or, more likely, by bringing more men from Asia Minor. Antigonos had to double the size of his force, more or less, which meant another 20,000 men. Eumenes had spent all the winter of 318–317 in recruiting half that. Yet Antigonos was in sufficient strength to venture into Susiana by June [29].

On the way he had called on Seleukos and Peithon at Babylon. They had no difficulty in agreeing that Eumenes had to be suppressed, though how much further their mutual agreement went is unknown. At a guess, not very far. Peithon for one had made his ambition to be lord of the east quite clear more than once. It may be that he thought that Antigonos would be content with the west, in which case Seleukos would be the unlucky one; he was certainly the weakest of the three. All Seleukos could do was to perform the services demanded of him by Antigonos and to trust that a chance would come in the confusion to establish his own unhindered power base. For the present, alliance with Antigonos, as equal as he could make it, was his necessary policy. He provided troops for Antigonos' army, which meant in fact that he lost virtually all the troops he had, apart from the necessary garrison for Babylon. Peithon was in the same situation. Seleukos also provided a bridge across the Tigris for Antigonos' army; there was no need to flush this army out. One hopes Antigonos appreciated the difference; probably he simply noted it for future reference.

Antigonos moved swiftly to Susiana and occupied Susa itself. The citadel, however, was held for Eumenes and the allied satraps by Xenophilos and his garrison, to whom strict instructions had been given not to surrender nor even enter into negotiations with Antigonos. To these instructions (presumably in the first instance delivered by the satrap Antigenes) Xenophilos adhered. He had in the citadel the remains of a huge treasure, so much so that he is called the treasurer by Diodoros, though he was clearly first and foremost the commander of the garrison.

Antigonos wanted that money. Eumenes' plan – presumably it was his, but it could have been a committee decision for the royal tent was in use again – was to make Antigonos divide his forces. Antigonos might sit down in the heat of a Susian summer to besiege the citadel. Earlier Eumenes had had trouble with supplies, and he had laid out a picket line along the Pasitigris river to prevent any supplies reaching Antigonos from the rest of Susiana; and, after feeding two greedy armies in the last year, Babylonia can have had little to spare. So if Antigonos' need for money was great enough to make him attack the citadel he would starve, and if he decided to attack Eumenes, he would do so at the end of a long line of communications, in a land stripped of food by Eumenes' troops, and with only a part of his army, for he would need to leave some to mask Susa's citadel. And without the money. Or he could withdraw, of course, but presumably no-one seriously expected that.

Antigonos decided to attack. The money problem was not yet acute, and Peithon had cash at Ekbatana if required. Seleukos, the weakest of the three commanders, was given the job of masking Susa, with the title of satrap of Susiana [30].

This is an important moment. Antigonos' legal position, if anyone at the time cared, was highly ambiguous. He had been appointed by Antipatros to suppress Eumenes, but since then Polyperchon had in effect cancelled that appointment by commissioning Eumenes to raise an army to aid him against Kassandros. It was this commission which had persuaded the allied eastern satraps to join Eumenes. Antigonos, thereby, became the outlaw, if law can be said to have entered into the matter. Now, by appointing Seleukos as a satrap, Antigonos was in effect claiming that his original appointment was still in force, and that Eumenes, the allied satraps, and Polyperchon were the ones who were outlaws. This incidentally vindicated Peithon's ambitions as well. The reality, of course, was a civil war with, as usual in such a situation, some of the right on each side. Also in such situations propaganda was a valuable and well-used tool, a fact which Antigonos learned from Polyperchon and Eumenes but which he eventually exploited much better than either. Allies were also important, but they could never be trusted, since inherent in the situation were so many factors that changing sides was a matter of apparent ease to some and to others of immense psychological difficulty. Both flexibility and stubbornness were problems.

Antigonos marched directly at the enemy, but was defeated in the attempt to cross the well-guarded Koprates river, and replied with a masterly strategic move. He took his army, less Seleukos and his siege force at Susa, north into Media [31]. His soldiers grumbled but the move put enormous pressure on the allied satraps. In the same way that Peithon's move into Parthia had threatened them, so did Antigonos' move into Media. Their alliance with Eumenes came under great strain. Those whose satrapies were east of Persis were now directly threatened; indeed, Sibyrtios of Arachosia returned to his satrapy, though he left his troops with the allies under a commander called Kephalon. Eumenes could only see that the route back to the Mediterranean and Greece was now open again, except for the small force under Seleukos [32]. For a time the allied force threatened to break up. If that happened, Antigonos was in an excellent position to deal with any threat or any opportunity. If Eumenes went west, Antigonos could intercept him in Babylonia by a march through the Zagros passes; and Antigonos would be warned of the move by

Seleukos at Susa, who might even fight enough to delay Eumenes' move, though past form suggested that he was more likely to lie down and let Eumenes walk over him. A fight between Antigonos' army of 40,000 and Eumenes' of less than 20,000 would surely settle the issue.

The allied satraps had shown before that they were reluctant to move into another man's satrapy. After all, their quarrel with Peithon was that he had done just that by intruding his brother into Parthia. They had fought to recover Parthia, but not to push Peithon out of Media. They had gone into Susiana, but the satrap Antigenes was one of them, even though he was then with Eumenes. If Eumenes now moved into Babylonia, the allied satraps would be invading Seleukos' satrapy, and at the same time leaving their own satrapies open to attack by Antigonos and any other enemy. Their shaky alliance could only hold together on the basis of satrapal autonomy. Therefore Eumenes had to dance to their tune, and stay in the east.

Eumenes, in fact, was prevailed on to move further east, into Persis, where supplies existed and which had communication with the rest of the east. Seleukos was thus left as a very distant satrap at the gates. He and Xenophilos settled down in comfort to watch the contest between the greater forces. One suspects that an agreement was reached between them. When next we have news of their activities, Xenophilos is out of Susa and acting as Seleukos' deputy [33]. No doubt the news of the defeat of Eumenes and the death of Antigenes induced Xenophilos to reflect on the probable fate of a man in charge of 20,000 talents who persisted in supporting a lost cause. Seleukos proved here, as later again and again, that he was a man who would not stoop to execution and murder in a civil war (or in any other war), that he was prepared to wait, using time as his ally, and that battles and bloodthirst were not his methods.

So Eumenes' and Antigonos' armies battled it out during the autumn and winter of 316, first in Paraitakene and then in the winter-battle in Gabiene. At the end, after fascinating manoeuvres and tricks and marches, Eumenes' army broke up and Eumenes fell a prisoner into Antigonos' hands. The news of this will have been the trigger for Xenophilos' submission to Seleukos. Among Eumenes' forces mutual recrimination made Antigonos' task easy. These recriminations had begun even during the battle, for Peukestas withdrew his forces as soon as he was attacked, the Argyraspides then loudly blamed him for the defeat, and the other satraps talked of withdrawing to their satrapies. Having others conveniently to blame, the Argyraspides then changed sides, ostensibly because Antigonos had captured their baggage. Rather later than he can have hoped, Antigonos' move to Media had finally had its effect [34].

Antigonos killed Eumenes and Antigenes almost at once. Antigenes was burnt to death, presumably as one who was guilty of faithlessness. Eumenes was soon executed as well, being too dangerous to have around, and as the man who, after all, was the only one present who could claim royal sanction for his acts. Eudamos, the usurper of power in India, who had joined the allied satraps at some point, and was reputed to be the murderer of King Poros, and had been the commander of Eumenes' elephants, was executed. Any one of these qualities could have earned him the hatred of others, and he was clearly an unpleasant fellow to have close by, treacherous and powerful. No-one seems to have been either surprised or sorry at his death [35].

Antigonos returned to his Median winter quarters, placing his troops mainly in the area of Rhagai [36]. This was the strategic key to Media, and gave Antigonos the option of moving east or west, and especially gave the appearance of a threat to the satrapies further east. Presumably the formerly-allied satraps also went to winter-quarters, each to his own satrapy, perhaps as a move to avoid seeming to threaten Antigonos. Their alliance had been effectively shattered at the Gabiene fight, and most did not co-operate again.

During the winter Peithon's suppressed ambitions reappeared. He had been a valued and valuable commander under Antigonos, and it was in his satrapy that Antigonos now wintered. But Peithon intrigued to seduce parts of Antigonos' army from its allegiance. He had powerful cards, for the old royal treasure at Ekbatana was under his control, and Antigonos' winter quarters at Rhagai were well away from that city. But, just as Eudamos had been treacherous too frequently, so Peithon had intrigued too often. Antigonos had no difficulty in luring him into his grasp by putting out a rumour that he intended to make him general of the upper satrapies, a position Peithon had claimed before. Once in Antigonos' headquarters, a council of officers obediently sentenced him to death, and the sentence was carried out at once [37].

Peithon and Eudamos and Antigenes had all been satraps as well as commanders and faithless men. It was perhaps high time that someone took a strong line with such men. But Eumenes had been conspicuously faithful, and this was the characteristic for which he was remembered, even above his military ingenuity. Antigonos was credited with remorse for his death, and respect for the dead, and he must have known that his reputation would suffer from the killing of Eumenes. The word was spread that 'the Macedonians' had clamoured for his death, and this may be the origin of the later emphasis on Eumenes as a Greek, an emphasis which has rung all too true to nineteenth- and twentieth-century ears. But which Macedonians? And when did Antigonos ever pay attention to the clamour of any of his soldiers? If any soldiers were consulted it was, as in the case of Peithon, a council of officers. In Peithon's case these men could be counted on to condemn him, for it was their own men whose loyalties he had been tampering with. The story of 'the Macedonians' demanding Eumenes' death is propaganda, put out no doubt by Hieronymos of Kardia, who was captured in the Gabiene battle, and earned his reprieve by putting his pen to the service of Antigonos, the killer of his fellow citizen. The execution of Eumenes was necessary to Antigonos as an act of state; the fact that it would hurt his reputation was of less consequence than that it would increase his power. In particular it was clearly designed to impress the local satraps. This it did.

All resistance to Antigonos now ceased. He marched to Persepolis, where he deposed Peukestas, who had become locally too powerful for Antigonos' peace of mind. He had provided the largest eastern contingent in the allies' forces, largely of local Persian recruitment. This independent power base clearly made him dangerous. Peukestas was not helped by a Persian (called Thespios by Diodoros) who stood up and proclaimed his loyalty to the satrap. This was precisely the problem from Antigonos' point of view. Thespios was instantly murdered, Peukestas was removed from power, and a new satrap with an 'adequate' force of troops was installed in

Persis — adequate, that is, to control Persis without local recruitment [38].

Peukestas had clearly governed his satrapy well, but he had always been ill-at-ease in the society of his Macedonian fellows. He was one of the very few Macedonians ever to rise from among the common people to a position of power. This was largely due to his bravery, and to the favour of Alexander. But among the Macedonian nobles who provided the corps of satraps, he was liable to dither. Antigonos really had nothing to worry about. He could have left Peukestas in safety in his satrapy, and Peukestas would have been quiet and loyal. But Antigonos needed to make an example of someone. Thespios' death would suffice as a warning to the Persians; Peukestas had to go as a warning to the other satraps. He was the obvious victim, not because he was non-noble, but because he was militarily the most powerful of the satraps. Excuses could be found for the elimination of the other satraps — faithlessness, rebellion, intrigue — but Antigonos had to demonstrate his power over these satraps of the east who had so nearly beaten him in battle, and who had joined Eumenes because Eumenes was the representative of the king. They could have argued that he owed his victory to their withdrawal from the Gabiene battle, and that would never do. So Peukestas was deposed, though, for a mercy, not executed. That would have been going too far, and Antigonos knew it. Without office, and away from Persis, Peukestas was a danger to no-one. He could be allowed to live. From all points of view, the removal of Peukestas served Antigonos excellently.

He also thereupon dealt with the rest of the east. At bottom Antigonos was no more interested in the east than Antipatros had been. All he required of it was that it should be quiet, that the satraps govern, so that he could concentrate on the west. Hence he went no further east than Persepolis. He sent for only one of the satraps who were actually in post, Sibyrtios, whose merit was that he had quarrelled with Eumenes and deserted him before the great battles. The fact that at the time Sibyrtios had left his troops behind to continue fighting in Eumenes' army was carefully ignored. Sibyrtios was welcomed, confirmed in office in Arachosia, and given the poisoned chalice of a sizeable detachment of the Argyraspides, with instructions to use them up in penny packets. Antigonos, sensibly enough, wanted nothing more to do with those turbulent geriatrics [39].

Also confirmed in office, without actually meeting Antigonos, were Stasanor of Baktria and Oxyartes of the Paropamisadai, neither of whom had joined Eumenes in person, though both had sent soldiers to fight with him. Both are said by Diodoros, and so probably originally by Hieronymos, to have been too powerful to remove without a major campaign. This may be true, though not judging by the size of their contingents with Eumenes. The real problem for Antigonos was not their strength but the distance, and the sheer irrelevance, to him, of removing them. Tlepolemos was also confirmed as satrap of Karmania, and he had been present in person at both battles. There is no mention of Stasandros of Aria, but a new satrap was appointed, Evitos, who soon died, to be replaced by Evagoras. This last name is very suggestive, for it is above all a name connected with Cyprus. Stasandros and Stasanor were both from Soli in that island, possibly brothers, certainly related. Speculation suggests that Stasandros had died – there is no mention of an execution – and had been replaced by another relative in Evagoras [40]. Further speculation, without any foundation, leads to the thought that the appointment of three Cypriots to the one satrapy should indicate something about the satrapy, possibly that it had been settled by a contingent of Cypriot mercenaries. But this is to pile a possibility on top of two speculations, and one must not do that. Yet a few inscriptions from Areian cities might prove to be very interesting.

The matter of the origins of these satraps would be unimportant, but for the fact that two other of Antigonos' appointments are interesting for the same reason. In Media, a rich satrapy capable of producing large numbers of troops (Peithon had raised 2,500 horses in a few days), the satrap appointed to succeed Peithon was a Mede, Orontobates. He was given an infantry commander, Hippostratos, who had 3,500 mercenaries under his command, but it appears that Orontobates was to command the local cavalry. These two worked well together and suppressed a rising of two of Peithon's old officers who had collected a force of unattached troops to dispute control of the satrapy [41].

The second appointment was to Susiana. Antigonos

marched from Persepolis towards Susa, and was met at the crossing of the Pasitigris by none other than Xenophilos, now operating as Seleukos' deputy. Carefully keeping Xenophilos with him, just in case, Antigonos occupied the citadel from which Xenophilos had defied him the year before, and happily counted the money he thereby acquired. It came to 15,000 talents worth of art objects, 5,000 talents in coin and crowns to add to the 5,000 talents of silver he had collected from Ekbatana after removing Peithon. Enough, he must have thought, to finance the conquest of the west. He had it all packed in wagons and on camels for transport westwards. As he left he appointed a new satrap, Aspisas, a native of the satrapy [42]. In his new appointments Antigonos looks to be pursuing a deliberate policy [43].

He moved on to Babylon. Seleukos had not been present in Susiana, but he cannot have been surprised to hear that a satrap had been appointed to replace him there. The appointment of Aspisas was not in any way a threat to Seleukos, whose own appointment to Susiana had been a wartime measure. Similarly there was no reason to believe that Antigonos' earlier actions in replacing and confirming satraps contained anything ominous for him.

At Babylon, the returning victors were feasted by Seleukos, and Antigonos was presented with costly gifts; Seleukos was clearly trying to ingratiate himself. To no avail. Antigonos' suspicions had been aroused. Appian reports that Seleukos punished a subordinate governor without consulting Antigonos, who was annoyed, and who then demanded that Seleukos present his accounts for inspection [44]. Diodoros simply has Antigonos suddenly demanding an accounting [45]. If the story of Antigonos' interference in Seleukos' administration is correct, then he was obviously doing so in order to weaken Seleukos' authority, for in effect he was encouraging Seleukos' subordinates to look to him, Antigonos, in the event of a dispute. Perhaps this happened; perhaps not. If Antigonos went straight to a demand for a view of Seleukos' accounts, it amounted to the same thing, for this implied that Antigonos had a right to approve of the way in which Seleukos disposed of the revenues of the rich province of Babylonia. Not very courteous behaviour after a slap-up feast.

Seleukos took the point at once. His reply, according to

Diodoros, was that he had been appointed satrap by 'the Macedonians', by which he meant the assembly at Triparadisos, that is, the council of senior officers who had met there and who had appointed Antipatros to be *epimeletes*. It will not have escaped those listening that Antigonos owed his authority to that very same meeting. Indeed some of those present will have witnessed the scene where Antigonos and Seleukos together leapt on the dais to protect Antipatros from the wrath of the aroused and wage-less soldiery. Seleukos, however, went further. He claimed that the satrapy had been given him in recognition of his services under Alexander. This was truly one-upmanship, for everyone knew that Antigonos had remained in the west as satrap of Phrygia during Alexander's great expedition. Seleukos was in effect declaring his effective independence of Antigonos' authority, by appealing not just to 'the Macedonians', but to service under Alexander; by implication he was challenging the legality of Antigonos' deposition of Peukestas and even his execution of Peithon and other satraps. Seleukos was adopting the political stance of the defeated eastern satraps, though it was rather late in the game for that.

It seems doubtful that all this was said at once. Diodoros says that the argument went on for several days, and Seleukos' reference to Alexander, since it was both an insult to Antigonos and unanswerable nonsense, has all the hallmarks of a statement made in anger, or, more likely, of a final statement designed to force Antigonos into some act which Seleukos could then claim to be illegal.

If this is so, Seleukos was also ready. With an escort of fifty cavalry, he rode out of Babylon northwards, through Mesopotamia and Syria and into Ptolemy's lands, which he would have reached in mid-Syria. Antigonos is said to have been warned by some 'Chaldaean astrologers' that to let Seleukos escape would mean eventual disaster to himself. Antigonos hardly needed such a warning; if it really happened, it might be a sign that there were opponents of Seleukos among the Babylonian priesthood [46].

There remains the problem of why Antigonos should have picked a quarrel with Seleukos just at that time. He had really nothing to fear from the Babylonian satrap, who had few troops at his disposal. He was rich, no doubt, and he may well have dipped his hands into the treasure at Susa while he was satrap there. (Maybe this is one origin of the rather odd demand for a rendering of accounts.) Seleukos had just proved his ability to swing with the tide in a disturbingly survivalist way, but that was no problem for the winner Antigonos. So why bother chasing Seleukos out? It may be, of course, as one reading of Diodoros suggests, that this was a quarrel which built up from very little and grew because two proud Macedonian noblemen simply would not agree with each other. But both were politicians and did not quarrel without good political reasons, which meant that it was Antigonos' decision to force a quarrel, since Seleukos had nothing to gain.

It is a political quarrel, then, and so something in the political situation called it forth. Our sources will not necessarily explain this background. Diodoros, in particular, used a method which divides events into geographical areas, each dealt with in turn over short periods of time, usually a year. In the section before the dispute at Babylon, he covered the events in Greece which had resulted in the deaths of King Philip Arrhidaios, his queen Eurydike, and old Olympias, the widow of Philip II, and had left the boy-king Alexander IV and his mother Roxane, Alexander the Great's widow, in the hands of Kassandros, and Kassandros in control of Macedon and most of Greece. Diodoros had no need to repeat all this. His readers had seen it for themselves. What is in question is whether Antigonos and Seleukos knew of these events. The Babylonian chronicler didn't know of the death of King Philip, which occurred in October of 317, and he recorded the start of Philip's eighth year in March of 316 [47]. Nor was he alone in this, for there are other documents in Babylonian cuneiform which suggest that Philip's death was not publicly known in Uruk until after Seleukos' flight [48].

This is not to say that Antigonos was equally ignorant. If anyone in Babylonia knew, he did. Kassandros and he were allies, fighting against those – Polyperchon and Eumenes – who were acting in the name of King Philip. The king's death would cancel that authority. But Kassandros did not get control of the persons of Alexander IV and Roxane until he took Pydna, though he had them and Olympias penned up in the city and under siege for a year [49]. Olympias had proved in the past how dangerous she was, and how she could break up a coalition by bribing or encouraging a single member to pursue his own interests. I suggest that it was the news that Philip was dead and Olympias incommunicado which stimulated Antigonos to act against Seleukos as he did. If Olympias, holding Alexander IV, got free, she could use that authority against Antigonos, and Seleukos was an obvious target for her wiles, as were the other eastern satraps, former allies of her protégé Eumenes. If Kassandros captured Pydna and Alexander IV he held the whip hand, and could easily turn from an ally into an enemy. But for a time there was a gap. No inconvenient orders could come in the name of Philip or Alexander or Olympias. Antigonos could use this gap to clear up the east finally by removing the only man close enough to both eastern and western satrapies to have an influence on both. By installing his own man in Babylonia, Antigonos knew he had nothing to worry about in the east. He would then have his own men in Babylonia, Media, Susiana, and Persis, a solid block of territory which could cut off the disaffected farther eastern satraps from any problem in the west. The situation of the year before when Eumenes could join with the allied satraps would be unrepeatable. So Seleukos was chivvied out. Probably Antigonos did not intend Seleukos to escape in such a spectacular fashion, though he could scarcely expect another tame submission like that of Peukestas. Hence the attempt to put Seleukos in the wrong, and hence the deliberate loud-voiced appeal to Macedonian public opinion which Seleukos subsequently made.

Antigonos vented his annoyance by dismissing the satrap of Mesopotamia, one Blitor, who thus appears in history only at the moment of his disappearance – when was *he* appointed? – and then marched to Kilikia, where, as a consolation prize, he laid his hands on yet another royal treasure, another 10,000 talents [50]. Meanwhile Seleukos was telling his story to Ptolemy.

4
ADMIRAL AND SATRAP (315–312)

Seleukos reached Ptolemy's territory somewhere in Syria, and went on from there to Egypt. It is a commentary on our sources that, despite the fact that Seleukos was well known, even notorious, for being the only Macedonian officer to have kept the wife married to him at the great ceremony at Susa, no source considers it worth mentioning what happened to her, or their son. Diodoros does mention Seleukos' escort of fifty troopers, and the whole affair is made to seem very sudden, almost spontaneous [1]. In fact, it was carefully planned by Seleukos, since the final argument was deliberately brought to a head by him, and the escort was ready, so it must be assumed that he had arranged for Apama and Antiochos to set off earlier, or he took them with him. A number of people who were in Seleukos' employ are said to have been released when he returned to Babylon four years later [2], but his wife and children are not mentioned. Since Seleukos professed to fear the fate of Peithon, he could hardly leave his family to the tender mercies of Antigonos. So it is best to assume that they accompanied him, or were sent off earlier.

In Egypt, Seleukos' tale was that he feared the fate of Peithon, that is, execution after a rapid and private trial by Antigonos' own officers. By implication he claimed that such a proceeding would be illegal. He expanded on this, adding in Peukestas' fate and claimed to see evidence in these cases that Antigonos had a special animus against those who had served with Alexander. This was delicate ground, for one of the people he and Ptolemy would need to convince was Kassandros, who not only had not served with Alexander but was reputed to hate his very memory. And Kassandros was also, at present, Antigonos' ally. So the story was expanded still further. Peithon, Peukestas, and Seleukos had all, it was said, performed great services out of friendship. The implication here was that these services were performed for Antigonos, and that they had been waiting patiently and trustfully for their rightful rewards, when Antigonos executed or deposed them [3].

This was, of course, nonsense. Peukestas had never performed any services for Antigonos, indeed he had opposed him to the end – unless his withdrawal from the Gabiene battle meant that Peukestas was acting as Antigonos' man. Hardly a creditable event, if so. The whole story, however, relied on the fact that the precise course of events in the east was little known in the west. The battles had taken place in winter, deep in Iran; no doubt the overall results were known quickly enough, but hardly much in the way of detail. The deaths of Eumenes and then Peithon and perhaps the deposition of Peukestas were probably known, but perhaps neither the reasons nor the processes. It would be natural for people in Greece to think in terms of them being killed in battle. Seleukos was concerned to alert people to the danger which was now posed by Antigonos, and the very fact that he had to do this presupposes a lack of detailed knowledge of the winter events on their part. His purpose was best served by relating carefully selected details, so that the whole story became essentially a propaganda version.

Kassandros and Lysimachos would scarcely be roused by the news of the fates of either Peithon or Peukestas, but that of Seleukos was more disturbing. He, like Lysimachos and Antigonos, had been appointed during the last distribution of satrapies at Triparadisos. This was perhaps the last event which could be regarded as a legal enactment of a united Macedonian government. If Seleukos was to be held accountable to Antigonos, then so was Lysimachos. As for Kassandros, he did not even have the fig-leaf of the Triparadisos act to cover his naked usurpation of power. He had acquired power by fighting and beating the man appointed as *epimeletes* by the previous regent [4]. If Antigonos should turn on him, Kassandros would likely have little support, and Seleukos' story made it seem very likely that Antigonos would turn on him.

Yet quite probably none of these men paid much heed to

such stories, beyond a generalized sympathy for Seleukos which would have been of no use at all to him. These were men of power, who respected only power, and whose touchstone was possession of power. Seleukos was, as his very presence in Egypt showed, powerless. What electrified them into alliance with Ptolemy against their former ally Antigonos was the news that Antigonos was now possessed of a formidable new power. Friends of Seleukos – presumably those cavalry troopers who had escorted him to Syria and who now begin to look increasingly like a carefully selected group of diplomatic agents – were sent to the Aegean to spread the news [5]. Antigonos, they reported, was returning westwards surrounded by huge armies and carrying immense quantities of treasure.

Soldiers and silver. These were the measures of power at the time. Antigonos had recruited large numbers of Eumenes' soldiers who had willingly re-enlisted once Eumenes was captured and dead. He will have also recruited any stray soldiers in the east – such as those with whom Orontobates had had trouble with in Media [6]. But above all, Antigonos had the Persian silver. It had not perhaps been realized in the west just how immense this treasure was, nor perhaps had it been appreciated that Antigonos would be able to lay hands on it. Even Antigonos seems surprised. Diodoros quotes some figures which suggest that Antigonos got someone to make an inventory. It was calculated that Antigonos' lands would produce an annual revenue of 11,000 talents, upon a base of 25,000 brought from the east and with the 10,000 he appropriated at the treasury of Kyinda in Kilikia [7]. These were quantities far beyond those of Kleomenes or of Harpalos. Even Ptolemy could not deal in those terms from Egypt's resources.

So Seleukos' friends went off to alert Kassandros and Lysimachos. Antigonos, meanwhile, when he had digested the implications of Seleukos' flight from Babylon, also sent out his messengers, emphasizing the need to continue the alliance [8]. He could scarcely do anything else, but he could certainly have done more. A redistribution of satrapies was one possibility, and a division of the loot was another. He offered neither. This gave the deprived allies their opening. While Antigonos, having replaced Seleukos in Babylon by Peithon, son of Agenor, was making his slow way westwards, encumbered by his camel train and his laden wagons carrying the treasures of the east [9], the resentful and fearful four co-ordinated their responses. They worked quickly, which suggests that Seleukos and Ptolemy had sent Seleukos' friends off with more than just warnings and tales, but also with concrete proposals for an alliance.

Antigonos met envoys of the four conspirators when he reached northern Syria. This was in October, most likely, since we know he was in Kilikia 'after the setting of Orion', in November [10]. It seems that he intended to collect the treasury at Kyinda first, then cross into Asia Minor, and there overwhelm Lysimachos and Kassandros with his power, adding Macedon and Thrace to his lands, before moving against Ptolemy. Instead he was presented with an unexpected ultimatum before he reached the Taurus. At once Ptolemy began to seem the more menacing and perhaps at the same time the more vulnerable of the conspirators. So Antigonos stopped in Kilikia, then moved back to winter in Syria and prepared to deal with Ptolemy first [11].

The ultimatum he was given was designed to be rejected, but it was not without its own logic, and deserves some consideration for itself, rather than the swift enumeration and dismissal it generally gets [12]. Since Antigonos had not offered lands or loot, the allies demanded them in such a way that, if he agreed, Antigonos would be ruined. His lands in Asia Minor were to be dismantled for the benefit of Lysimachos and Kassandros. Lysimachos' satrapy of Thrace was to be joined by Hellespontine Phrygia to make a solid block of territory straddling the Straits. Kassandros' control of Macedon was to be expanded across the Aegean, to Lykia and Kappadokia. This would encircle Antigonos' main base in Phrygia in the same way that Antipatros had designed after Triparadisos. Indeed the Triparadisos settlement was clearly the basis of the allies' demands.

It was the same with the east. Seleukos was to be allowed to return to Babylon, of course, and 'the rest of Syria' was to go to Ptolemy. Ptolemy already controlled Phoenicia and Palestine, so 'the rest of Syria' meant that he would expand his control north to the Taurus and the Euphrates. Thus Ptolemy and Seleukos together would neatly slice Antigonos' territories in half, separating Kilikia from the eastern lands. Thus the satraps of the Iranian lands would cease to be Antigonos' men, and would resume their earlier status. And, of course, the treasures which Antigonos had collected after the battles with Eumenes, that is the Susa and Ekbatana and Kyinda treasures, 35,000 talents, were to be divided among all the five.

Antigonos' rejection of all this will have been automatic, and probably angry, and his reply was effectively a declaration of war [13]. The timing was important, for the winter was now available to the allies for preparation. Antigonos had thus lost the first round, and it was all due to Seleukos' escape and his subsequent busy diplomacy. If he had not escaped, if he had been kept in Babylon, or like Peukestas had remained under Antigonos' thumb, Antigonos could well have arrived in western Asia Minor before the others were able to make any serious preparations to resist him. Lysimachos, for one, in Thrace, could scarcely have resisted at all. Once Antigonos was established in Thrace, Kassandros' position in Macedon, facing Antigonos' Macedonian veterans returning home at last, would have been wholly untenable. And without the distraction of war in Europe, Ptolemy would hardly have survived.

Instead Seleukos' messages had roused the westerners and Ptolemy was able to prepare. All of them spent the winter arming [14], and so Antigonos' huge strength was much less overwhelming by the spring than it had been in the autumn. In addition, the existence of the alliance compelled him to divide his forces. Kassandros attempted to rouse Kappadokia, perhaps by appealing to memories of Eumenes, more likely by appealing to memories of the Persian satraps defeated earlier by Antigonos. He also economically sent a general who laid siege to Amisos, on the Black Sea coast, and also threatened to invade Asia Minor across the Bosporos, presumably in concert with Lysimachos. So Antigonos had to send an army north and then west to deal with all this. The commander of this force was Antigonos' nephew Ptolemaios, and his final instructions demonstrate that this move was primarily defensive, despite its great geographical extent, for he was to camp at the Hellespont to deter Kassandros' invasion. Thus one major portion of Antigonos' strength was detached [15].

A more economic use of his resources was to send Artemidoros of Miletos, one of his followers, to the Peloponnese with 1,000 talents. This highly successful move distracted Kassandros' attention for over a year [16]. An even better move was to send another man, Agesilaos, to Cyprus. Several of the city-kings in that island, Nikokreon of Paphos, Pasikrates of Soli, and Androkles of Amathos, had been allies of Ptolemy since the crisis with Perdikkas [17], but Antigonos had been in the island at that time as well [18], and his contacts had clearly survived. The allies of Ptolemy effectively dominated the island, and the other kings no doubt were apprehensive. This provided Agesilaos with his entrée. In short order he collected the alliances of Praxippos of Lapethos, Stasikarenos II of Marion, Pumiathon of Kition, and the king at Kerynia (perhaps called Themison). Of these only Pumiathon had any serious pretensions to much power, and he, as a Phoenician, had been victimized by the rest in the past. But control was not Antigonos' purpose, at least not yet. His envoy's success was to be measured by the disruption caused to Ptolemy's alliance, a good investment by Antigonos [19].

Antigonos' own move was against Ptolemy directly. He marched south into Ptolemy's area of Syria, masked Tyre with a detachment, and then cleared Ptolemy's garrisons out of Palestine, replacing them with his own. But his main objective was ship-building. He aimed at a fleet of 500 ships, organizing a large labour force to cut wood, and concentrating on four shipyards: at Sidon, Byblos, and Tripolis in Phoenicia and one in Kilikia. He did not build anywhere near 500 ships, so, unless this is just a Diodoran guess, the number is likely to be an inspired rumour, designed to strike terror into the hearts of his enemies, and awe into the hearts of his followers [20].

The siege of Tyre was a minor matter in comparison with the building of the ships, but it served to keep his troops occupied until the ships were ready. This explains the length of the siege, a year and a quarter. One cannot expect a fleet of new ships – whatever the intended number – to be built in much less than that length of time. It also demonstrates that the siege was relatively unimportant: Antigonos' purpose was to acquire a naval capability which he had not possessed earlier.

To a potential fleet and a foothold on Cyprus was added an

alliance with Rhodes. The city agreed also to build ships for Antigonos from timber which he would supply [21]. This alliance with Rhodes was a key to the whole campaign. If the island was hostile to Antigonos it could effectively interrupt his quickest communication route between the Aegean, that is, Artemidoros in the Peloponnese and Ptolemaios on the Hellespont, and Antigonos himself in Palestine. By contrast, if it was friendly, Rhodes could equally well interrupt the allies' communications. So the alliance was a notable *coup* for Antigonos [22].

Ptolemy was the only ally who could reply, since he was the only one with a fleet. In addition, he was the one who was directly threatened and he fully appreciated the value of distractions. He sent a fleet of a hundred ships on a cruise to the Aegean, and put Seleukos in command [23]. This cruise and the size of the fleet were designed with definite purposes in mind, one of which was Rhodes. A hundred ships was too big a fleet for Rhodes to tackle alone, yet it was no real threat to a city as relatively powerful as Rhodes. It was a convincing demonstration of the potency and reach of Ptolemy's power, and it successfully attracted into the alliance the satrap of Karia, Asandros.

This was Seleukos' doing. He sailed ostentatiously along the Phoenician coast, demoralizing by his very presence the workmen and soldiers who were busy producing Antigonos' ships and besieging the city of Tyre [24]. He will have called at Cyprus, thereby encouraging the allies of Ptolemy, who held the predominant power in the island. At some point Ptolemy sent a reinforcement of 3,000 soldiers to the island [25]; possibly Seleukos was the delivering agent. His route was then along the south coast of Asia Minor, past Rhodes and Karia, and it is likely that contact with Asandros was made then. As a demonstration Seleukos sailed into the Aegean, landed at Erythrai, and laid siege to the city [26]. Why Erythrai in particular is not clear; possibly it was merely a display of the usefulness of sea power, quite likely it gave Seleukos' men something to do while he pursued the negotiations with Asandros. It is also possible that the siege was designed to do exactly what it did do: attract the attention of Antigonos' military nephew Ptolemaios, who having relieved Amisos, was guarding the Hellespont against a possible invasion from Europe by

Kassandros or Lysimachos. Seleukos' siege brought Ptolemaios down to relieve the city, and then to attack the defecting Asandros [27]. The Hellespont was thus, at least to some extent, open for an invasion from the west. But Kassandros was busy in Greece, dealing with Aristodemos, whose 1,000 talents had quickly conjured up a mercenary force of 8,000 men, with which he was making a good show in the Peloponnese [28].

Seleukos took the fleet back to Cyprus. This suggests very strongly that the Erythrai venture was merely a distraction, that the demonstration voyage was now over and everyone from Tyre to the Hellespont had been duly impressed. Now the real business was about to begin.

Ptolemy had sent a further armed force to Cyprus to reinforce his initial 3,000 men and the armies of his Cypriot allies. When Seleukos returned to Cyprus from Erythrai, he was soon joined by a further hundred ships from Egypt commanded by Polykleitos, who brought 10,000 soldiers under the mercenary captain Myrmidon of Athens. There also arrived Ptolemy's brother Menelaos, as commander of the whole force [29]. Seleukos commanded two hundred ships, and Menelaos had up to 20,000 men in his army. This was a formidable force, strategically placed between Antigonos and his western forces, and so stationed as to exert a major threat to the whole coast from Karia to Tyre.

Meanwhile Antigonos had made a major political move at Tyre. His envoy in Greece, Aristodemos of Miletos, having recruited his mercenary army so as to give his words clout, had contacted Polyperchon, who had been appointed *epimeletes* by Antipatros just before the latter's death. Since he had commissioned Eumenes to act for him in the east, in 318, Polyperchon's fortunes had steadily sunk, and he was now a refugee in Aitolia; his son Alexander, however, held a few places in the Peloponnese. The breach between Antigonos and Kassandros was to their advantage, and Aristodemos signed them up for Antigonos [30]. Alexander went over to Tyre, mainly, it appears, to collect his fee, 500 talents. He also, or rather his father, had a less tangible contribution to make to the alliance. One of Polyperchon's moves against Kassandros had been to announce that he regarded the Greek cities as now free [31]. It had never been more than a propaganda ploy, but it had its uses in that area. And now Antigonos was able to use

Alexander's presence at Tyre to annex the ploy for his own use.

He adopted the method which had become a pseudo-legal means of promulgating policy and personnel changes since the death of the great Alexander. He called a meeting of the Macedonians at Tyre, the vast majority of whom were his own soldiers. To them he made a series of complaints about the conduct of Kassandros. The crowd dutifully cheered. Antigonos then demanded the release of Roxane and the child-king Alexander IV and claimed the position of *epimeletes* for himself. Further cheers. Finally he declared that the Greek cities should be free and without foreign garrisons. Attention has usually been directed at this last point, but it was clearly the least important, especially when the earlier points are considered, one of which demanded the re-destruction of Thebes, which had recently been founded anew by Kassandros [32]. It was an exercise in propaganda, not a serious programme to be put into effect. The really important part was Antigonos' claim to be *epimeletes*, an office which implied the possession of the persons of Roxane and Alexander IV. The cheers which dutifully greeted all this were Antigonos' ratification. The fact that he made the claim meant that he was claiming the power and authority originally wielded by Antipatros and Perdikkas. And that meant that he also claimed the power to depose his rivals. It was, therefore, a ratification also of his eastern settlement [33].

It may well have been accompanied by propaganda of a different sort. One of the media of propaganda used by all three competitors was the anecdote, featuring some event which redounded to the credit or discredit of one or more of the men involved in the struggle for power. Seleukos was perhaps the master at this game, but he had earlier teachers, of whom Antigonos was one. The central figure in the coalition against Antigonos was in fact Seleukos, who, though overshadowed by the others in power and resources, was the one who held the others together. A story was floated, probably at this time, which was designed to denigrate him and to reduce the persuasive powers he evidently possessed. It was the story of the vigil in the temple at Babylon.

This is contentious ground. The story has been taken to be true by later historians and Arrian and Plutarch relate it in its chronological setting, on the night before the death of Alexander [34]. Yet, as so often with propaganda, a single detail has caused disquiet among modern historians – the vigil is said to have taken place in the Sarapis temple at Babylon. There was no Sarapis temple there in 323, for the very good reason that the cult of Sarapis did not get developed until later. Ptolemy I invented it some years after 323 as a transparent attempt to provide a divine sanction for his rule in Egypt [35].

If one takes the reference to Sarapis in the story, however, to be an analogy, whereby Seleukos has gone to Ptolemy (i.e., Ptolemy = Sarapis) then the Sarapis reference is explained. Some attention can now be directed at the companions Seleukos is said to have had with him in the temple, a factor not yet taken account of by any other student. They are a very strange, heterogeneous bunch of men, but some tentative conclusions as to their common characteristics can be reached. One group – Peithon, Menidas, Peukestas, Attalos, and Seleukos himself – had all recently been enemies of Antigonos. Another permutation produces Seleukos and Peithon as murderers of Perdikkas, their lord. Kleomenes was the name of the notorious satrap of Egypt during Alexander's expedition, whose greatest exploit was to manipulate the corn market in a time of famine to produce a huge fortune for himself. Menidas was one of the murderers of Parmenio, a mercenary associated with Peithon, willing to take on any task so long as he was paid. Demophon was a seer who had been involved in subversion of Alexander's army in Egypt; Attalos was Perdikkas' brother-in-law, who had attempted to subvert the army at the time of the Triparadisos meeting. As a group therefore they emerge as untrustworthy, even treacherous and subversive. (For details of these men, see the Appendix.)

The story is clearly directed at those who have heard of the scandalous exploits of Alexander, those whose knowledge of recent events is based on anecdote, rather than detailed analysis, particularly since it seems that the story of Alexander's campaigns and adventures was only just beginning to be retailed as a complete entity. At first it was the exotic adventures which were told, and the most violent events – largely, it seems, in the words of Kallisthenes, the executed Greek philosopher [36]. The main target for these stories was the Greek reading public. In the temple-vigil story it was, for example, the Greeks who were likely to be annoyed by Kleomenes, and so he was included, even though he had never been at Babylon, and a moment's thought would have shown this. The Macedonians are also the target for the story, since Menidas, the murderer of Parmenio, is included. There are so many of these details that it is clear that the story is invented, though it may well have a factual basis or origin. The date of the invention must be at some point where it will discredit Seleukos with both Greeks and Macedonians, that is, in the year or so after his flight to Egypt, the land of Sarapis. It would have been circulating in Greece when Seleukos was commanding Ptolemy's fleet and attacking the Greek city of Erythrai. As a guess, the man who circulated the story might be Artemidoros in the Peloponnese.

This was by no means the only such story which circulated [37]. At least ten others have been recognized concerning Seleukos alone. Another, embroidering on events surrounding Alexander's death, survives as a pamphlet [38]. Other stories accused Kassandros' family of being the murderers of Alexander [39]. This was clearly the favoured method of political propaganda at the time, inevitably so when no clear principles separated the various contenders for power, and so personal denigration was likely to be the most effective weapon. In a way Antigonos' proclamation of Greek civic freedom was a serious attempt to move the level of political dispute out of the slough of invective to the hill of principle. But few bothered to follow him – though Ptolemy also proclaimed Greek freedom [40] – because all knew full well that Antigonos would swiftly reveal that his new-found enthusiasm for Greek freedom. would be tempered by personal ambition at the first obstacle

Antigonos – if it was he who saw to the dissemination of the temple-vigil story – was therefore making a variety of appeals to a variety of audiences by several methods. He was denigrating Seleukos. He was condemning Kassandros for being cruel to the family of Alexander. He was claiming the position of royal protector, as the man with the right to raise the boy Alexander. By implication he was stating that he would hand over to the king a united empire, when the boy was fully grown. This was to be at some time in the fairly distant future, but the inference was clear enough. He was harking back to the days of unity by his use of Macedonian assembly, with its echoes of similar meetings in the last years of Alexander and under Antipatros. He was appealing to the Greeks by adopting Polyperchon's slogan of freedom for the Greek cities. But let there be no mistake about all this activity. It was propaganda, not a programme he expected to be implemented. Antigonos had no serious hope of acquiring control over the upbringing of Alexander IV, since Kassandros would not give him up. Antigonos had no real intention of freeing Greek cities, but at that moment it was a useful stick with which to beat his enemies. And so on. The one tangible result of the meeting at Tyre was an alliance with Alexander, son of Polyperchon, who took his 500 talents with him to continue the war against Kassandros in Greece.

In Cyprus the gathering of the Ptolemaic forces led to a conference on what to do with the force now assembled. The arrival and presence of Ptolemy's brother Menelaos is a sign that Ptolemy himself had sent instructions, but what these were precisely is not known. It seems reasonable to assume that what the conference did broadly followed what Ptolemy wanted it to do, though Diodoros states that it was the conference of commanders which made the precise distribution of forces [41]. This is perfectly credible.

There were two overriding necessities: to support allies and to secure Cyprus. So some of the force had to be kept on the island to eliminate the allies which Antigonos' agent Agesilaos had collected. Asandros of Karia, under attack by Antigonos' nephew Ptolemaios, had also to be assisted. Asandros was the most urgent problem, so the land commander Myrmidon of Athens was sent there with a force of mercenaries [42]. How large this force was is unclear. Ptolemy had sent 10,000 soldiers with Menelaos and had earlier sent 3,000 to add to whatever troops were on the island already. Myrmidon will have had several thousand soldiers, since anything less would have been pointless.

Fifty of the ships were sent under the command of Polykleitos to the Peloponnese, to help against the combination of Alexander, Artemidoros, and the Aitolians [43]. This left Seleukos in command of the ships at Cyprus, probably his original 100, for Myrmidon's soldiers will have required transport to Karia. The remaining soldiers were also placed under Seleukos' command in order to sort out the Cyprus problem.

What Menelaos did is unclear, possibly he was henceforth the governor of the island, leaving the fighting to Seleukos, who would thus acquire the odium pertaining to a conqueror and then sail off, leaving Menelaos with clean hands to rule the island.

This was the first time, so far as we know, that Seleukos had a large force under his personal command with which to wage war – for the siege of Erythrai was not serious. It seems likely that he had several thousand of Ptolemy's soldiers, and an equivalent number of Cypriots from the kings. Previously he had never commanded more than two or three thousand troops. Nor had he ever actually commanded an army on campaign, unless he had been active in Babylonia, with the exception of the unfought siege of Susa and Erythrai.

It is conceivable that, had Seleukos been unsuccessful in Cyprus, he would have vanished from sight as thoroughly as Myrmidon the Athenian, who is never heard of again. It was essential that Seleukos succeed if he was ever again to be more than one of Ptolemy's generals. It was also up to Seleukos to ensure Ptolemy's control of Cyprus, for it is clear that Menelaos could not do it: when he actually did undertake military operations he was always beaten.

There were two aspects of the Cypriot problem: ensuring the loyalty of Ptolemy's allies, and conquering Antigonos' allies. Of the former, the ruler of Amathos, Androkles, was compelled to give hostages for his good behaviour, but it seems that the rest were judged to be trustworthy. Of the enemy rulers, one, Stasikarenos of Marion, isolated in the north-west corner of the island and cut off by Ptolemy's allies at Paphos and Soli, was easily enrolled in Ptolemy's system by diplomacy and perhaps threats. Two other of Antigonos' allies, the ruler of Kerynia on the north coast and of Lapethos on the long north-eastern peninsula, were taken by siege, probably without much difficulty.

Kition was another matter. King Pumiathon was an old problem for the island's Greek kings, for he was a pugnacious Phoenician, and he now stood a siege with the same tenacity as his compatriots of Tyre had shown against Alexander. (Thus there were two Phoenician cities under siege at the same time, by opposing Greek armies in the eastern Mediterranean; the Phoenicians must have wondered if they could survive this further bout of Macedonian warfare.) It must be presumed that Kition was eventually captured, for when next heard of its ruler, still Pumiathon, was being arrested for intriguing with Antigonos, which means he was subject at that time to Ptolemy's overlordship. Presumably when he saw that Antigonos was not going to rescue him, Pumiathon made terms. It would be like Seleukos to wish to end the fighting on Cyprus having negotiated terms, partly because he was a man who rarely pushed his enemies to extremes, preferring to let them destroy themselves, and partly because it would release forces for other theatres of the war [44].

It would be useful at this point to know just what pressures there were from other combatant areas. Yet it is very difficult to fit events together. Diodoros' notorious chronological ambiguities are difficult enough, and modern reinterpretations of his words are only usually successful in piling complications on top of confusion. The modern insistence on precision of dating has not helped, for what is most important is to knit together the various strands into which Diodoros has sorted his events. From the point of view of this study, also, the best of the recent reconsiderations of Diodoros' chronology, that of Errington, wilfully ignores events in Cyprus [45].

It is not often recognized just how difficult a task Diodoros has, nor that his solution is a perfectly reasonable one, and one which, with variations, and amid the clatter of complaints about his incompetence, is the one normally adopted by every student of the period. It ill becomes modern students to complain about him, then repeat his mistakes, and at the same time conveniently ignore chunks of evidence provided by their victim, because those chunks do not fit their own theory. No modern student has yet produced a satisfactory account of events covering both the East and the West Mediterranean, yet at least Diodoros made the attempt.

The essential problem is not to assign precise dates to events, but to get events in the correct sequence and to establish connections between the different theatres of events. In this particular case, for example, the problem is to establish the proper connections between events at Tyre, in Cyprus, in Karia, and in the Peloponnese. Diodoros suggests that the siege of Tyre was just about over when the campaign in

Cyprus was reaching its final phase, and that the capture of Tyre by Antigonos more or less coincided with the beginning of the siege of Kition. Further, he also suggests that the end of the siege at Tyre was the beginning of the accumulation by Antigonos of the immense fleet which he had been building for the past year. This fleet included, so Diodoros says, ships captured at Tyre, and though he does not say so, the implication must be that they were captured when the starving garrison capitulated [46].

The fleet was made up of these captured Tyrian ships together with those constructed in the past year or so in Phoenicia amounting to 120 ships in all. This number was doubled by two smaller fleets which were brought from the Aegean. There were 40 ships from the Hellespont under Themison. These will have been the ships left to guard the crossing point against Lysimachos when Ptolemaios marched south to rescue Erythrai. Then there was a fleet of 80 ships formed partly of Rhodian ships and partly by a group from the Hellespont guard. This group was commanded by Antigonos' nephew Dioskorides, who perhaps had collected some from Themison at the Hellespont and called at Rhodes on the way east. Dioskorides will have needed a substantial force with him when he collected those Rhodian contract ships just in case Rhodes decided that the ships were not in fact to be handed over. Dioskorides' force brought the total in Antigonos' fleet in Phoenicia to 240, and this total included 90 quadriremes and 10 quinqueremes. Diodoros also says that there were three 'nines' and ten 'tens', but it is difficult to believe in them. Antigonos had only been building for a year and a quarter, and to design and build those huge ships would surely take longer [47].

This fleet, whether the monster ships were built or not, was larger than anything else in the eastern Mediterranean. (It was also only half the planned, or rumoured, size of 500; this was clearly much too ambitious.) Dioskorides was sent to the Aegean with it [48]. To get there he had to pass Cyprus, which is why it would be useful to know if Seleukos' siege of Kition was over or not. Seleukos had at most 170 ships available, less those detached to Karia, plus any belonging to the Cypriot kings. This was probably not enough to challenge Dioskorides, and certainly it would be difficult for Seleukos to leave the untaken Kition in his rear while tackling a superior Antigonid fleet, for he would need many of the besieging troops in the ships. At all events, Dioskorides safely reached the Aegean, where he detached 50 ships to the Peloponnese, which exactly matched the fleet sent there by Seleukos and Menelaos under Polykleitos. Dioskorides took the rest, presumably 190 ships, on a flag-showing exercise, a circuit of the Aegean. Antigonos' propaganda, faithfully reflected in Diodoros' account, depicted this as an exercise in winning support and guaranteeing safety for the various cities and islands which lay in the fleet's path. No doubt the cities and islands thus 'guaranteed' and 'persuaded' had a different perception of what was going on; but a generation of war had taught most of them to feign a welcome in preference to being destroyed.

The Ptolemaic forces had become dangerously stretched in the attempt to distract Antigonos, and the ruse had only partly worked. Antigonos with most of his army was still in Phoenicia, and now that Tyre had fallen, he was free to strike elsewhere. Polykleitos with his 50 ships was recalled from the Peloponnese. He encountered an Antigonid fleet which was accompanying a small land force along the south coast of Asia Minor. He ambushed the land force and destroyed it; then he captured the fleet, including its admiral, one Perilaos. Polykleitos was effusively congratulated on reaching Egypt, where rather more was made of this victory than it really deserved [49]. But it was a success, a Ptolemaic success, and thus it was heartening, at a time when Antigonos was clearly winning.

Another possibility now opened up. Negotiations were begun for the ransoming of Perilaos and his senior officers, and these led on to a summit meeting between Antigonos and Ptolemy to discuss an end to the war. The scene was a desolate piece of coast called Ekregma, east of the Pelusian distributary of the Nile, and thus in the no-man's-land between Ptolemy's fort at Pelusion and Antigonos' garrison at Gaza [50]. Only guesses can be made as to the content or tone of the meeting, said to be between the two men alone. Some fairly safe conjectures can be made, however. It was in the interest of Antigonos to offer generous terms, but it was never in Antigonos' nature to do this. Ptolemy's interest lay in holding to the alliance with Kassandros and Lysimachos unless the terms he was offered were so good that he would gain protection from Antigonos even if Antigonos conquered the others. It is impossible to imagine what sort of terms Antigonos could have offered which would have reassured Ptolemy in such a way. It was clearly in Ptolemy's interest to insist on the restoration of Seleukos to Babylon. This demand had the advantage of both seeming to be altruistic and requiring the destruction of Antigonos' hitherto greatest achievement, the conquest of the eastern satrapies. Thus Seleukos, no doubt to his own considerable satisfaction, would have found himself the cause of the breakdown of these incipient negotiations.

One result of this meeting may well have been to persuade Antigonos to go north. He will have seen for himself, for the first time – he had never been to Egypt before – just how difficult it would be to get an army across the desert between Gaza and Pelusion. At the same time, if Ptolemy could be lured to talks in which he at least potentially considered betraying his allies, maybe those allies could be induced to do the actual dirty on Ptolemy. But to talk to them he would have to be in the north; it was not something which could be done by anyone else. In turn this would bring him closer to one of his armies, that under Ptolemaios, and would thus allow him to finish the campaign in Karia, thereby releasing that force as a further threat to Kassandros. He would also be closer to his fleet. Antigonos must have considered the possibility of invading Egypt, and Ptolemy must have been on his guard against it. The meeting at Ekregma, had it produced peace, would have been excellent propaganda for them both, and would have made good sense as well. Its failure, which cannot have surprised anyone, paradoxically meant that the participants virtually ceased to fight each other directly.

Antigonos now sent more of his fleet to the Aegean, and took most of his troops to Asia Minor, even moving through the Taurus passes in winter [51]. In this decision, he showed poor strategic judgement, for Ptolemy was by far the more worthwhile victim. The situation in Greece and Asia Minor was not so serious that it could not have waited longer for his personal attention. There was nothing there which would alter the situation very quickly, for so many different forces and commanders were involved that none was going to be decisive. On the other hand, Egypt was surely conquerable. The Persians and Alexander had both succeeded in doing so, and Perdikkas had almost succeeded – all within the past thirty years. If Antigonos had moved south he would in all likelihood have eliminated a major threat at his rear which, when it did become active, proved to be a decisive distraction to him.

Seleukos was in the Aegean during all this, having sailed there in the wake of Dioskorides' great fleet. He was involved especially in minor actions in the vicinity of the Karian war. At one point he was appealed to by Aristoteles, a commander in Kassandros' service who was trying to recover control of Lemnos. Diodoros implies that Seleukos sailed to Lemnos, and when their attempt to take the island failed, then sailed to Kos [52]. The further implication is that Kos was Seleukos' base, conveniently placing him between Rhodes and the main Antigonid fleet, and at the same time close to Karia, where fighting was still going on. Kassandros had also sent a force across to Karia to help Asandros and the Ptolemaic army sent from Cyprus. Antigonos' nephew Ptolemaios had come down with his own force, and all these armies constantly added to the misery of the Karians. Ptolemaios had not been strong enough to succeed alone and now Antigonos intervened in person. He won Asandros back to his side and crushed the enemy forces. Then he sent Ptolemaios across the Aegean to interfere in the campaign in Greece. If Seleukos was still at Kos he had not been able to help Asandros or to prevent his defection, nor could he prevent Antigonos and Ptolemaios between them capturing – 'liberating' – the cities of Miletos, Tralles, Kaunos, and Kasios, all of which were on the coast, nor had he prevented Ptolemaios from sailing across the Aegean from Karia to Euboia with a fleet of only 30 ships [53]. It seems likely therefore that he was elsewhere.

Exactly where is not known but the best guess is that he was back in Egypt. After the Ekregma meeting, Antigonos had moved north, but not without leaving problems for Ptolemy to attend to. There was a rebellion at Kyrene about this time [54], and, as soon as Ptolemy had suppressed that, he had to sail to Cyprus, where unrest had developed amongst the kings there. These events were, no doubt, Antigonos' parting gift, and they would have been in preparation even while the talks in Ekregma were being organized. Their occurrence at the same time as an invasion of Egypt from Palestine would have been very useful; they were just as useful to Antigonos when he did not invade.

It was, not surprisingly, the Cypriot kings who had been beaten by Seleukos who were unhappy. This time, however, there was little fighting. Pumiathon of Kition was caught red-handed in negotiations with Antigonos, and was executed. His elimination was the major factor in the subsequent pacification of the island. The kings and dynasts of Lapethos, Kerynia, and Marion were all deposed, and the inhabitants of Marion were bodily removed to a new city which Ptolemy established at Neon Paphos. He then appointed Nikokreon, King of Salamis, as his viceroy for the whole island [55].

Both of these upheavals betray Antigonos' methods, but without actual armed support from him both of the revolts were distinctly half-hearted. Inevitably Antigonos' reputation for getting others to sacrifice themselves for him was growing. His ostentatious refusal to garrison cities he had 'freed' in his next campaign was, no doubt, in part a deliberate attempt to counter that reputation. Meanwhile Ptolemy had been preoccupied for only a part of the campaigning season and was able to raid northern Syria from Cyprus, sacking two of Antigonos' garrisons on the coast, and Kilikia, where he allowed his soldiers to plunder in the area around the city of Mallos, which they had captured. In behaviour towards the civilian population, there was little to choose between the two kings [56].

Antigonos' attempt to negotiate peace with Kassandros and Lysimachos failed in the same way that the attempt with Ptolemy had failed, though the fact that the talks had taken place at all showed again just how weak were the ties binding the alliance. Antigonos, as before, could not bring himself to offer terms good enough to persuade the northern allies to give up the fight [57]. By now the failure of these negotiations can have occasioned no surprise.

Antigonos became heavily involved in the fighting in Karia and Ionia and Greece, and thereby neglected his rear. Ptolemy and Seleukos, apparently jointly, planned an invasion of Syria while Antigonos was busy in the north. To some extent Antigonos had not been negligent, for he had left substantial forces in Syria, had fomented trouble in Ptolemy's lands to keep him busy, and had left a gang of experienced generals to advise his young son Demetrios on how to defend Syria. None of this was sufficient in the event. The distractions were only minor, and the generals were out-generalled. Antigonos has to be convicted of underestimating his opponents, both in their power and in their imagination.

Ptolemy gathered an army in Egypt and marched it across the desert to Gaza. This called for careful organization, and large numbers of Egyptians were recruited – impressed, rather – as bearers to carry the supplies. No doubt food dumps and supplies of water along the route had been prepared as well. The move did not come as a surprise to Demetrios and his mentors for the Antigonid army was waiting at Gaza to do battle. Seleukos accompanied Ptolemy, and indeed Diodoros repeatedly refers to 'Ptolemy and Seleukos' as being the commanders. But it was Ptolemy's army, and he will have been in overall command. The joint reference may well have taken the sting of defeat from Demetrios' and Antigonos' wounds, though it is perhaps more a tribute to Seleukos' later fame than to his actual authority at the time. It is worth remembering that neither of these men had been in a battle of this size since Alexander's Indian campaign, twelve or thirteen years before, while Demetrios had been in a great battle much more recently, for he had commanded cavalry in both the Paraitakene and the Gabiene battles under his father's command. And he had as advisor the satrap of Babylon, Peithon, son of Agenor, who assisted in laying out the battle line. No doubt Peithon's presence gave an added zest to Seleukos' participation.

Ptolemy had come prepared to deal with Demetrios' elephants, with an iron-tipped *cheveaux-de-frise*, and a large supply of missiles. But this entailed allowing Demetrios to dictate the disposition of forces. The army of Ptolemy was posted with the phalanx of 18,000 in the centre, and the cavalry divided equally on either wing. But Demetrios and Peithon, being heavily deficient in infantry (with a phalanx of only 11,000), massed their cavalry on their left, 3,000 strong, with 30 of their elephants, and put only 1,500 cavalry on the right, angled back defensively. Thus Ptolemy had to switch part of his own cavalry to *his* right to face Demetrios' mass, leaving only

1,000 on his left. The battle was therefore determined by the cavalry-and-elephant fight on the Ptolemaic right. Since Demetrios and Peithon had failed to disguise their intentions, the cavalry battle was between equals and was for a time indecisive. The elephants advanced, only to meet the *cheveaux-de-frise* which many of them refused to tackle; they and their mahouts were assailed by arrows, darts, and javelins in a constant hail from the well-equipped light forces posted behind the impenetrable stakes. In the end it was the elephants, many of whose mahouts were killed, who backed away, apparently towards their own cavalry, still heavily engaged with Ptolemy's horse. Diodoros does not bother mentioning if the phalanxes were engaged, but it does seem that the infantry waited until the cavalry battle was decided, perhaps because neither Ptolemy nor Demetrios had time to set them in motion.

Demetrios' cavalry left the field, his elephants were captured, and most of his infantry surrendered. Ptolemy followed up the cavalry retreat as far as Gaza, where the formation of the Antigonid horse finally broke up. Ptolemy captured Gaza in the confusion, and Demetrios finally took to his heels and headed north at speed. Having successfully outdistanced the pursuit, he then admitted defeat [58].

What part Seleukos actually played in the battle is unknown. Diodoros' use, more than once, of the phrase 'Ptolemy and Seleukos' [59] is not convincing in its suggestion of a joint control of the battle. It may, in fact, be the relic of one of Seleukos' propaganda stories which circulated later, but Ptolemy would never have allowed it. It does suggest that Seleukos was both present and prominent in the battle, which is very likely. Perhaps he was in charge of the phalanx, or of the right wing. It is, however, quite certain that Seleukos was active soon after the battle.

Peithon, son of Agenor had been killed in the battle [60]. This meant that Babylon was without a satrap, and the troops there were perhaps now uncertain of the chain of command, particularly since Demetrios was beaten and Antigonos was still in Asia Minor. At the very least Peithon's death introduced an element of uncertainty into the situation in Babylonia. It may have been this which prompted Seleukos to suggest a swift ride to Babylon with the aim of extending the war and capitalizing on the confusion [61].

That it was Seleukos' idea seems certain enough. That it was as spontaneous as our sources make it appear is a good deal less certain. The fact that Seleukos was greeted warmly by the inhabitants when he reached Babylon rather suggests that he had been preparing the ground in advance. Indeed it would have been surprising if he had not kept up his contacts in Babylon all the time. He did, after all, claim to have been wrongly deposed, and therefore he also claimed to have been the rightful satrap all along. There were people held prisoner in the citadel in Babylon because they were his supporters [62], but there is no indication as to how long they had been there. Some of them could have been caught in communication with Seleukos at any time in the past four years.

So Seleukos had in all probability prepared the ground for his return. Psychologically he was ready to go back, and was waiting for a suitable moment. Until the aftermath of the Gaza battle Syria had been full of Antigonos' troops and garrisons. It would have been most incautious to have tried to reach Babylonia through that hostile thicket of soldiers, and everything we know of Seleukos goes to suggest that caution was one of his major political characteristics, and that he only hazarded himself or his power on certainties. After Gaza, however, for a brief time, Syria was effectively without garrisons. Demetrios' retreat did not stop until he reached Tripolis, from where he sent news to his father and at the same time summoned help from troops in Kilikia. Some forces had been left in the Phoenician coastal cities, but otherwise the land was open to penetration [63].

Ptolemy marched northwards through Palestine and into southern Phoenicia without meeting opposition until he reached Tyre, where the Antigonid commander Andronikos defied him briefly before his troops threw him out and, presumably, surrendered to Ptolemy to avoid a siege or a storm [64]. Ptolemy also captured Sidon, but seems to have gone no further north, Demetrios being at Tripolis in sufficient force to stand a siege. It is at this point that Seleukos was detached. He was given a force of 800 infantry and 200 cavalry, together with his friends (perhaps these are the survivors of the original 50 horsemen who had fled from Babylon with him) and his slaves – which may account for the different figures given by

Appian, who says he had 1,000 foot and 300 horse. With these he moved on Babylon [65].

It was not a particularly large force, but then neither was it all that small. In the circumstances it was clearly powerful enough to deal with any opposition it encountered in Syria, whether mobile or static, while the shock of Gaza lasted. It was not, however, actually intended to fight, at least not until it reached Babylonia. Thus, assuming Seleukos was detached at Tyre or Sidon, his route would carefully avoid Tripolis, which in terms of Syrian geography, means that he went inland, perhaps along the Biqaa valley, and north along the Orontes. The land east of the Orontes was at this period barely settled, but would provide grazing for his horses. The villagers of the Orontes valley, indifferent no doubt to which Macedonian ruled over them, would be able to provide food, especially if Seleukos could pay for it – and he was strong enough to seize it if they refused. A supply of hard cash would surely be a first priority for this expedition, partly to pay his men, partly to bribe the enemy, and partly to smooth his passage by such elementary means as paying for food which he might otherwise never get. He would not wish to leave the countryside behind him in too much of a turmoil since this would alert Demetrios to what he was doing, and at the start relative secrecy was a requisite.

Across the Euphrates a different secrecy was required. He stopped at Karrhai to recruit soldiers from the settlers there, and to make sure the rest did not rush on ahead to warn the wrong people of his approach. But the inhabitants of Babylonia clearly knew he was coming, and welcomed him. More reinforcements, a thousand strong, came in under one Polyarchos, a local governor who would seem to have been suborned beforehand. Seleukos' force now was perhaps 3,000 strong, quite enough at least to persuade Diphilos, the late Peithon's commander at Babylon, to shut himself up in the citadel rather than dispute in the open; and quite enough to besiege and storm that citadel. The whole operation clearly depended on speed and dash, on keeping Diphilos off balance, and it succeeded for that reason. The friends of Seleukos imprisoned by his enemies were released before they could be used as hostages; it would seem that siege and storm followed very quickly upon Seleukos' arrival in the city [66]. In possession of the citadel he controlled the city; in control of the city, he could once more plausibly claim to be satrap of Babylon, and this time he owed it all to his own efforts.

5
GENERAL AND VICTOR
(312–308)

Seleukos' journey to Babylon was undertaken just in time. Demetrios recovered his military balance quickly. Ptolemy pushed an army detachment forward from Sidon, under a general called Killes, possibly in order to cover Seleukos' movements. By this time Demetrios had gathered troops from garrisons in the north in sufficient quantity to attack Killes successfully, and this persuaded Ptolemy to withdraw from his conquests. He did not hurry, as is sometimes said, but took his time, carefully destroying the fortifications of several Palestinian towns and cities on his way [1]. Demetrios advanced in time with Ptolemy's retreat. Any further support which Seleukos might have expected or needed from Ptolemy would no longer be available. He was now clearly on his own, though it is likely that he never expected any more assistance. His small original force, his almost excessive care to recruit enemy soldiers, and his insistence on his welcome among the Babylonians all argue strongly that he knew all along that Ptolemy's support would be strictly limited to his original force.

Antigonos came down from the north to check on Demetrios' activities, bringing reinforcements [2]. Perhaps he was reversing his previous strategy, now aiming to eliminate Ptolemy before returning to deal with Kassandros and Lysimachos. Peace talks with those two had failed, just as had those with Ptolemy. Once more chronology is difficult, but it is most reasonable to accept that Antigonos' move south took place in the spring of 311, after the Taurus passes were reopened, though he and Demetrios had been in regular contact during the winter. It is difficult to believe, however, that neither Demetrios nor

Antigonos knew of Seleukos' adventure by that time. Seleukos, by the spring of 311, had been in control of Babylon and Babylonia for a good six months, since he had set off not long after the Gaza battle in the previous autumn.

That both Antigonos and Demetrios knew of Seleukos' conquest of Babylon is therefore so probable as to be taken as certain. That they did nothing about it is equally improbable. The extent of Seleukos' victory is not to be exaggerated. The area of land he controlled was one satrapy, and the number of troops under his command was, as was to be shown in the spring, less than 4,000. Most of them had switched sides to join him on being defeated and could be expected to switch back again at the cost of no more than their worn pride and some well-chosen sarcasms from Antigonos. In the larger scheme of things, therefore, Antigonos did not take Seleukos very seriously, simply because Seleukos' military power was negligible. He could be regarded as a distraction mounted by Ptolemy, on the same sort of level as the Nabataeans, whose power and wealth had attracted the attention of Antigonos and Demetrios [3]. Maybe Ptolemy was responsible here too. Antigonos had mounted the same sort of distraction himself a year or so before, in Cyprus and Kyrene. The practitioner no doubt thought he recognized a similar ploy.

On the other hand, Seleukos was not being totally ignored. Orders were sent to the satraps of the east to deal with him, thus leaving Antigonos able to concentrate on the west. When the orders reached the east is, of course, unknown, but what is quite clear is that a considerable period of time passed between Seleukos' success in retaking Babylon and Babylonia and the actual response from the satrap of Media, who had been given charge by Antigonos of the operation to recover Babylon [4].

This satrap, Nikanor, had presumably been given or had acquired the sort of supervisory position to which the late Peithon had aspired with such disastrous results for himself and others about him. Nikanor collected troops from his own satrapy and also from the neighbouring satrapies, of which Diodoros names Susiana and Persis and to which Aria can be added since its satrap was involved in the subsequent events.

Now this process of gathering troops will have taken time. Nikanor cannot have begun doing so until the late autumn or early winter of 312, and taking into account the winter conditions in the high Iranian plateau, the difficulty of moving an army through the Zagros passes, and the fact that he had an army of 10,000 infantry and 7,000 horse in the campaign he mounted, it becomes clear that his invasion of Babylonia came in the spring of 311. So at about the same time that Antigonos moved south through the Taurus passes into Syria, Nikanor was moving though the Zagros passes into Babylonia.

Nikanor had 17,000 men against Seleukos' 3,000 foot and 400 horse. Antigonos therefore had good reason for confidence that he could leave the eastern problem to his eastern supporters. Nikanor was just as confident and as a result he became careless. Seleukos, on the other hand, was on his mettle as an ingenious commander, and almost all his experience had been in handling small forces. Seleukos seems to have trailed his coat, pretending to flee. He crossed the Tigris, so the campaign took place away from Babylon and between the Tigris and the Zagros. Seleukos could not afford to allow Nikanor to gain the psychological advantage of capturing Babylon, so he led the pursuing army along the east side of the river. Nikanor, confident of victory, relaxed his guard when camped at an apparently secure site, one of the royal posting stations. Seleukos' small army had hidden in nearby marshes. The existence of the posting station told Seleukos exactly where Nikanor and the high officers were, naturally in the best accommodation; perhaps also, with marshes in the area, the camp was spread out, maybe along the road and on the drier islands. The precise spot is not known. To conceal his small numbers and to create maximum confusion, Seleukos took the risk of a night attack. He will have had the advantage of knowing the ground, quite possibly having actually chosen it, with his general's eye for ground. He had the further advantage of commanding a group of men who really do seem to have been won over by him. He used the familiar devices of messing with them, rewarding them, and assessing and using their individual capabilities; above all, he had been successful so far. He could, and did, talk of it all as an adventure, and shared the risks – in fact, he risked more than they, for if he lost again, Antigonos would scarcely allow him to escape this time, while the soldiers would be likely to be simply recruited back into Nikanor's forces.

GENERAL AND VICTOR

So the night attack went in, and one of Nikanor's commanders, Evagoras, the satrap of Aria, was killed early on. Nikanor seems to have become separated from his command. The news that Evagoras was dead spread through the larger army, and perhaps in the absence of any other competent commanders, the soldiers gave in. 17,000 surrendered to 3,400. And almost all enlisted with Seleukos. Nikanor himself escaped with just a few men [5].

So, once again, a defeated satrap fled west with a handful of followers, but this time *to* Antigonos, not from him. Nikanor sent a messenger in advance with news of his defeat [6]. Seleukos therefore had some time in which to exploit his victory, before an army came from the west. He could not know how long he had, nor could he know how powerful the counter-attack would be, but he would be quite certain it would come during the summer of that year. Once more he had to gamble, and once more he succeeded.

Exploitation eastwards was clearly indicated [7]. His army, even it was now 20,000 strong, was no match for that which Antigonos could bring, so there was no point in marching west to meet his attacker half way, only to be beaten in a great battle. It was much more sensible to push east, into the satrapies from which his new troops had come, at least two of which had now lost their satraps. Further, there is some indication in Diodoros' words that the battle was lost by Nikanor at least partly as a result of Antigonos' own personal unpopularity among the troops from the east. It is quite likely that these were men who had been in the army of Eumenes five years before, or in the army of the allied satraps. They might be men who had been left in the east by Alexander. In some cases they were Persians, Peukestas' old recruits; Evagoras, the Arian satrap, was in command of a group of Persians when he was killed. None of these men had any love for Antigonos, nor had Antigonos done anything to win them over. He was always only interested in the east in so far as nothing happened there. His attention was always on the west. And now Antigonos' satraps were either dead or gone, and Seleukos' men could spread the word about the kind of commander they had, cheerful and gracious and accessible.

The propaganda stories were spreading too. One of them was the story of how popular Seleukos was among the native population of Babylonia [8]. No doubt there was a strong basis of truth in this – it will have been obvious to the soldiers left behind by Antigonos as his garrison in Babylon, for example – but no doubt also the story lost nothing in the telling. Then there were the stories which Seleukos himself is said to have told to his original fellowship on the march from Syria. One story was that Seleukos had originally been prepared to set out with even fewer men than the thousand provided by Ptolemy. Only his own friends and his own slaves would suffice, it was said, so confident of victory was he [9]. So a thousand men was over-insurance, and victory would be correspondingly easier. It sounds like the sort of story told after victory had proved to be so much easier than expected.

Seleukos had a dream, so he said, that Alexander stood beside him, and showed that Seleukos was a future leader [10]. Generals were in the habit of calling up Alexander in support of their enterprises, but it could only be done by those who had been with Alexander, and it could only convince those who had marched with Alexander. Eumenes had worked the magic, and Lysimachos, later, put Alexander on his coins [11], but neither Antigonos nor Kassandros could do it. Seleukos, like Eumenes, clearly had the knack of appealing to the Macedonians in a way which gained their confidence and loyalty. He had the advantage over Eumenes in this, in that he himself was a Macedonian, and the effect did not wear off, as it tended to with Eumenes when the troops remembered that Eumenes was a Greek. No doubt Ptolemy could do it too, but Ptolemy did not have that spark of recklessness which leavened Seleukos' basic caution.

The reason for Seleukos' inspired recklessness in 312–311 is surely the four years spent as one of Ptolemy's generals. After a five-year spell as lord of Babylon, demotion to someone else's commander, no matter how highly regarded, will have hurt. It left Seleukos with the desperation required to bring out all his innate military and political ability.

Seleukos' move further east won him a huge territory. Media and Susiana were his eastern neighbours in Babylonia. Diodoros adds that he took over 'some of the adjacent countries' [12]. Like Antigonos, Diodoros does not know much about the eastern countries, and was not much interested in them, but his words can only mean Persis and Aria and probably

Parthia. Aria because its satrap had been killed, Persis because it was apparently Persian troops who had begun the surrender in the night battle, and Parthia because it seems to have regularly gone with Media since Peithon murdered its satrap back in 316. Baktria-Sogdiana had conspicuously not provided troops for Nikanor's army; the satrap there, Stasanor, was clearly semi-independent; there is no sign of Seleukos disturbing him.

Control of all Iran went with the acquisition of Nikanor's army. There were few local forces left to dispute Seleukos' take-over, and in the cases of Aria and Media, no satraps either. And this was a ticklish matter for Seleukos to deal with. The dead satraps had been appointed by Antigonos, a move which Seleukos and his allies claimed to be illegal. Seleukos had always based his claim to rule in Babylonia on his appointment there by the conference at Triparadisos. By now, however, this ideology was looking rather careworn, nor did it cater for deaths in office. It could hardly be acceptable to him to apply to the designated successor of Antipatros for replacements, for this was Polyperchon, the ally of Antigonos. On the other hand, Seleukos himself could scarcely appoint any successors, since this was the action of Antigonos which he complained of. There is no indication that new satraps were appointed yet, neither is there any sign that Seleukos refused to appoint replacements. Perhaps the matter simply did not occur to the authors of our sources, or to their sources, but it is important and it must not be ignored. It seems possible that Seleukos himself took over Media, and Appian says that he 'acquired the kingdom of Media'; as an emergency measure, at a time of conquest, he could well have ruled Media himself along with Babylonia, but the more distant areas must have needed some delegated authority. Aria, for example, clearly needed an on-the-spot government because of its size and its frontier situation. There were several possibilities – appoint no-one and just let the matter slide; appoint a new governor but don't call him satrap; hand a province over to another *in situ* satrap; appoint sub-satraps, men who would rule part of the satrapies. Whichever device Seleukos adopted it was clearly successful, in that it kept the east quiet for the present, while he and his army turned back to face the attack from the west [13].

It all took time, and by the time Seleukos had secured the east he was under attack in Babylonia. Antigonos had received the message of defeat from Nikanor, sent on ahead of the fleeing ex-satrap, while he was licking his wounds and contemplating the next move in a losing contest with the Nabataean Arab nomads [14]. If these people really had been one of Ptolemy's ploys to distract Antigonos, it had been very successful, for Antigonos' reaction to defeat had been to persist, and his reaction to a drawn fight had been to make yet another move, indirectly, to attack his tormentors [15]. All this lasted into the summer, until he was told of Nikanor's defeat, and the loss of the whole of the east. Antigonos' primary purpose for being in southern Syria had originally been to attack Ptolemy in his home base of Egypt. He had delayed over the Nabataeans; now he postponed the attack on Egypt once again in order to deal with Seleukos.

It is difficult to understand Antigonos' plan in this case. He gave Demetrios a force of 15,000 foot and 4,000 horse with which to march to Babylon, recover that satrapy, and then return to Syria [16]. It is also clear from subsequent events that Antigonos imposed a time limit on Demetrios' operations [17], which required Demetrios to be back in Syria in time to go into winter quarters. It must be assumed that Antigonos simply did not know the extent of Nikanor's disaster – indeed perhaps Nikanor himself did not know its extent for some time. Demetrios' force was only equal to that now under Seleukos' own control, and Seleukos will have been recruiting more troops. A time limit on such a campaign will impose haste and superficiality. It may become known, thereby demoralizing one side and encouraging the other. Unless Demetrios captured Seleukos himself, or defeated Seleukos' army so comprehensively as to destroy his credibility as a leader beyond recall, then Demetrios' withdrawal into Syria would simply allow Seleukos to recover any of the conquests Demetrios had made. These conditions were so unlikely to be fulfilled that it is necessary to believe that Antigonos thought that Seleukos still had control over an army of only a few thousands, and over Babylonia only. Nikanor either did not tell him of the loss of the whole of the army of the east, or left the clear impression that it was still fighting under other leaders, or perhaps never mentioned it. It seems clear enough that

Seleukos' move into Media and Persis and Aria was quite unknown and quite unexpected. The east always was one of Antigonos' blind spots.

When Demetrios and his army reached Babylonia, therefore, Seleukos was out of reach, somewhere in the east. The march, from the borders of Nabataea to Damascus, where the army was assembled, north to Thapsakos, where Alexander's bridge still served as the crossing point of the Euphrates, and then east to the Tigris and south along that river, cannot have taken less than a month, perhaps double that. The partisans of Seleukos had plenty of warning, for Demetrios could move no faster than a marching man, say a maximum of twenty miles a day. Seleukos' governor in Babylonia, Patrokles, was warned of Demetrios' approach when he was still in Mesopotamia, well to the north.

Patrokles was clearly expecting an attack, and had pickets out to provide warning [18]. He had also prepared measures to deal with the attack. Further, from the nature of the measures, it very much seems that he had the co-operation of the native Babylonian authorities, that is, the priests. For the resistance to Demetrios' attack took the drastic form of using the city of Babylon itself as a fortified barbican, and holding it in sufficient strength to force Demetrios to assault it. This meant moving out the whole population and leaving the two citadels with strong garrisons. The civilians were scattered over all southern Babylonia, some going off into the desert, and some being sent as far as Susiana and the shores of the Persian Gulf, where Alexander's cities no doubt received them, willingly or otherwise.

Patrokles was clearly an intelligent general, or he was coached and trained by one, that is, by Seleukos. Seleukos also deserves credit for selecting Patrokles, and above all for trusting him and letting him get on with his task. For the fight in Babylonia was one of attrition. In case Demetrios was intent on a methodical conquest, then this had to be made as slow and difficult as possible, and his army had to be used up, either as casualties or as garrisons. Babylonia with its cities, its canals, its rivers, its marshes, was ideal country for defensive warfare, and for causing casualties among the assaulting troops. Patrokles had to avoid pitched battles on any real scale, since he would lose, for Demetrios had the stronger force. In addition Patrokles' movements were to some extent restricted by his need to keep in contact with the garrisons left in Babylon and with Seleukos, who was in Media [19].

What Seleukos was actually doing in Media is something of a mystery. It is possible that he was simply keeping out of Demetrios' way, in the knowledge that the only way to lose this phase of the war was for him to be captured or killed. The size of Demetrios' army will have told him that Demetrios could be beaten by Fabian tactics without risking the lives or loyalty of his newly acquired forces in a stand-up knock-down battle. But there is another possible explanation. In his account of Seleukos' rise to power, Appian includes a detail which is not recorded elsewhere, to the effect that Seleukos killed 'Nikator' in a battle in Media [20]. Since this 'Nikator' is further described as Antigonos' satrap of Media, it is usual to assume Appian is making a mistake for Nikanor. It may also be a mistake of his to say that he was killed, for Appian does not mention Evagoras, nor does he mention Nikanor's flight from the Tigris night battle. Yet it remains possible that Appian preserves a detail from a longer version of events in which Seleukos had to fight for Media and Nikanor was killed defending his satrapy. This in turn would help explain Seleukos' absence from Babylonia, and the relative lack of numbers in Demetrios' forces. In this scenario, Demetrios was still expecting to join forces with Nikanor, a junction which Seleukos and Patrokles between them prevented. Nikanor's death, therefore, was perhaps in a desperate fight to break through to join Demetrios. Perhaps if Appian had shown himself a more competent condenser elsewhere, this reconstruction might be more convincing. Diodoros gives no hint that Demetrios expected assistance, and his father's timetable rather suggests that Demetrios was expected to succeed quickly and alone. Plutarch, whose account is even briefer than Appian's, even omits Antigonos' role in originating the expedition of Demetrios, and he can no more be trusted in this than can Appian [21]. He does suggest, however, that Demetrios knew that Seleukos was away from Babylonia, and that Demetrios' raid was in search of an easy victory. This has a certain air of plausibility to it, for Demetrios was always a notably unsuccessful general, prone to defeat, and one whose victories tended to be sterile. A spectacular capture of famed Babylon might well be to his taste.

If so, he banged his head on another brick wall. His forces succeeded in capturing one of the citadels or palaces in the evacuated city, but not the second. With Patrokles roaming the countryside behind him, Demetrios will have rapidly run short of supplies, and was reduced to drastic foraging, which was publicized by his enemies as ravaging the country – in obvious contrast to Seleukos' normal behaviour. In short order, Demetrios will surely have realized that his task was an impossible one. Ruthlessly he cut his losses, left a quarter of his forces – 5,000 foot and 1,000 horse under one of his officers, Archelaos – besieging the other Babylon citadel, and marched away back to Syria [22].

There Demetrios discovered that his father had been negotiating for peace once more. This time he made sufficient concessions to entice Kassandros and Lysimachos into a treaty. The terms are not clear, as usual, but must have included the renunciation by Antigonos of any aspirations to overlordship, and thus a recognition by both sides of each other's effective autonomy. Having made peace with Kassandros, and with Lysimachos included at Kassandros' insistence, Antigonos could then turn to Ptolemy and Seleukos. His policy now was to stand on guard against one of these, and use overwhelming force against the other. So he would either make peace with Ptolemy and attack Seleukos, or accept Seleukos' position for the moment and attack Egypt. Quite possibly he decided on personal grounds, quite possibly on technical. It was easier for him to contact Ptolemy, and he had already discussed peace with him. Ptolemy was also, now, distinctly the more vulnerable of the two. Egypt was the easier conquest from Antigonos' point of view, and Ptolemy could see this well enough. By contrast, against Seleukos he had a personal grudge, not surprisingly after the confrontations at Babylon in 315 and 311. The fact that a small army of Antigonos', under Archelaos, was in occupation of half of Seleukos' city at the time that peace was under discussion with Ptolemy may also have weighed with Antigonos, for peace with Seleukos would have certainly involved withdrawing that force.

In the event Ptolemy accepted Antigonos' peace proposals at once. He was, in effect, asked to add his name to the treaty which had been negotiated with Kassandros. Without the alliance of Kassandros and Lysimachos, Ptolemy had no choice but to accede, since to fight on alone against the might of Antigonos was for him quite impossible [23].

There was nothing which Seleukos could do to assist if Ptolemy was attacked. Seleukos, apart from the sheer distance involved, was simply not strong enough to attack Antigonos. Even if he tried to attack, he would have to eliminate Archelaos' force in Babylon first, and that was large enough to be awkward. On the other hand, Ptolemy certainly could use his power to distract Antigonos if the latter turned on Seleukos. This would, of course, entail breaking the peace, but Ptolemy will not have taken that seriously except in the short term. The purpose of making peace, for Ptolemy, was to avert an imminent attack on Egypt. Once the attack ceased to be imminent – that is, as soon as Antigonos was preoccupied elsewhere – then Ptolemy could restart the fighting. But then and there, if he wished to retain Egypt, he must bow to necessity. Antigonos had won the war.

Or so it may have seemed. He had regained the territory which had been lost to Ptolemy after Gaza; he had gained some territory in Asia Minor; he had, as part of the peace treaty, trumpeted his policy of 'freedom' for the Greek cities, and thereby he had gained allies, if not actual territory, in Greece and in the islands of the Aegean. But all this was in the west. In the east, he had lost control of everything from Babylon eastwards. In exchange of territory he had lost decisively, though it is likely that no Greek or Macedonian considered Babylonia and Boiotia, say, as equivalents: all would imagine the latter the more important. Probably Antigonos did. There is also, in the end, some evidence that Seleukos did too.

The peace treaties left Seleukos fighting alone against Antigonos. Betrayal has been charged against Ptolemy and Kassandros, though we have no evidence that they had agreed to fight on until Antigonos was destroyed [24]. They had put forward a set of demands at the start of the war, in 315, all but one of which were quite outrageous; the only one not outrageous was the restoration of Seleukos to Babylon [25]. Kassandros could not, surely, have seriously expected Antigonos to give him Kappadokia. Ptolemy, however, clearly did want to control Palestine and Phoenicia and repeatedly made attempts to do so, but at no time, even when he had the opportunity did he attempt to establish control over northern Syria. These demands had been included, therefore, only to compel Antigonos to fight. But now, since the aftermath of Gaza, Seleukos had regained Babylon. That is, the one realizable demand had been realized. During the course of the war at no time had Seleukos made any serious attempt to assist Kassandros, still less Lysimachos, even when he had charge of the fleet in the Aegean. Their joint ventures, in Karia and in Lesbos, had both failed. From the viewpoint of the Europeans, Seleukos had been merely Ptolemy's agent. They can have had no possible reason to go on fighting Antigonos, except to assist the growth of Ptolemy's or Seleukos' lands. That is to say, Kassandros could see that the object of the war had been achieved, and that any further fighting was likely to cost him control of those parts of Greece which he still held, while Ptolemy consolidated his own gains, and Seleukos expanded his power over enormous eastern territories. Kassandros, carrying Lysimachos with him, cut his losses. And so did Ptolemy, though his losses were less dangerous to him. Seleukos could, if Antigonos let him, make peace too, but none of the others was obliged to help him any more.

In arguing thus, of course, if they did, Kassandros and Ptolemy were missing the point. The character of Antigonos was the real issue. He aimed at the empire of the world, just as had Alexander, and just as, later, did Seleukos. But neither Ptolemy nor Kassandros seem to have accepted that Antigonos' ambitions were different from their own smaller aims, though he had provided evidence enough in his original demands for their submission. Or perhaps they did know, and made peace because they perceived that they were losing, and a brief peace would stave off the evil moment of final defeat. In that case, Seleukos was their salvation, both in the short term and in the long. In the short term because it was his success in regaining Babylonia and holding it against Demetrios which had induced Antigonos to make peace in the west; in the long term because Seleukos, against all the odds, actually won his war against Antigonos.

This war is one whose detail is almost entirely gone from knowledge [26]. Its dates, its events, its battles, have escaped from the record. Those parts of the ancient historians' accounts in which the war was discussed have not survived. But this does not mean that nothing has survived. Indications do exist. The existing records can be interpreted to yield a story of sorts. And more information will turn up, as excavations in areas such as Iraq, Iran, Soviet Central Asia, and Afghanistan are made. After all, it is not so long since it was argued that Seleukos must have been included in the general peace of 311, because no information about fighting in the east after that date existed [27]. Now it is clear that fighting in the east did take place, so the interpretation of the peace has changed.

Further, the absence of source material should not delude us into diminishing the importance of this war. It was, in fact, the crucial phase of the post-Alexandrine fighting. Had it gone the other way, had Antigonos won, he would have returned to the west refreshed and strengthened; instead he was cruelly weakened, and, in the event, mortally wounded.

The situation when Ptolemy joined in the peace process was that Antigonos, aged 71, controlled all the land from the Hellespont to Gaza, and east into the satrapy of Mesopotamia. He had a force under Archelaos in position in Babylon, but that force was neutralized by an inferior force under Patrokles which held one of the citadel-palaces of Babylon and controlled the open country nearby. Eastwards Seleukos was in control of Media, Susiana, Persis, Aria, and probably Parthia. To the west of Antigonos' lands were those of Ptolemy, Kassandros, and Lysimachos and the usual Greek cities and confederacies, independent, dependent, insurrectionary, and allied. All of these were actual or potential enemies of Antigonos. To the east of Seleukos' lands were satrapies, tribes, kingdoms, and cities stretching, for practical purposes, north into the steppes of Central Asia and east to the valley of the Ganges. All of these kings, peoples, cities, and tribes were involved, in one way or another, in the fight waged by Antigonos and Seleukos, and the result of the war was to be decisive for all of them.

Ptolemy probably made his peace late in 311, say in the late summer. It was possible for Antigonos to mount his assault on Seleukos in the autumn of that year, and it would seem that he did so. The Babylonian Chronicle records a campaign of fighting between the two from the month of Ab, say

August, until the month of Tebel, say December [28]. This fighting, unrecorded in western accounts, clearly took place in Babylonia, but few if any of the people actually fighting were Babylonians. They suffered, but otherwise did not participate, though their preference for Seleukos over his enemy never seems to have wavered.

Seleukos was in communication with Ptolemy even while in Media. Diodoros records that, having acquired Babylonia, Susiana, and Media, Seleukos sent word to Ptolemy of his success [29]. By that time Ptolemy was back in Egypt, facing a possible invasion, while Antigonos controlled all Syria as far as Gaza and beyond. But Antigonos did not control the desert, and his attack on the Nabataeans provides evidence of this. Arrian mentions in his book on India that Ptolemy sent men to Babylon on camels across Arabia [30]; the journey could as easily be reversed, particularly as at the western terminus there were friendly nomads who could be employed as guides and expert camel-men. When he made peace, the least that Ptolemy could do was to warn his old friend and client what he was about. That is to say, Seleukos will have been warned that the whole might of Antigonos was about to fall on him.

Seleukos had made his preparations, even more thoroughly than for meeting Demetrios' raid. This time Seleukos could expect, not a detachment of Antigonos' army, but most of it. Antigonos disposed of about 80,000 soldiers [31]; even if he left half of them facing any dangers in the west, he would march east with an army double the size of Seleukos'. So Seleukos' basic task when he had news of the peace in the west was to recruit. He would be able to call up some Greeks and Macedonians from his satrapies, though it seems unlikely that he would still find many, and there were none available from farther east. The Babylonian Chronicle, however, records on successive lines the word 'friendship' and the term 'the army of the Guti' [32]. This was the archaic scribal name for the Kossaeans, old enemies of both Alexander and Antigonos (and of Babylon – they were the latest manifestation of the Kassites, who had ruled in Babylon before the Assyrians). Antigonos had carved a path of blood through their land in his campaign against Eumenes, and, as usual, he had done it in such a way as to leave a solid resentment behind [33]. Seleukos, that is, would seem once more to have been able to capitalize on his opponent's mistakes, and to have been able to recruit his army up to something nearer parity by enlisting these redoubtable hillmen.

It also seems that Seleukos used the brief moment of calm between the invasions of Demetrios and Antigonos to retake Babylon from Archelaos. Such, at least, is a possible understanding of the Babylonian Chronicle's fragmentary sentences [34]. It would make sense to eliminate a weak enemy first, and it would not be surprising if in the process he captured and recruited some or all of Archelaos' 6,000 men. This was another mistake of Demetrios', who, when he saw that he could not succeed with his 20,000, should not have left 6,000 to try to do the same job. Demetrios' military education was likely to cost his father a great deal before he began winning.

When Antigonos moved into Babylonia, then, he probably found that Seleukos was fully in control of the city, of the countryside, and of the Zagros hills to the west and north, and that the Median and Susian satrapies were under his firm control. Further, he will have found that Seleukos' army, though smaller than his own, was larger than the year before, and was animated by a spirit of hostility to Antigonos personally, and by a corresponding devotion to Seleukos. Beyond that, Antigonos will have found, or rather will have rediscovered, that the Babylonian population, priests, townsmen, and peasantry, were hostile as well. Seleukos had everything on his side, except numbers, and Antigonos' superiority in numbers could be whittled away by an active defence, and by his need to leave garrisons in captured towns. Seleukos probably had less need to release men for garrison duty, partly because he did not have to hold down a restive population, and partly because he may well have been prepared to evacuate towns, or, more subtly, abandon them to Antigonos, people and all.

The course of the war is lost. The Babylonian Chronicle records fighting, apparently more or less continuously, by which we should understand manoeuvring and Fabian tactics, until the winter of 311–310. The rest of 310 seems to be lost, in a gap in the Chronicle, and when the intermittent thread can be picked up, it seems that Antigonos had captured Babylon, but not the whole city. A building called the Bit

Haru is explicitly said not to have been captured. By this time it is Shebet of 310–309, that is, January–February 309 [35].

Antigonos, to be sure, had not been able to concentrate fully on affairs to his front. Constant incidents occurred in the west. Ptolemy discovered yet another intrigue in Cyprus, as a result of which King Nikokles of Paphos, hitherto one of Ptolemy's constant allies, was compelled to commit a spectacular suicide with his whole family. Menelaos then ruled the whole island as Ptolemy's viceroy, with the royal title which had been Nikokreon's. It seems that Ptolemy, probably correctly, blamed Antigonos [36]. As a reprisal Ptolemy sent a raid into Kilikia Tracheia, which captured and held a few places until Demetrios came along to expel the Ptolemaic forces [37]. Then Ptolemy sailed along the coast, captured Phaselis, raided into Lykia, and then sailed into the Aegean, where his son was born at Kos in 309 [38]. Ptolemy also began making propaganda noises about the freedom of the Greeks. None of this necessarily meant open war, unless Antigonos reacted rather more strongly, but it was a situation in which the initiative very definitely lay with Ptolemy, and which Antigonos had to watch, and for which he had to keep troops available in the west, which were thus unusable in the east. It was clearly a situation closely related to what was happening in the east, and Ptolemy's move in Kilikia was obviously designed to relieve the pressure on Seleukos, just as much as to gain revenge for Antigonos' Cypriot intrigues. It seems that Demetrios was charged with a general defensive role covering the whole Mediterranean coast. He had been in Kilikia to clear up after Ptolemy's raid, and it may be now that he relieved a Ptolemaic siege of Halikarnassos (though it is as easy to place this earlier) [39]. From the point of view of the campaign in the east, it is clear that Demetrios needed substantial forces under his hand. Ptolemy's use of sea power was highly effective, and very economical of manpower.

Similarly there was a move even further off and in an even more sensitive area, when Antigonos' nephew Ptolemaios became disaffected and threw off his allegiance. He then emplaced a friend of his as satrap of Hellespontine Phrygia, meanwhile concluding an alliance with Kassandros. Surely we may see in this the delicate intriguing hand of Ptolemy, all the more likely since Ptolemaios appealed to Kassandros, who was not at all pleased at the prospect of another fight with Antigonos. The episode was only potentially serious, for Kassandros was no more ready for a full-scale conflict than was Ptolemy, but the Hellespont was a danger point and it had to be recovered, a task which Antigonos entrusted to another of his sons, Philip, who was successful [40]. But, again, this employed a force in the west which could not thereby be used in the east [41].

All this had to be watched by Antigonos while he fought Seleukos. It is clear that it was Antigonos, and not a subordinate, who was campaigning in the east. Not only does the Babylonian Chronicle say so, but he is not personally recorded in the west at all during these years. At every problem he sent someone else to attend to it, but it was clearly Antigonos himself who controlled all the reactions to events. For a man in his seventies, who in 311 was referring to the fact that he might not live long, he was very spry.

But Babylonia was being wrecked. The Chronicle talks of 'weeping and mourning' and describes Antigonos plundering both the city and the country. He attacked the city of Cutha, which was unsuccessfully defended by its own citizens, and at least part of the temple there was burnt. Antigonos, amid the ruin, considered he was winning, and appointed someone as satrap. Famine struck. The Chronicle recorded the enormously high prices being paid, or at least being charged, for the staples of Babylonian diet, barley and dates. Fighting continued. Seleukos took, or was at, Borsippa in the spring. There was more plundering and weeping and mourning. Appropriately, the end of the Chronicle is even more fragmentary than usual, as though in reflection of the fact that the whole society was disintegrating [42].

The fighting went on at least until August of 308, for a battle in Ab (August–September) of the ninth year of Alexander IV is noted on the left edge of the Chronicle tablet [43]. As it happens, this may well be more or less the end of the war. In 307, Antigonos was active in the west again with most of his forces under Demetrios' command [44]. This suggests that soon after the August battle, some sort of peace was made with Seleukos. It may be, in fact, that we have a brief account of that last battle. Polyainos included a stratagem of Seleukos' in his collection, in which Seleukos' army fought for a day against that of Antigonos. The two drew apart for the night and Seleukos kept his men in fighting kit all night so that they appeared ready to attack in the morning before Antigonos' men were dressed in armour or had eaten their breakfasts [45]. Something like this may have finally broken Antigonos' will to continue fighting, and made him admit defeat. The stratagem makes it clear that the armies were fighting stubbornly but on more or less equal terms. Antigonos had lost whatever advantage of numbers he had had at the start.

In the west, Ptolemy had raided Antigonos' cities in Lykia and Pamphylia, and was now with his fleet in the Aegean. Lysimachos moved out of the interior of Thrace to the coast and built a new city, named after himself, on the Hellespont[46]. He could scarcely have made his ambition plainer. Kleopatra, Alexander's sister, whom Antigonos kept under lock and key in Sardis, tried to escape and was killed on Antigonos' orders [47]. The murders of the boy Alexander IV, and of his mother Roxane, became known [48]. Ptolemy moved into mainland Greece at Corinth and Sikyon [49]. Too much was going on here for Antigonos to ignore. Sometime after August of 308 he made peace in the east, leaving Seleukos in control of all his conquests, and brought his army back to the west.

Antigonos' strategic mistake was to assume that a central position gave him the advantage in the war against the allies. In fact it simply meant that he had to fight all the time, and if he concentrated on one enemy, the others could attack him elsewhere. Ptolemy turned out to be the true strategist, keeping Antigonos busy in Asia Minor, in Greece, in the Aegean, in Babylonia, while he picked up small but useful conquests. Seleukos proved to be the best fighting general of them all, fighting off an attack which may have seemed overwhelming at first. It is also clear that Ptolemy did not actually 'betray' Seleukos in the peace of 311, any more than Seleukos himself betrayed Ptolemy by making peace in 308. It seems likely that neither regarded such agreements with any seriousness, any more than did Antigonos. The situation was constantly developing, in a fluid state, with no-one knowing at any one time whether the condition of the world was one of peace or war. Antigonos made peace with Ptolemy but felt that he could intrigue in Cyprus; Ptolemy felt he could send a force into Kilikia and later into Pamphylia and Lykia, without breaking whatever peace he had agreed to.

The most important result, in fact, for the future, was the victory of Seleukos. He had beaten off attacks, by Demetrios and now by Antigonos. The cost in life and property in Babylonia was undoubtedly very great, perhaps more than in any other of the wars of the successors of Alexander. But Seleukos had shown himself to be so formidable that Antigonos and Demetrios never seriously contemplated an attack on him again. And having beaten off this attack from the west, Seleukos was free to turn east.

6

CONQUEROR AND KING
(308–303)

The war with Antigonos proved Seleukos as a general. After the peace, both sides recoiled from the combat and turned their arms in opposite directions. Antigonos sent Demetrios to Athens; Seleukos took himself to the east. That is not to say that they ignored each other. Antigonos spent the next years in north Syria. Earlier, his favourite headquarters had been in the Asia Minor lake country at Kelainai, which had looked as though it might develop into his capital. Now he needed better communications, so as to be in touch with the sea, with Egypt, with Asia Minor, and with the frontier over against Seleukos to the east. By 306 he had founded a new city in north Syria, naming it after himself, and it was under construction when he received news of his son's great naval victory at Salamis [1]. The new Antigoneia was a suitable place from which to watch all his enemies.

To the east it seems that Antigonos did not have to look very far. The frontier of his and Seleukos' lands was probably not very far across the Euphrates. The evidence here is awkward to interpret and highly disputable – even more so than normal. The land across the Euphrates was the ancient Mesopotamia, a satrapy which had been under Antigonos' control in 311 and 310. Seleukos had travelled through it in 311, seducing the allegiance of the garrison at Karrhai as he passed. It seems unlikely that this was the only garrison in the satrapy, but no others are locatable. However, Seleukos made no attempt to control Karrhai itself at that time, being interested only in taking away the soldiers [2].

Elsewhere in Mesopotamia there are two Macedonian cities which appear to share the same founder: Nikanor is said to have founded the city of Europos, on the Euphrates at the site of a town with the Aramaic name of Dura [3], and another city called 'Antiochia Arabis' [4]. This latter is not known by that name outside the pages of Pliny. Both Nisibis and Edessa were also called Antiochia [5], and either of them could be thought of as 'of Arabia', though Nisibis is marginally the better candidate.

The name Nikanor is, of course, most intriguing. This was the name of Antigonos' satrap of Media, who was defeated at the Tigris night battle by Seleukos in 311. One source, the unreliable Appian, claims that Nikanor was killed later in the fight for Media, and Diodoros only says he fled from the night battle, sending word to Antigonos of his defeat [6]. The name, unfortunately, is very common at this time, but it is difficult to accept a multiplication of Nikanors, when we have here a Nikanor active in the same area, in the same office of satrap within the brief period of fifteen years. It is quite probable that this is the same man. This does not end the matter, however. Appian, though not to be relied on, does say he was killed in Media in 311. If so, his foundations of 'Antiochia Arabis' and Dura-Europos took place before that date. In which case, we have a problem over names, for he is scarcely likely to name one of his cities 'Antiochia'. So what was the name Nikanor gave it? Europos is also awkward, for it was Seleukos' birth-place. No Antigonid satrap of Babylon would name a city after Seleukos' birth-place.

So an alternative reconstruction must be essayed. Assume Appian is wrong, and Nikanor did not die in Media in 311. He therefore lived on. In Antigonos' service? Unlikely, after his catastrophic failure. In Seleukos'? Surely this is possible. It would explain these cities as being his foundations, after 311. He would not be the first, nor the last, to switch sides and join Antigonos' enemy. After all, his whole army had done that. It would also be characteristic of Seleukos to put such a turncoat on the spot, by putting him in charge of the frontier over against his old master Antigonos, while Seleukos himself went off to the east. Those who deserted Antigonos did so wholeheartedly, for very good reasons, for he was a hard and at times an unjust master. Seleukos' reputation is very much the opposite, and Seleukos seems to have made a habit of giving great responsibility to his subordinates, and then trusting them, for which they rewarded him with conspicuous loyalty. He had entrusted the defence of Babylon to Patrokles in 311 [7], and later he gave the whole eastern part of his kingdom to his son Antiochos [8]. Nikanor would fit into this sort of pattern well enough. It is noticeable also, while on this subject, that Seleukos never suffered from rebellions by these subordinates. Ptolemy was always having trouble in Kyrene and Cyprus; Antigonos lost men regularly, even his nephew Ptolemaios; Lysimachos' kingdom collapsed in a welter of rebellion and disloyalty; Seleukos, on the other hand, commanded loyalty from all – until the very end, that is, when one he trusted turned on him, but the traitor, proving the point, was a Ptolemy.

To return to Nikanor. The two cities his name is associated with, Dura-Europos and Antiochia-Nisibis, are tellingly placed geographically. Dura-Europos is on the Euphrates, in desert land, blocking the route along that river from Syria to Babylonia. Antiochia-Nisibis (if Nisibis is the correct identification) is also placed to block a major route, from the Euphrates bridge to the upper Tigris, and then to Babylonia along that river. It is, in fact, this dual geographical situation which is the best reason for assuming that Antiochia-Nisibis is the correct identification, just because it blocks that route; Antioch-Edessa, the alternative, is too far east to be similarly effective, as well as having, as will be seen, towns nearby which seem to be foundations of Antigonos [9]. Hence both Dura and Nisibis block routes from Syria to Babylonia in such a way that an army commander advancing from Syria will be halted in the desert if he decides on a siege, or he will have to leave an enemy-held fortified city in his rear. These routes had both been used by invading armies: that along the Euphrates by the army of Kyros the Persian in 401 which included Xenophon among its officers; the northern route was Alexander's in 331, and that of Demetrios in 311, and perhaps that of Antigonos just after. Nikanor's foundations were thus sited as the result of the experiences of those invasions.

An alternative interpretation would be that Nikanor, the founder of these settlements was still working for Antigonos, and that these places were in fact settlements, thrown out from the direction of Syria so as to control the approach routes for Antigonos in preparation for a later attack. If that was the case one would not expect them to be given names closely connected with Seleukos (his father and his birth-place), and one *would* expect traces of Seleukid works facing them, and in the context this would be other fortified cities. There was room for them, east of Nisibis and further down the Euphrates from Dura. But they are not there. However, there is a line of settlements to the west of these two, which looks very much like a line established to block a possible attack from the east, from Babylonia or from Media. There are three of these settlements along the line of the Balikh river, which flows southwards to join the Euphrates 100 kilometres east of the Thapsakos bridge. One of them was Karrhai, which is known to have existed as a fortified site under Antigonos' control before Seleukos recaptured Babylon, and which presumably continued to exist, with a new garrison, after Seleukos had left it stripped of soldiers. Karrhai was an old city, and one worth controlling for its own sake; on either side of it to north and south there were settlements with Macedonian names, at Edessa near the source of the Balikh, and at Ichnai, near its junction with the Euphrates [10].

It is not possible to prove that these places were founded by or on behalf of Antigonos, but they have the appearance of a centrally planned line of defence. Their Macedonian names suggest a foundation date earlier than the coronations of the Macedonian generals, for cities founded after that tended to be given dynastic names. The assumption behind the whole theory, of course, is that it is inherently probable that Seleukos and Antigonos, in recovering from their mutual conflict, and recoiling from their collision, would automatically take measures to guard themselves against a surprise attack by the other. Seleukos' measures, in this interpretation, included the founding of military posts to block the two possible routes leading from Antigonos' lands into his own. Antigonos will have done the same, and, since Karrhai already existed, a guard-post on either side of it made military sense, since the line of three forts would provide a powerful advance guard for the bridge. At a guess Seleukos began the process, since he was the weaker of the two; and Antigonos then developed his own line from Karrhai outwards in reply.

There is also one other place in this area which has to be considered. South of Ichnai, at the actual junction of the

Balikh and Euphrates rivers, is the site of the city of Nikephorion [11]. This is generally attributed to Seleukos, partly by analogy with his nickname of Nikator, and partly on the evidence of Appian, who explicitly states that Seleukos was the founder [12]. There is no reason to doubt the fact. The problem is to find a suitable date for the foundation of the city. Seleukos could not found a city commemorating his victory before 308, since he was only assured of victory then. He could have founded and named such a city at any date after that, but 308–307, 301–300, or 281 are the three obvious dates, since those are the times following his three great victories. Working on the assumption – not necessarily valid – that Seleukos would be present at the official foundation ceremony for his cities, then the third is the least likely, for he was in western Asia Minor at the time; the first seems equally unlikely, since he was in the east at the time. The middle period is perhaps the most likely, for it was then that he was founding cities at a great rate in Syria nearby. The argument is, of course, very tenuous. The first victory is hardly likely to be commemorated by a city which was placed on the very doorstep of Antigonos' territory, by a ruler who then went off to the far east. That would be asking for the humiliation of losing the city named for his victory almost at once.

But suppose he really did found the place after beating Antigonos in Babylonia in 308. Nikephorion in that case would be a statement of intent, a boundary marker, and, with such a name, a deliberate provocation to Antigonos. Suppose Nikephorion was the first of the Mesopotamian foundations of either of these men, except for the pre-existing Karrhai. Then in that case Ichnai was a deliberate blocking foundation by Antigonos, pushed up close to Seleukos' town, to prevent Seleukos from exploiting north along the Balikh. It would explain the strange placing of Ichnai, whose logical site would have been at the river-junction, which the earlier theory left unoccupied.

The trouble with these theories is that they make unlikely assumptions about the characters of the two lords. If Nikephorion was a foundation of Seleukos in 308–307, it was a most uncharacteristically reckless manoeuvre, and every move Seleukos made in his rise to power suggests that he was a fundamentally careful and cautious man who waited for his opportunities until they had become virtual certainties. Equally unlikely is the response to such a challenge which is imputed to Antigonos. Everything about his conduct suggests that, had Seleukos pushed a foundation so far forward, Antigonos would have found it intolerable and would have attacked it rather than simply reacting by founding Ichnai close by. Of course he was old by this time, and partly preoccupied with events in the west, but his acquiescence seems most uncharacteristic. It is most likely, therefore, that Nikephorion was one of Seleukos' foundations to be dated about the year 300, and so it is one with the cities he founded in Syria.

Having thus mutually guarded their backs, Antigonos and Seleukos then proceeded to ignore one another for the next five years. Antigonos sent Demetrios to Greece and to his usual mixture of victory and defeat. Seleukos turned east. Antigonos, however, did not move his main force westwards until 307, when Demetrios with a fleet and an army arrived at Athens [13], so it was not until this move began that Seleukos could afford to make his own move. That is, he did not move east until the spring of 307, or perhaps even the summer; Demetrios was at Athens by June, so Seleukos could have been on the move by then.

Not that he would have been idle. The extensive destruction in Babylonia required his attention. The city of Babylon had changed hands at least twice during the fighting, each time as a result of direct attack, and it had undoubtedly suffered damage. It is at this point that the foundation of the new city of Seleukeia-on-the-Tigris would most happily fit, though its precise foundation date is not actually known [14]. The prospect of rebuilding the old city, encumbered with the physical and psychical remains of the long past, and politically dominated by the assertive and greedy priesthood of Esagila, would have been daunting, to say the least. To a Macedonian lord, the logical answer would have been to establish a new city. Lysimachos and Kassandros had already adopted this course, with Lysimacheia and Kassandreia. Antigonos was by 306 doing the same with Antigoneia in Syria, and most likely he began building earlier. The example of Alexander was always before them, and the example went back to Alexander's father, who had chosen Pella, only twenty kilometres from Seleukos' home town, as his new capital.

Seleukos, however, had a greater problem. He had to contend with the Babylonian priests who had already emerged victorious in a contest with Alexander. Seleukos' approach was different from Alexander's, for he was not as superstitious as Alexander – after all, he didn't have Olympias as his mother. The priests of Esagila – or, at least, some Babylonian priests – were consulted as to the most propitious day for founding the new city. They are said to have worked it out, then to have told Seleukos a different date, so as to curse the new city at birth with an unlucky foundation date, and hence, no doubt, to preserve the size and influence of Babylon and of themselves. This is quite a credible scenario. When the real date came, however, so we are told, an irresistible impulse took hold of the troops who were being used to begin the laying out, and the men began work spontaneously. When anxiously consulted, the priests confessed their lie [15].

This seems to be an account of events which may very well have happened. But it does need to be explained. The 'spontaneous' impulse is highly suspicious. A large number of troops may get all sorts of spontaneous impulses, but digging the foundations of a new city is unlikely to be one of them. If this dubious spontaneity is ignored, then there are other possible explanations for the event. One of the priests might have let out the real date; the 'spontaneity' was then so well organized that the priests lost face. Or the priests were browbeaten afterwards into agreeing that the actual date was really auspicious after all. It is necessary to accept that the priests did agree in the end that the day was auspicious, for if they had gone on claiming that the day of actual foundation was unlucky, then Babylonians could well have stayed away from the new city, whereas in fact many of them shifted to it within the next generation. If the city was to flourish the Babylonians would have to be attracted to it, for purely economic reasons.

This is probably an example of Seleukos' ability to manipulate religious belief to his own purpose and advantage. Ptolemy was doing the same with his promotion of the cult of Sarapis. Kassandros and others honoured Delphi and other shrines. All this is in strong contrast to the simple-minded credulity of Alexander, who was taken for a ride and then browbeaten by those very Babylonian priests whom Seleukos was manipulating in such a satisfactory manner. Perhaps it was a quality that was inherent in Seleukos, perhaps one inherent in all of Alexander's successors, who were, after all, mostly older and more cynical than Alexander had had a chance to become; perhaps it was simply a matter of increased familiarity with the forms and methods of Babylonian priestcraft. It is a fact, though, that Seleukos clearly comes out on top in this contest with the Babylonian priests, and by ensuring the success of his rival city, he had successfully sapped the foundations of their power. Babylonia would never be the same again.

The founding of a new city might be regarded as an act of royalty, and thus the founding of these cities – Kassandreia, Lysimacheia, Antigoneia, Seleukeia – might be thought of as acts of usurpation. But there was no king. Alexander IV had been killed in 310, and it is noticeable that none of these new cities predate his death. Even the first are technically refoundations – Thebes and Olynthos-Thessalonike by Kassandros, Kardia-Lysimacheia by Lysimachos. But Antigoneia and Seleukeia were as new as Alexandria.

Thus, even before taking the royal titles, Antigonos and Seleukos may well have been acting as kings. It is, in fact, specifically of these two men that it is recorded that they dealt with the populations of the east as the kings did. The peoples of the east, pragmatically, ignored Alexander IV, though in Babylonia the scribes continued pedantically to date by the years of his reign. Instead, they referred to Antigonos, as early as 315, after the elimination of Eumenes, as king [16]. Since he was disposing right and left of satraps and satrapies, collecting the royal treasure, and demanding a rendering of accounts, to call him king was a mere detail, a simple recognition of the location of power. The Greeks and Macedonians appear to have been a little shocked at this, and Antigonos, no matter how tempted he might have been, did not claim the royal title then. When Antigonos was beaten back from Babylonia by Seleukos, therefore, it was only logical for Seleukos to receive the acclamations of the same eastern peoples as king [17]. Ptolemy was disposing of the local kings in Cyprus, giving his own brother the title of king and employing the services of Philokles the king of Sidon; that is, Ptolemy was acting as an overlord of the local kings, which was a position previously only held by Alexander and his Persian predecessors.

The death of Alexander IV was public knowledge by 308. The peace agreements of 311 had sealed the boy's fate, for their practical effect was to recognize that each war-lord was independent. The only threat to that independence came from the growing king, who would soon be old enough to claim his inheritance. The murder was done secretly, of course, and only slowly did the word of his death spread [18]. It was not until this knowledge was in the public domain, until, that is, 308 or possibly even later, that any of the inheritors could publicly claim the title. And even then there was another prerequisite: military victory. From 315 onwards, no one had achieved a sufficiently spectacular victory to put him in the same league as Philip or Alexander. Even the one clearly decisive military success – Seleukos' resistance to Antigonos' attack – was defensive in nature. Also, since the fighting was in the east, no Greek or Macedonian would consider the victories worth very much. Yet from 308 onwards, the royal title was available for the man who won a sufficiently large victory, and all the great lords will have considered their chances. It was an ingredient in the constant fighting.

Seleukos' move to the east requires more of an explanation than this. The general opinion in the west seems to have been that the east was of no importance. Certainly Antigonos behaved as if that was his opinion. The east was clearly deficient in military resources, and its satraps were by now well entrenched – Stasanor had been in Baktria since Triparadisos. It could be that the attempt at conquest would merely absorb Seleukos' limited military manpower and add nothing to it. Comparing the troops he had in 312, before Antigonos' attack (about 25,000), and in 302, at the battle of Ipsos (about 32,000), it is clear that he did not gain much in a military sense from his eastern campaign – with the crucial exception of a corps of war-elephants.

Much of this was clear enough before Seleukos' move. Yet he had little choice but to make the attempt to conquer the east. Politically it made his name. It was a reminiscence of Alexander's conquest, and was thus a political statement of his ambition. It was also the only move he could make while Antigonos was too strong to be attacked. The only alternative to an eastern campaign was to do nothing, and it was politically impossible to do nothing. On a local level the wear and tear on the satrapal administration of the east had already left a number of vacancies, and this would only get worse as more time passed. This was therefore an opportunity for Seleukos to establish himself as *hegemon* of the east, the position to which his old colleague Peithon had aspired. If he did this, it would be one more sign of his actual power, one more statement of his ambition, one more sign that he was capable of wielding royal power. It also meant recreating Alexander's empire. Seleukos, of all the generals, was the one who now had the opportunity to do this. Antigonos could not, now. Ptolemy, Kassandros, and Lysimachos would not. Seleukos, by conquering the east, was also proclaiming his ambition to be Alexander's true successor.

At the end of his war with Antigonos in 308, Seleukos was lord of only that part of the east which he had acquired in 312: Babylonia and western Iran as far as, probably, Persis and Parthia; eastern Iran and India were still out of his grasp. The death of the satrap Evager, who was probably the satrap Evagoras of Aria, in the Tigris night battle, and the known submission of Susiana and Persis, allow the presumption that Seleukos' authority reached as far as the eastern borders of Aria and Persis. The fact that Antigonos himself, in his moment of triumph at Persepolis, had not attempted to displace most of the eastern satraps, means that one can equally assume that those men were still firmly established in the eastern satrapies and must by now have considered themselves virtually independent. In particular Stasanor, the satrap of Baktria and Sogdiana, had contributed only small forces to the joint satrapal army back in 317–316, and Oxyartes in the Paropamisadai had seemed similarly unenthusiastic. Antigonos had simply left them alone without, it seems, extracting even a token submission, and had simply confirmed others in office.

It has to be presumed that the satraps employed or confirmed by Antigonos in 315 remained in office to face Seleukos in and after 307. It seems quite likely that at least one of them will have been killed or otherwise removed in that time, given the reasonably high satrapal casualty rate, but without new evidence, it is impossible to know. In fact, there is only one sentence which is directly relevant to the events of 307–

305: Justin says that Seleukos 'first took Babylon, and then, his strength being increased by his success, subdued the Baktrians'[19]. Since the first two parts of the sentence are accurate, if somewhat excessively compressed, it seems reasonable to accept the third part as a summary of a longer account. It implies a war between Seleukos' forces and an opposing force in Baktria. The last satrap we know of is Stasanor of Soli, who was transferred to Baktria as far back as Triparadeisos, and left in office by Antigonos. If still in power, he was by now well entrenched, and it will have taken fighting to shift him. He could claim, after all, an equal status with Seleukos, for both appointments were of the same date, and equally he could refuse obedience since he owed his office to the Macedonians, just the argument Seleukos had used against Antigonos. Stasanor's difficulty, if he did use this argument, was that no-one was listening. Apart from his fellow-satraps in the east, no-one would now be impressed by such a legalistic argument. Certainly not Seleukos' troops. Seleukos controlled the communications to the west, and Stasanor's only hope lay in gaining help from a western potentate, which could only mean Antigonos. In effect Stasanor was on his own.

'Baktrians', however, in Justin's brief notice, might also mean the native inhabitants rather than the forces of the Greek satrap. In fact, on the face of it, this would be the natural meaning one would assign to the phrase. Yet all warfare at the time had consisted of fighting between Macedonian lords and their armies and it has seemed reasonable to assume that this war was similar. There is, however, some evidence to suggest that Stasanor's grip on his large satrapy had loosened with time. Some coins were produced in the name of two men, Sophytes and Vakshuvar, who are otherwise not known. Since the findspots of the coins are confined to Central Asia, and since they bear resemblances to other coins of this period, they are assigned to this difficult gap in Baktrian history, between Alexander and Seleukos [20]. Many assumptions are involved. The interpretation is that these men ruled, in Akhaimenid-satrap fashion, over parts of Stasanor's satrapy in rebellion against him [21]. And this multiplies the possibilities available to Seleukos on his way east.

He could arrive in Baktria as one coming to rescue the Greek-speaking settlers; he could claim to be coming to help out the hapless Stasanor; he could come proclaiming his disinterested pursuit of peace and reconciliation, pointing all the while to his Baktrian wife and half-Persian son, and his own Macedonian-ness. Whatever he said, his words were perhaps more likely to be accepted at their face value by the Greeks and Macedonians, and certainly Justin states explicitly that he had to fight the Baktrians. He would be helped to a victory if there was at the time also a threat from the nomads across the northern frontier – and it is a safe bet that the confusion in Baktria had encouraged them to become threatening, if not worse. He could then proclaim the identity of interest of all peace-loving sedentary folk over against the wild horsemen of the steppes.

As well, Seleukos will have arrived in full force, and his army included, not just Macedonians and Greeks but Iranian hillmen as well, such as those 'Guti' the Babylonian Chronicle noted. This was exactly the mixture of peoples existing in Baktria, though from a smaller geographical area, on a smaller and weaker economic base, and having that constant anxiety of an open nomadic frontier. Seleukos, then, had political advantages which Stasanor could not match. Above all, perhaps it was Apama's presence which was decisive. She was no nonentity, if we may judge from her apparently autonomous participation in gift-giving to Apollo at Didyma later [22]. Her existence made it very likely that Seleukos would be a kindly and generous ruler of Baktrians, as his reputation will have already attested. He could show he was open to his Baktrian subjects, and that he was likely to be careful of their interests; above all, he was likely to allow them to participate in the defence of the nomad frontier, which meant participating in local government. He could show that his power, added to that of the Baktrians, would be a powerful reinforcement of their security. This would form a clear contrast to the destructiveness of Alexander's visitation, which cannot have been recalled with any pleasure by the Baktrians, and to the inevitable partiality of Stasanor's rule. If he and the coin-producing Persians had been fighting each other, the claims of reconciliation might be even more persuasive.

A good deal of all this is speculative, but not overly so. The fact is that Seleukos conquered Baktria with relative ease. He did not have to fight as hard or as long as Alexander, and he did not fail, as Antiochos III did later. The fact of his success is emphasized by the additional fact that he could afford to move on to war in India immediately afterwards, apparently without any serious fear of revolt to his rear, and then, after his failure in India, he could move back to the west, to another war, again without fear of a Baktrian rebellion. This confidence powerfully suggests that he knew full well that Baktria was safe, that his conquest in 307–306 had resulted in a strong weld between the two halves of Iran. And in fact it took the physical separation of Baktria from Iran by the successful thrust of the Arsacid Parni into the province of Parthia fifty years later to compel the Baktrian satrap to become an independent king [23].

So Seleukos succeeded in conquering Baktria. He thus doubled the size of his lands, and the conquest brought him into contact with India, which proved to be his most formidable enemy. The Indian provinces of Alexander's empire had gone through an even more violent series of changes than the rest. Virtually all trace of Alexander and his conquests had vanished. His progress through India had been the nastiest episode of his career of destructive violence, with scarcely a redeeming feature [24]. Like all purely destructive episodes, it had left almost no trace. One by one the men he had left to rule in the Indus valley had disappeared, by assassination or by desertion [25]. In their place came the force which had so frightened the Macedonian soldiers that the mere threat of facing it had moved them to defy even Alexander.

Those hard-bitten veterans had been frightened by the rumours of the power of the dominant state in the valley of the Ganges, the kingdom of Magadha [26]. Soon after Alexander, power in Magadha was usurped by two men. The new king was Chandragupta, a general and the first of the Maurya dynasty; the planner of the military *coup* was his minister, Kautilya. Between them, these two went on to plan and execute a huge expansion of the power of Magadha, overthrowing all the other local states in the Ganges valley and those of the Indus as well [27]. When he also incorporated the lands of the Narbada valley, Chandragupta had articulated the classic Indian imperial configuration, which was repeated constantly until the British invasion finally broke the mould. The Greeks claimed later, in their usual arrogant way, that

Chandragupta had been inspired to his conquest by seeing Alexander during his meteor-like passage [28]. This was quite possible, of course, but in truth there was nothing about Alexander's career in India that was inspirational for any Indian, and the story entirely neglects the facts of Indian history, Chandragupta's earlier life, and above all it ignores the central political role of Kautilya.

It comforted Greeks and Macedonians to suggest that Chandragupta was a surrogate Greek, because in his conflict with Seleukos, Chandragupta was a clear winner. Once he had conquered Baktria, Seleukos, emulating Alexander all too predictably, moved on India. He must have been expected, having been fighting in Baktria already for some time. Perhaps he achieved a sort of tactical surprise, since Appian mentions that he crossed the Indus river [29]. Yet even this need not mean much, even if it is true. If Seleukos marched through Oxyartes' satrapy of Paropamisadai and down the Kabul river, as is so likely as to be a virtual certainty, he would find the Indus at the end of that valley, just as Alexander did. Getting over the river was no great trick, but holding on to any territory there was a different matter. There was no reason for Indians in the Indus valley to welcome a Macedonian army, and many reasons for them to unite against it. Chandragupta only had to let Seleukos cross the Indus, and Seleukos would find himself in a trap, with a large river at his back and a hostile continent before him.

So Seleukos can have got little or no further into India than the banks of the Indus river. Such fighting as there was produced a decisive Indian victory, with Seleukos reeling back through the passes as far as Baktria, and with Chandragupta's armies moving up through the hills to remove from Seleukos' control all the high Afghan plateau which is the *glacis* of India. With that land under Indian control, no invasion is possible. If it is under the control of a powerful non-Indian state, then the invasion of India from the region of Afghanistan is facilitated, is in fact almost inevitable, because Afghanistan is poor and India is rich.

It has to be admitted that there is little or no evidence for the above account. Appian is the only ancient source to mention Seleukos' crossing of the Indus, and Appian is not very reliable. The career of Chandragupta is as unclear as that of Seleukos in the east [30]. Yet the central fact of Seleukos' defeat is inescapable, for he surrendered not only the Indus valley to Chandragupta, but Arachosia as well [31]. This can only mean that Seleukos ended up facing an Indian army west of the Hindu Kush. Equally inescapable is the fact that Seleukos invaded India in the first place. He had to. He was in effect claiming the mantle of Alexander. Presumably he did not expect it to fit quite so well as to include defeats for both of them in India. But both his invasion and his defeat are clear. Beyond that, it is not possible to go without further evidence [32].

Seleukos made an agreement with Chandragupta, a good old-fashioned peace treaty as between equals, between kings. By this time, in fact, he was probably calling himself king and wearing the diadem. By the treaty Seleukos surrendered all control over India's approaches. Not only did he give up any interest in the Indian satrapies themselves, but he allowed Chandragupta to take over Arachosia and Gedrosia as well. There is no reason to believe Strabo when he includes Aria in the list; given Seleukos' continued control of Parthia and Baktria, he must, geographically, have held Aria as well, and Seleukos' son Antiochos was active there fifteen years later [33]. In return, perhaps relieved that the war was over, and probably well informed about the situation in the west, Chandragupta gave Seleukos a force of elephants. The size of this force is said to be 500, a figure which has been widely doubted, even explained away by reference to traditional Indian mathematics [34]. Why that should dictate a figure only found in Greek sources is not clear. If Seleukos did not get 500 elephants, we do not know how many he got. But there seems no real reason to doubt the number, other than its suspicious roundness. In propaganda terms, of course, the '500' is a good clear, round, and memorable figure. And, it may have seemed, frightening and overwhelming, too. The number had already been used by Antigonos, in his preliminary propaganda over the construction of a fleet [35]. Perhaps Seleukos had learnt the lesson.

The question is worth pursuing, however, for it sheds light on a series of connected matters, and thus on Seleukos himself. First, there is the matter of whether Chandragupta could afford so many elephants, together with attendants and mahouts. The rumour credited by the Macedonian army in 326 put the elephant forces of the kingdoms of the Ganges at 4,000 [36]. Since Poros, the king they had just beaten, who ruled over a section of the Punjab, had had 200 elephants [37], 4,000 in the Ganges valley is not an unlikely figure. It was a time of intense political conflict in which armed force was the deciding factor, and the greater a king's army the more powerful the king. By 303 the forces of all the various competing kingdoms in northern India had fallen to Chandragupta. He was credited by Pliny with an infantry force of 600,000 men, and an elephant force of 9,000 [38]. In the history of Rome, the equivalent period is after the final victory of Octavian, whose army, made up of his own, Antony's, and Lepidus', numbered about that figure. So both 600,000 infantry and 9,000 elephants are quite credible as a force for the ruler of all north India, a land equivalent in size and resources with the Roman Mediterranean. Chandragupta could well have afforded 500 elephants. The army he had was undoubtedly too big now that all his enemies were vanquished. It would be eating up the economic resources of northern India at a quite unacceptable pace. One of Chandragupta's and Kautilya's priorities must have been to reduce the army, so that giving 500 of the elephants to Seleukos, who would then have to feed them, was an admirable and economical solution. It was, after all, most unlikely that Seleukos would ever again attack India, after the drubbing he had received. And if he did, a force of 500 elephants would hardly be decisive against the remaining 8,500. And, anyway, no doubt Chandragupta and Kautilya made sure that Seleukos got only the oldest of the elephants. There were certainly none of them left thirty years later.

So from the point of view of Chandragupta this was a good exchange. He reduced his over-large elephant park, and at the same time enlarged his empire by the addition of provinces beyond the Hindu Kush, provinces which were an admirable barbican to interrupt any attempted invasion from that direction. In addition Chandragupta could claim both a victory and a peace. There were benefits, military, political, and economic, for Chadragupta in all aspects of the treaty with Seleukos. In that sense it is an entirely reasonable and credible transaction.

The second aspect of the problem is the relationship of

those 500 elephants to warfare in the west. Elephants were reasonably familiar as war animals in western armies by 302. Not only had Alexander met them at the battle by the Hydaspes (at which Seleukos, Ptolemy, and Lysimachos had all been present) but he had even met a few of them at Gaugamela before that. All Macedonian armies in every battle since then had possessed or had met elephants, at Gabiene, at Paraitakene, and at Gaza. In no battle had they been decisive. Their methods and tactics were quite familiar by now, and they could be beaten, as Ptolemy had shown at Gaza (or, indeed, as had Alexander at both Gaugamela and the Hydaspes). But no one since Poros had ever had so many. Eumenes had 85 at Paraitakene and Antigonos 65 [39]; at Gabiene the numbers were 114 and 65 respectively [40]; at Gaza Demetrios had 43, and Ptolemy none [41], which stimulated the latter to work out a successful set of tactics for dealing with them. So a force of 500 was much bigger than anything seen by a Macedonian army, bigger even than the largest force they had seen in India. And at the one battle which counted, Ipsos, Seleukos' elephants were, for once, decisive.

That is to say, Seleukos knew what he was doing when he accepted defeat in India, and took away his consolation prize. On the one hand, defeat in India would hardly affect his prestige in the west, since Seleukos himself would be the means by which the news was disseminated, and he was a good propagandist. On the other hand, he gained a weapon which would, properly handled, win him a battle in the west which would efface any doubts about the war in India. No doubt his own troops were partly annoyed at losing and partly relieved at not having to fight longer in India against the huge, efficient, and war-hardened Indian forces. There could be no dishonour in failing to beat such enormous armies. Added to which, the presence in the Paropamisadai and Arachosia of a powerful Indian empire would help to keep the Baktrians in order, since their secession from the Seleukid state would then open their southern flank to a possible Indian attack. The benefits to Seleukos of this treaty were not, therefore, confined to 500 elephants, and he was of agile enough an intelligence to see it. Peace in his eastern lands was now as necessary for his western ambitions as peace in the west had been before he moved eastwards.

Seleukos was in the east, probably continuously, from 307 to 303, four years. Peace was probably made with Chandragupta in 303. During that time, developments in the west had again reached a crisis. Seleukos was never out of touch with events in the west, and, despite his eastern preoccupations, he was ready at all times to react to events in the west. Thus, in 306 he was apprised by Ptolemy of the defeat of the joint land and sea invasion of Egypt by Antigonos and Demetrios, which had followed on the destruction of Ptolemy's fleet at Salamis in Cyprus and the loss of that island [42]. No doubt the desert route to Babylonia was used again. Seleukos did not have to do anything but rejoice on this occasion, no doubt appreciating the irony that the first ventures of the newly proclaimed kings had resulted in defeat. Antigonos had taken the title after Salamis and had conferred it on Demetrios also. Their next venture was a failure as well, for Rhodes resisted Demetrios' siege, helped by Ptolemy, and as a result Ptolemy also took the royal title.

This triggered off the rest. Seleukos [43], Lysimachos, and Kassandros all became kings, and Agathokles in Sicily soon joined in [44]. This all took place while Seleukos was on his eastern campaign. It was the custom to delay taking the title until a victory made the deed seem blessed. The conquest of Baktria would be a most satisfactory moment for the deed.

The Babylonians, however, were not fooled. The scribes there who recorded events both in the heavens and on the earth recorded the matter prosaically: 'Year 7, which is [his] first year, Seleukos king' [45]. They knew that he had been effectively king in Babylon since 312, no matter what title he actually chose. So did all the east, towards whom Seleukos had habitually acted as king. So did Chandragupta. So the Babylonian scribe's contradictory dating makes perfect sense, and no doubt he sighed with relief at having an easy formula to use once more.

The barrage of title-taking only highlighted once more the extensive ambiguity of the positions of all these Macedonian lords. They were all kings of the Macedonians [46], by implication, of all the Macedonians, though by 303 B.C. there were only two men in a position to realize that ambition, Antigonos and Seleukos. So the stage was set for another fight. Seleukos began to move back to the west. He had recoiled from the last collision to acquire new lands in the east. He now recoiled from a collision in the east to seek new power in the west.

7
VICTOR AND ORGANIZER (303–298)

The new war in the west was, once again, an attempt by Antigonos to expand his power. Demetrios' failure to conquer Rhodes had been spectacular but, as it turned out, unimportant. By moving at once from Rhodes to the relief of Athens, which had been beleaguered for a year by Kassandros' forces, Demetrios had gone from an attempt to suppress a free city to the rescue of another. It seemed that the old policy of promoting Greek civic freedom was reinstated. The Greeks fell for it yet again. In a year Demetrios had cleared Kassandros' forces out of all of Greece south of Thermopylai. Then he set about fastening his and his father's control on the freed peninsula.

Demetrios revived the old Hellenic League, which had been Philip II's and Alexander's instrument of imperial control in Greece, but now with Demetrios himself as *hegemon* [1]. This meant that so long as the war lasted, he controlled Greece. Kassandros, seeing what was about to happen to him, sued for terms from Antigonos. Again the old man threw the substance away for the sake of a shadow, and demanded unconditional surrender [2]. It was now Kassandros' turn to send out appeals for help combined with warnings. He also prepared to resist attack by seizing the initiative.

Kassandros appealed for help to Lysimachos and Ptolemy [3]. Since he had done nothing to assist Ptolemy's forces in Greece while they were being overrun by Demetrios, no doubt Ptolemy reacted coolly. He certainly did not do anything active, though he did send on the message to Seleukos [4]. Lysimachos, on the other hand, was alarmed, since if Kassandros was beaten, he would be next. He was willing to fall in with Kassandros' plan to seize the initiative, but required some of Kassandros' soldiers to implement it. Kassandros supplied these, plus a general, Prepelaos, to command them [5] and presumably to secure part of the conquests for himself.

In all this there is the usual difficulty of divining the actual intentions of any of these men at any particular moment, and it is in this instance compounded by the difficulty of deciding just when everyone did everything. It is reasonable to assume that all four were looking after their own interests first, and that they allied because they could see no other way of surviving. No particular surprise need be evinced that the alliance lasted until the day after the defeat of their joint enemy, and no longer. This was inherent in the situation.

When exactly a clear alliance had been formed is difficult to say, since it depended on Ptolemy and Seleukos. Ptolemy scarcely moved. Seleukos was miles away, but was moving west, elephants and all. Diodoros states that they agreed to assist Kassandros as soon as they were told of the new war [6]. But this cannot be so, partly because of their great physical separation, and partly because this is exactly what they did not do. No co-operation can have taken place until the winter of 302–301, since only then was it clear what had to be done. The alliance was one purely of convenience and opportunity, and was determined as much by the actions of Antigonos and Demetrios as by the intentions of the allies.

Kassandros was the man under immediate attack. He stood on the defensive in Thessaly, in a fortified camp which successfully hypnotized the attentions of Demetrios' larger army [7]. Lysimachos, with a detachment of Kassandros' army, now successfully drew the attention of Antigonos by a surprise invasion of Asia Minor. He penetrated deep into Antigonos' lands, as far as Synnada in Phrygia, where he persuaded the ever-pliable Dokimos to change sides. Kassandros' detachment under Prepelaos ranged along the coast of Ionia as far as Ephesos. Several of the cities in Ionia, including Ephesos, were captured [8].

Lysimachos' activity was eye-catching and spectacular, though it was not really solidly based. Yet it stung Antigonos into immediate activity. He was at his new city of Antigoneia in northern Syria when the news of Lysimachos' invasion arrived. That the news was a surprise is shown by the fact that he was in the middle of celebrating a city-festival. He broke these celebrations off, scattering 200 talents among the professional artists in attendance, and marched off to war [9]. It is also clear that Antigonos' army was instantly available. He had in other words already concentrated his army in northern Syria, ready for war.

Who Antigonos had been intending to fight is, however, less clear. Since he was surprised by the move made by Lysimachos, Antigonos must have been expecting to fight someone else, and that must mean either Ptolemy or Seleukos. For this he was in a good position, between their two armies, and so able to march against either, or each in turn. Yet he was hardly going to chase Seleukos through Babylonia and Iran, nor can one seriously expect Antigonos to be intent on yet another attack on Egypt. The most likely hypothesis is that he was intending to stand on the defensive, blocking the junction of Seleukos and Ptolemy, while Demetrios eliminated first Kassandros and then Lysimachos. Demetrios' immobility in Thessaly and Lysimachos' move into Asia now made this impossible. Antigonos now had to change his plans, though his aim was still to deal with his enemies one by one. He took his main army with him to face Lysimachos in Asia Minor [10], presumably aiming to eliminate him first, but he also left some troops behind in garrison to hold up any awkward invasions by Ptolemy and Seleukos. This certainly worked on Ptolemy, but not on Seleukos.

Seleukos' precise position and movements while all this was going on are unknown, as usual. In general terms he was moving westwards from Central Asia, but since his starting time, his point of departure, and his speed are all unknown, any precision is impossible. He had made peace with Chandragupta Maurya during 303, so he had been free to move west at any time since then. It is clear that he spent the winter of 303–302 in the east. Possibly the Indian treaty was concluded so late in the year that he could not travel west before it was necessary to put his army into winter quarters. Maybe he had to make his presence felt in Baktria after his defeat in India. The elephants perhaps took some time to reach him, and he would certainly need time to collect the vast quantities of food they would need for the journey west. There is plenty here to have kept him and his army in the east during that winter.

The message from the west cannot have reached him before the summer of 302. Kassandros' appeal to Ptolemy and Lysimachos was made after the formation of the League at Corinth early in that year. Kassandros then asked terms from Antigonos, who replied from Syria, and only then did Kassandros appeal to Ptolemy, who passed on the news to Seleukos, across their desert line of emergency communication. If the League was formed in, say, March, then it does not seem likely that Kassandros can have sent his appeal to Ptolemy before May at the very earliest, or for Seleukos to have received Ptolemy's message before June or July. The middle of 302 for Seleukos' first move west certainly helps to explain the subsequent course of events.

Seleukos probably had already reached Iran. He will have travelled by the normal route, between the Elburz mountains and the Dasht-i-Lut, through Hekatompylos and Rhagai, heading for Ekbatana. While he travelled, Lysimachos moved into Asia, Demetrios attacked Kassandros, and Antigonos moved from Antigoneia to face Lysimachos. It seems probable that Antigonos' reaction to Lysimachos' invasion occurred at more or less the same time as Seleukos heard from Ptolemy.

Seleukos took up headquarters at Ekbatana. (The other possibility is Babylon, but it was scarcely on the main route from Iran to Asia; and it was August, not royalty's favourite month in Babylonia.) Ptolemy reacted as Antigonos had expected. He invaded Palestine, and steadily re-took all the towns and cities as far as Sidon, which he besieged [11]. Since he eventually abandoned the siege when everyone else was into winter quarters, he probably began his invasion more or less as soon as he heard the news of Antigonos' move north, say in July or August.

Seleukos faced a more difficult and complex logistical and geographical problem. His natural route from Ekbatana to join with his allies was through Mesopotamia and Syria. Yet this, for him, was impossible. He would be able to travel through his own territory as far as Nisibis, but then there would loom before him a sequence of increasingly difficult obstacles. First were the cities – Edessa, Karrhai, Ichnai – planted by Antigonos for the very purpose of warding Seleukos off. He would have to capture at least one of these. Then there was the Euphrates to cross, at Thapsakos. The bridge, we can be sure, would not have survived by the time he reached the river. In Syria were garrisoned strongpoints, as in Mesopotamia, of which he would need to capture at least some. He would have to cross the Amanus, by a difficult pass which could be blocked, and then maybe (depending on the pass he used) break through to Kilikia along the coast at the Pillars of Jonah, where there were old fortifications. Finally, if Antigonos had not by this time eliminated Lysimachos and returned to the east, Seleukos would have to cross the Taurus by the Kilikian Gates, notoriously easy to block.

Such a sequence – which Seleukos will have known and discussed with his advisers – was what Antigonos had planned for him. It was, in a way, what Ptolemy was doing, and he had got stuck at Sidon, only a quarter of the way to the Taurus. If Seleukos did the same, the war would be lost, all the allies defeated in isolation.

So he went a different way. The actual route is, as always, not known, but he did winter in Kappadokia [12]. This suggests that he had marched from Media by one of two routes: by way of the basin of Lake Urmiah and Lake Van and then by the valley of the Kara source of the Euphrates, or through the northern Tigris valley and into Kappadokia in the area of Melitene. Both of these routes debouch into Kappadokia, and both are slow and difficult, though the second traversed territory which was under Seleukos' control for part of the way. It would not be at all surprising to find a large army, encumbered with elephants, taking several months on either route. Seleukos probably did not start from Ekbatana until August, and would find his route in these high altitudes blocked by snow by December at the latest, possibly by November, quite apart from any problems with fodder and supplies. A thought may be spared for the logistical feat which Seleukos accomplished, of moving a large army into Kappadokia together with the supplies required to keep that army alive for several months. The longer one contemplates this move, the greater must be our appreciation of the difficulties and of the magnitude of the achievement.

By the time Seleukos was in winter-quarters in Kappadokia with 32,000 men, 12,000 cavalry horses and remounts, several hundred elephants, and thousands of pack-animals [13], Lysimachos himself was wintering his own forces in the Salonian

Plain [14], 400 kilometres away in the north west of Asia Minor, and Antigonos was in his old base of Phrygia [15]. Antigonos had been baffled by Lysimachos' tactics, just as his son had been baffled by Kassandros'. Both allies had built formidable fortresses and stayed inside them, defying their enemies and neutralizing the Antigonid numerical superiority. Lysimachos had occupied a succession of camps, slowly drawing north from Sardis until the winter closed in. By that time Antigonos was weary of the game and pulled his forces back into Phrygia [16]. It was news of an incident in this intricate and difficult campaign which, magnified into a battle by the rumour, persuaded Ptolemy to move back to Egypt for the winter [17]. Otherwise it was likely he would have maintained the siege of Sidon all through, unlike Antigonos, who gave up his sieges.

Lysimachos was able to draw supplies from the coast behind him, for he had a working alliance with the city of Heraklea [18], and he received some more reinforcements from Kassandros by that route, though a large part of the force died in crossing the Black Sea in the winter storms [19]. Lysimachos had, with Kassandros' troops, about 45,000 men [20]. Antigonos also called in reinforcements from Greece under Demetrios [21], who recaptured much of Prepelaos' conquests in Ionia when he arrived [22]. Antigonos concentrated an army of 80,000 men plus 75 elephants at the plain of Ipsos [23]. He therefore still had the advantage of numbers, and he also had the chance of interposing himself between the two armies of Lysimachos and Seleukos and thus of defeating them in detail so long as he moved fast enough and early enough.

He did not do so. By a move which is completely lost to us, the two allies succeeded in joining their forces and marched to attack Antigonos. This is clear from the fact that the battle took place close to Antigonos' winter camp. Seleukos must have broken his winter quarters early and marched to join Lysimachos before Antigonos could move to intercept him. However it was done, it was a masterstroke. It is also a cause for wonder. The winter in Kappadokia is colder and longer than in the west of Asia Minor, and Antigonos was in the area where, in the interior, winter ends as early as anywhere. He really should have been able to block the allies' junction. But he was 81, probably too old for what he was about [24].

Demetrios was there, but he was always subservient to his father, losing all initiative when they were together. Despite this, Seleukos must be given the credit for getting under way as soon as he did, marching 400 kilometres in the last days of winter to join his ally. If Antigonos during the winter was in a position which anticipated that of Napoleon before Waterloo, Seleukos' march was a vastly greater achievement than that of Blücher. The fact that Seleukos and Lysimachos successfully joined their forces perhaps persuaded Antigonos not to move from his own base, where he was close to supplies and to his treasure, and where he could prepare the ground for the battle.

The battle took place in the early summer of 301. The allies were slightly outnumbered in infantry, 70,000 to 64,000, but had more cavalry, 15,000 to 10,000, and more elephants, 400 or 480 to 75 [25]. They therefore planned to use their strengths and to refuse an infantry fight. Antigonos' elephants were neutralized by an equal number of Seleukos' beasts; Demetrios' cavalry was induced to charge at the allied cavalry commanded by Seleukos' son Antiochos, and was then enticed away from the field by a retreat which seems to have been planned; the remaining elephants, over 300 of them, then blocked off Demetrios' return. With the rest of his cavalry, Seleukos rode around behind the infantry phalanx, issuing threats and promises alternately until Antigonos' force began to break up and desert. In the final fight Antigonos was killed. Demetrios fled [26].

Lysimachos had been in charge on one wing, Seleukos on the other; neither could have won the battle alone. Yet the plan looks very much like something produced by Seleukos. It involved especially the elephants and the cavalry, and those were mainly his own troops, for Lysimachos' cavalry was only a quarter the numbers of Seleukos' [27]. Yet Lysimachos' infantry had been the solid foundation around which all the manoeuvring had been based [28], and Lysimachos had a better control of his infantry than almost any other general of the time. The battle was thus a joint victory for the two generals.

In addition Kassandros had assisted with his timely reinforcements at considerable risk to his own position. It was only reasonable that these three kings should share the loot.

What was not so clear was that Ptolemy should be allowed a share. He had duly invaded Syria and besieged Sidon. He *could* have done more, such as delivering reinforcements to help Lysimachos, though this would have been very hazardous for Demetrios' fleet held control of the Aegean and his troops had regained control of the Ionian ports. In Syria it seems unlikely that Ptolemy could have done much more than he did. His problem was the same as Seleukos' had been when summoned to Asia Minor from Media: in Syria he was cut off from the main area of action, and he had no means of reaching it. Furthermore, there was no point in his marching to the Taurus mountains, for he would not get through. Not that there was ever any prospect of his doing any such thing. Ptolemy had never, over a period of twenty years, shown any interest in acquiring any part of Syria north of the line of the Eleutherus river, and he was not about to change now. His move into southern Syria in late 302 was designed to conquer that area and annex it to his existing possessions.

The rumour of the defeat of Lysimachos led Ptolemy to make a four-month armistice with the Sidonian commander and return to winter-quarters in Egypt. This was entirely sensible. He could disperse his troops for the winter, and they were not exposed to a sudden attack by Demetrios or by Antigonos by sea or by land. Since he had made a truce with Sidon, he clearly intended to return.

And so he did, in the spring, well before the great battle. The news of Ipsos reached him in his old camp at Sidon [29]. So did the news of the division of Antigonos' kingdom agreed on by the other allies. Ptolemy was not included on the grounds that he had not taken part in the final decisive battle [30]. Lysimachos took Asia Minor, Seleukos Syria and Mesopotamia. Kassandros' brother Pleistarchos, who had brought in the reinforcements by sea in the winter, and who had fought at Ipsos, was given Kilikia [31]. This division was sensible and simple. It did not give much to Kassandros, but he gained a good deal in Greece, where the Antigonid position had begun to crumble as soon as Demetrios was recalled by his father and which now collapsed when the news of Ipsos arrived [32]. Above all, Kassandros ceased to have any fear of Demetrios. And, of course, Kassandros had not been present at the battle.

It had presumably been intended that Seleukos' share would

extend as far south as Gaza and Raphia, the borders of Egypt. But Ptolemy had returned and was in occupation of land he had conquered. He was besieging Sidon, and controlled Palestine. He clearly felt entitled to keep these conquests. In addition, it was in his interest to occupy a good forward position in Syria, and this interest did not depend on the result of the fighting in Asia Minor. If Antigonos won, Ptolemy at some stage would come under attack, and a position well forward of the River of Egypt would be a useful defence; if the allies won, the occupied area would be his share of the spoils. He must have heard the comments which come through in our sources, that he scuttled back to Egypt at the first word of a rumour [33]. Those comments were the first moves in the diplomatic game which followed the destruction of Antigonos. The allies were allies for one purpose only, to beat their common enemy; after that, they ceased to be allies. And meanwhile all were looking for ways to improve their positions.

The swift defeat of Antigonos meant that Ptolemy had done little more than resume the attack on Sidon when he found that the situation had changed. He could not now concentrated on Sidon (or Tyre, which also still held out for Demetrios, in case Seleukos decided to enforce his claim to all Syria. Ptolemy clearly marked out his limits, by occupying the land as far north as the Eleutheros river [34]. Then he sat tight.

One part of the loot of which Ptolemy did not get his share was the Antigonid army. This was perhaps the most valuable part, though there was also the fleet, as well as the land itself. The army was partly concentrated at Ipsos, but also there were garrisons, small and large, scattered from Thessaly to Mesopotamia and Tyre. The Ipsos army had surrendered in batches, some to Lysimachos, some to Seleukos, perhaps some to Antiochos [35]. Part of it marched off with Demetrios, almost 10,000 men [36]. The forces in Greece seem to have melted away. Since they were mercenaries, perhaps the men were simply hired by the places in which they were stationed. No doubt Kassandros collected some men, and Demetrios himself was able to collect some from the Corinth area, with which he resumed the war by attacking Lysimachos [37].

The rest of the Ipsos army must have been divided between

Lysimachos and Seleukos, but upon what basis no source so much as provides a hint. Since the troops were partly mercenaries and partly 'Macedonians' it would seem reasonable to assume that they themselves would choose their new employer. Yet it is probably not so simple as that, for these soldiers were not all uprooted wanderers. Some of them had families and homes. The king who became the lord of the land in which their home was would be the most likely new employer for them.

Antigonos' kingdom, like all kingdoms, had been held together by military force. His soldiers were a mixture of Greek mercenaries, Macedonians from Alexander's and other armies, and Asian mercenaries recruited from his own territories. Their common language was Greek. These men, by 301, had been in Antigonos' employ for up to twenty years, possibly even longer, and many of them will have felt a loyalty to the old king, and possibly also a loyalty to Demetrios. But their service will have been made mostly in garrisons. The wars and campaigns were spectacular but brief. Antigonos himself does not seem to have stirred from Syria for five years (307 to 302); Demetrios operated with the same army, recruited up to strength locally, in Athens and Rhodes and Greece and Thessaly during those years. Therefore, the army which surrendered at Ipsos was largely composed of men whose loyalties lay partly with the kings and partly with their homes. Many of those men had become domiciled in the garrison towns to which Antigonos had assigned them. Their families will often have been left there when Antigonos concentrated his forces; in defeat, no doubt, many of the soldiers simply wanted to go home.

Where those homes were is, in some cases, known. Not directly, of course, but certainly by implication. For example, Antigonos' city of Antigoneia in Syria had a population of some tens of thousands, a substantial proportion of the males being in his army [38]. Other cities supposedly founded by Antigonos are usually, in fact, not so much new cities as old ones interfered with. He established Antigoneia in the Troad by sweeping the people of several small and some not so small cities into his new one [39]. He compelled the synoecism of Teos and Lebedos [40]. In both cases the act remained unpopular with significant numbers of his victims. Smyrna was a new foundation [41], probably by Antigonos' agency, and there was emphasis on his freedom propaganda at other places in Ionia – Erythrai, Miletos, Kolophon [42]. But the record is spotty, and when the time came he was unable to prevent these places falling to Lysimachos' attack. Thus either he had to garrison the cities to defend them, and so deny his own pretensions, or he had to leave them ungarrisoned and therefore vulnerable to attack.

In the interior of Asia Minor the rhetoric was unnecessary since Greek cities were absent. But there were urban centres, and so far as can be seen, these were garrisoned. Synnada held part of Antigonos' treasure, Kelainai was a royal residence, Sardis a provincial centre; all will have required garrisons [43]. Elsewhere Sidon and Tyre had garrisons [44], as Ptolemy discovered, and the three cities of the Balikh valley, Edessa, Karrhai, and Ichnai, will have contained troops since they were Antigonos' frontier guard. No doubt the Euphrates bridge at Thapsakos was protected by an army detachment as well.

These preliminaries are by way of considering the situation in Syria, which was Seleukos' main prize in the division of Antigonos' kingdom. They establish the fact – which is obvious to any who know the habits of rulers and conquerors – that garrisons existed in that kingdom, though the impression is sometimes given that Antigonos' army went into limbo between campaigns, to be conjured up again, fully armed and trained, at a moment's notice. The garrisons within Syria are not attested in the written sources, with the exception of Antigoneia [45], but there is another sort of evidence which seems to indicate where those garrisons were.

Within Syria-Palestine, there are a number of places which acquired Greek and Macedonian names and which were given such names before Seleukos and Ptolemy took over. Pella, for example, was an alternative, and so an earlier, name for the great city of Apamea in Syria, which was founded in 300. Larissa was another early settlement, especially associated with a group of Thessalian cavalry from Alexander's army. Chalkis and Kyrrhos seem to have existed also when Seleukos took control, and he used them as local headquarters for a time. All these names are taken from the Greek or Macedonian homeland. Places which owed their foundation to the work of the kings most often were given dynastic names – Antigoneia, Antiochia, Ptolemais, and so on – so these transferred Greek and Macedonian names were probably spontaneously awarded by the settlers, during the twenty or so years when Syria was ruled by Antigonos [46]. These are the places which the soldiers of Ipsos would have called their homes and where their families lived.

Thus we have here the basis of the division of the army which had been Antigonos'. Since Lysimachos and Seleukos each took about half of the conquered kingdom, by allowing a free choice to the surrendered troops they would get about half of the army each. Or rather less than half, considering casualties, and those who refused to serve either. Of the troops who re-enlisted, each king would get about half. Some men would, no doubt, go to Ptolemy or Kassandros, and some had gone to Demetrios.

All this has been necessary to account for the policies pursued by Seleukos when he reached Syria. He surely considered that he was entitled to a major reward. He had been the only one to stand up to and beat Antigonos when all the rest had made peace. He had brought up his army to force Antigonos to a final battle. It was true that Lysimachos had fought the old man for nearly a year by himself, but the decisive blow had been struck by Seleukos' forces. And his reward was, in territorial terms, a major disappointment.

He had been awarded Mesopotamia and Syria. But Ptolemy had occupied half of Syria and refused to budge, and Seleukos was not strong enough to risk a fight. Seleukos was, however, able to make some diplomatic and propaganda capital out of his situation. On the one hand, he made it clear that he did not accept that Ptolemy had any right to southern Syria, and that he maintained his own claim to it. At the same time, Seleukos managed to sound hurt and bewildered by Ptolemy's theft, thus recalling Ptolemy's scuttle the year before. And finally, Seleukos loudly refused to attack, giving as his reason his old friendship with Ptolemy [47].

The fact remained that Seleukos' reward for being in on the death of Antigonos consisted of two provinces of distinctly poor aspect. The richest part of Syria was Phoenicia, almost entirely in Ptolemy's hands, though Tyre and Sidon were held by Demetrios' forces. All Seleukos got was the island-city of

Arados, and even this may have been held by Demetrios' sea power. Or, if not held by Demetrios, it was still only loosely attached to Seleukos' new province, for its island position, and its long history, produced a distinct and persistent feeling of separateness and independence, symbolized by the continued existence of an Aradian monarchy [48].

The rest of Seleukos' part of Syria was basically a peasant land, with some Macedonian–Greek garrisons, and one city, Antigoneia. The politically important people were the immigrant Greeks and Macedonians, who were scattered through the land, holding down and exploiting the peasantry. There is no suggestion in Syria that the native population welcomed Seleukid rule, as the Babylonians had. Instead, all the indications are that Greek rule was less welcome than that of the Persians, for it had been the Persians who had been the liberators of Syria, from, as it happens, the rule of the Babylonians. Syrians had fought for the Persian king until Gaugamela, long after their own land was under Macedonian occupation [49]. Arados' continued opportunistic hostility to Seleukid rule was only the most obvious example of Syrian dislike of that rule.

So Seleukos had to reckon with, at the least, sullen dislike from the Syrian population. He also had a major problem with the Greeks and Macedonians who lived there. Their settlements – Pella, Larissa, Chalkis, Edessa, and so on – were inhabited by men who, until Ipsos, had been the subjects of King Antigonos and King Demetrios. The latter was still very much alive, though characteristically he had chosen to make war on the wrong man (Lysimachos) in the wrong place (Thrace) [50]. Had he had the sense to sail to Syria, he may well have been able to call on the loyalty of the old soldiers of his father, summoning them to his side, or, better still, refusing to accept Seleukos' authority. As it was, Demetrios attacked Lysimachos at a place where he had ruled for twenty years, and he made no headway at all.

Seleukos was therefore given time to solve the extraordinarily difficult political problem of Syria. It was difficult because of the intricate connections between internal and external factors, and it had to be dealt with in a way which damped down internal tensions and warded off external dangers. The weapon which Seleukos chose to solve the problem was the city.

The practice of founding cities in unpromising surroundings had been begun by Philip II and was continued by Alexander. There were Alexandrias scattered all over Iran and Baktria, and these had been the basis of the rule exercised there by Stasanor, and which were now the support of Seleukos. In the west the custom had been revived after the murder of Alexander IV, and each of the new kings had his own name-city. Lysimachos was perhaps the first, when he reconstituted ruined Kardia into Lysimacheia; Kassandros had followed with two, Kassandreia and Thessalonike; Antigonos had founded Antigoneia in Syria and synoecized others in Asia Minor; Seleukos had his Seleukeia-on-the-Tigris; Ptolemy founded a Ptolemais, but was able to concentrate mainly on developing Alexandria-by-Egypt.

Seleukos therefore had precedents for founding cities, but there was really no precedent for the activity he now undertook in Syria. Within a very short space of time, probably less than a year, he founded four new cities spread out in a great quadrilateral, naming them after members of his own family, and developed four others, mainly named from places in Greece and Macedon [51].

These cities were of two types. The four with dynastic names were all roughly the same size, between 220 and 300 acres interior area. The smallest was Antioch, which was the replacement for Antigoneia. The largest was Seleukeia-in-Pieria, on the coast, stretching up the hillside of Mount Kasios, and down to an artificial harbour large enough for a fleet of ships. South along the coast was another city with an artificial harbour, Laodikeia-on-the-Sea, placed at the northern end of the land which had been under the direct influence of Arados. Inland from Arados and Laodikeia was Apamea, near to but not on the Orontes. These four cities were very carefully sited. They were not at all well placed in terms of economic resources, and in fact three of them died when they ceased to be able to count on government support; only Laodikeia has had a continuous history. The sites were, rather, all chosen for military reasons. The two ports, besides their artificial harbours, were given strong walls and large and dominating citadels. Antioch was protected by its high acropolis on a craggy hill, and by the river, on a slightly awkward site that was liable to flooding occasionally. Apamea was placed above the Orontes valley, on the spur of the plateau which stretched east and north, and with a detached acropolis which was an old Iron Age town, and is still the fortified town of Qalat al-Mudiq.

The other cities were a group of places selected from a larger range of possibilities, selected, that is, from the army bases which already existed when Seleukos arrived. Three of them – Beroia, Chalkis, and Kyrrhos – bear names which suggest that they were in that category. (Another, Pella, was the basis for the new city of Apamea.) The old bridge of Alexander across the Euphrates may have been a casualty of the war with Antigonos, or it may simply have become too old – it was made of wood, after all, and thirty years old by 301. For whatever reason, its site was abandoned and a new bridge built, and to guard that bridge a new city was founded. It was given the founder's name, Seleukeia, but quickly became Seleukeia-Zeugma, 'the Bridge', and eventually just Zeugma. The city spanned the river, with a suburb on the east bank [52]. It was a nice conceit to name the suburb Apamea, so that the bridge connected Seleukeia and Apamea as the marriage ties linked Seleukos and Apama. These four cities were all about the same size, about a third of the area of the four great cities, and like them they formed a quadrilateral of power between the greater dynastic grouping and the Euphrates.

This pattern bears the clear indication of careful central planning, though it is not the evidence of planning so much as the sheer size of the undertaking which is astonishing. This is a unique effort in the ancient world. Not even Augustus produced such a scale of colonization in such a brief time. Each of the four great dynastic cities was the size of contemporary Rome, the Rome of the Servian Walls. Each of the smaller cities was the size of contemporary Miletos. Alexander's work in founding cities, in any case often ephemeral, is puny by comparison, being perhaps twenty sites spread over ten years. For the other major difference is that Seleukos' cities actually survived, unlike many of the Alexandrias.

The size of the cities is one thing, however, and the size of the populations of those cities is something else. The figure of 6,000 citizens is often quoted, based on a misunderstanding, or a misquotation of several disparate sources. It is best to say that the actual populations of these cities is unknown. The figure of 6,000 is the number of men said by Polybios to have formed the army of the Kyrrhestai, in rebellion against Antiochos III in 221 [53]. It is assumed by many that this is the total citizen population of the city of Kyrrhos, which is not what Polybios says and which is in any case most unlikely, for some citizens will have stayed at home, due to illness, age, antipathy, and so on. It is, thus, only a minimum figure and takes no account of the non-citizens; here it will suffice as the basis for the following tentative and hypothetical calculations.

Supposing Kyrrhos had a citizen-population in 221 of 6,000, that would mean a total population of at least four times that – say 25,000 – in order to include wives and children, on top of which must be added slaves and non-citizens. 25,000 is therefore an absolutely minimum population figure for that city. Suppose, secondly, that the same calculation can be made for cities of a similar size. This would give Chalkis, Beroia, and Zeugma the same population – a total of 100,000 people for the four. But those cities are only one-third the size of the four dynastic cities, and the acreage within the walls surely bore some relationship to the size of the population. So we must suppose a population of, say, 75,000 at the start of each of the four greater cities – again, a minimum. That is to say, Seleukos was probably settling, at an absolute minimum, nearly half a million people in these cities. And they were all founded in the course of one year.

Where all these people came from is an equally uncertain matter. Some, perhaps most, were already living in Syria when Seleukos took over. The population of Antigoneia and the soldiers of Antigonos and their families were all available as settlers. But there is also evidence that more people were recruited from elsewhere. The account of Antioch given by the geographer Strabo divides the original area of the city into two parts, of which the second was peopled by 'settlers', and these were contrasted with the people from Antigoneia who were already in Syria [54]. The implication must be that the settlers came from elsewhere than Antigoneia and elsewhere than Syria. If such people settled at Antioch, no doubt others immigrated to settle at the other cities as well.

This achievement is enormous in itself, but it also had profound effects on the political geography of the

Mediterranean area and the Middle East, and hence on the history of those areas. In an immediate sense, it changed the power-balance in the post-Ipsos world. The internal aspect of the Syrian problem was the fact that the Greco-Macedonian population was fairly small, scattered, and potentially disloyal. The new network of well-fortified and well-populated cities largely solved this internal problem. The new cities could claim Seleukos as their founder, an intangible but nonetheless powerful position of influence. Those Greeks and Macedonians who were residually loyal to King Demetrios had been diluted, even perhaps swamped, by a mass of new settlers who had no loyalty to Demetrios, but did owe their new positions to Seleukos. Thus Seleukos had converted a potentially hostile population into one which was potentially loyal, and was certainly a source of military strength. The potential of loyalty to Demetrios, however, was still present, and certainly affected Seleukos' actions for the rest of Demetrios' life. And, finally, the mass of Greeks and Macedonians in Syria effectively stifled any expression of discontent by the native Syrians.

All this was not accomplished without the usual Seleukid myth-making. The accounts we have of the Ipsos battle, poor though they are, bear all the marks of a version which emphasized the roles of Seleukos and Antiochos [55]. The same emphasis appears in the stories concerning the foundations of the cities. Seleukos decided to destroy Antigoneia. This city clearly had to go, since its presence would be a constant reminder of its founder, and of Demetrios. It was not just a matter of renaming the place, as happened with more than one of the Alexandrias, and with the other Antigoneias, but a matter of physical destruction, so that the very site is now unknown. Seleukos is then portrayed as needing to decide on the site of his own new foundation, which was to take the place, geographically, of Antigoneia. He sacrificed, praying for guidance. An eagle seized the meat of the sacrifice and flew off. Seleukos galloped off in pursuit and the eagle was discovered to have landed at the splendid site of Antioch, beside the Orontes, with its back to the steep crags of Mount Silpion, upon which the acropolis would be placed. Seleukos laid out the line of the walls, sacrificed a virgin to assure the city's future prosperity, and moved the homeless

Antigoneians to the new city [56]. The statue of the Tyche of Antigoneia was installed, along with various gods and goddesses to represent the various contingents of Greeks in the population [57].

Some of this is no doubt true, in the sense that it actually happened – though one hopes the sacrifice of the virgin is a later interpolation – but there is no doubt also that parts were carefully staged according to a prepared scenario. Seleukos would scarcely leave to the whim of an eagle the choice of a site of one of his most important cities. Yet the eagle is important, for it is Zeus' bird, and its participation in the role of an augur therefore suggested the participation of Zeus, and the god's approval for the whole series of events from the destruction of Antigoneia onwards. The same eagle story recurs in the foundations of the other three great cities. Once is just possible, four times is clear invention – or planning. The Greek and Macedonian public, however, was credulous enough to accept that Zeus was showing his favour to Seleukos, and that the new cities were beginning their lives under the best possible auspices.

Other aspects are not so believable. The virgin-sacrifice may be a rationalization of the appearance of a statue of the Tyche of Antioch. The transfer of the statue of the Tyche of Antigoneia to Antioch was a symbol of the reconciliation effected by Seleukos between his own followers and those of Antigonos. The whole story, therefore, is a skilful concoction, partly true, partly invented, wholly deliberate, which in total illustrates much of Seleukos' Syrian policy. Added to which it was a good story, and it is once more clear that Seleukos was a master of propaganda.

Internally therefore, Seleukos' strenuous city founding was a policy which successfully fortified his new province and also established in it a new population which had a predisposition towards loyalty to him. These 'fortifications' were, of course, still only potential for some time, since it would take some years for the walls and forts to be physically constructed, though the public announcement of the foundation of the cities and the very public ceremonies involved will have created their own pattern of assumptions among those who were not actually there. For Seleukos' policy was only partly an internal one: it was also directed at his actual or potential external enemies.

Seleukos was, in effect, diplomatically isolated after Ipsos. His one active ally was Lysimachos, who was soon heavily involved in warfare against Demetrios in Thrace [58]. The sea was dominated by Demetrios' fleet, which had bases in Cyprus, at Tyre and Sidon, and possibly at Arados. Kassandros, as always, showed no interest in anything beyond Greece and the Aegean and his own narrow interests, which left his brother Pleistarchos in a thoroughly uncomfortable situation in Kilikia. Pleistarchos could not be considered a friend to Seleukos, and his friendship was of little political value anyway. And to the south was Ptolemy, in control of land which Seleukos claimed as his by right. Thus there were enemies or potential enemies all round his newly acquired land.

Further, Ptolemy and Lysimachos, both of whom regarded Demetrios as their main enemy, concluded a marriage-alliance within a year of the Ipsos battle: Ptolemy's daughter Arsinoe married Lysimachos [59]. It was Demetrios' active naval power, combined with his possession of Cyprus, Tyre, and Sidon, all of which were coveted by Ptolemy, which was the element which brought the two together. Ptolemy got little or nothing out of the alliance, and, characteristically, contributed little or nothing to Lysimachos' war [60]. But, for Seleukos, the situation was horribly dangerous, for he lost the alliance of Lysimachos, and saw him allied with his enemy. In Seleukos' likely estimation it was only Demetrios' warfare against Lysimachos which kept either side from attacking him in Syria.

The solution to Seleukos' difficulty was, in fact, obvious, but it took him three years from the battle of Ipsos and two years from the alliance of Ptolemy and Lysimachos to adopt it. This time lapse is a tribute to Seleukos' cool calculation of events. In that time he settled Syria and organized those new cities. During that time Demetrios alone kept the allies busy and preoccupied. Ptolemy, as Seleukos well knew, had no real wish to expand his power northwards in Syria, any more than Kassandros was interested in moving east. By 298, however, Demetrios' war with Lysimachos was petering out, and it was necessary for Seleukos to make his move. A marriage alliance was arranged, of Seleukos with Demetrios' daughter Stratonike. Demetrios came east to Cyprus in order to finalize the matter. Now it was Ptolemy's turn to be worried, and Lysimachos' turn to pay little attention to the alliance. Demetrios, however, had an easier victim in view. On his way to meet Seleukos he raided Kilikia, reclaiming the treasure deposited originally by his father at Kyinda. Pleistarchos fled, to Seleukos of all people [61]. If he expected Seleukos to help him, he was disappointed. If he even asked for it, he demonstrated his innocence and his ignorance of the political situation. This suggests a good reason why no-one ever paid much attention to him. He went off to his brother, but Kassandros paid no heed to him either.

Having swallowed Kilikia in a bloodless campaign, and fattened his treasury to the tune of 1,200 talents, Demetrios sailed to Syria. The meeting of the two kings took place at the small town of Rhosos, along the coast north of the newly founded city of Seleukeia-in-Pieria. Rhosos was, and is, a small port, at the mouth of a small but surprisingly deep river – a suitable place to meet a sea-king. The two kings put on a conspicuous display of friendship, and Stratonike was married to Seleukos. The political map had shifted again [62]. Just to emphasize the point, Demetrios went down to Tyre and Sidon and conducted a raid into Ptolemy's new province, reaching as far as Samaria with his forces [63].

Seleukos' gains in all this were not simply international, in that he had the alliance of a notable distractor of his enemies, and personal, in that he was now married to a nubile young woman; they were also internal-political. The alliance with Demetrios was a signal to any of his Syrian Greek subjects who were still unhappy at the result of Ipsos. The two kings competing for those men's allegiance were now friends, so there could be no disloyalty to Demetrios in serving Seleukos.

Seleukos' political conduct in the period since he had returned from the east had been masterly. His conduct of the Ipsos campaign and battle had brought a clear victory; his hard work and imagination had fastened his and his family's control over Syria for the foreseeable future; he had acquired the alliance of the one man who could keep his enemies away from his own territory; he had neutralized or removed the actual and potential enmity of Ptolemy, Pleistarchos, Demetrios, and the Greeks of Syria. It does not seem as though he had put a foot wrong along the way.

It is probable, however, that Seleukos' achievement was even more complex. It was one thing to found cities, but it was another to maintain control over them. There was, from the king's point of view, no advantage to be gained in founding cities in his territory if those cities were going to aspire to independence. All Hellenistic kings had problems with the old cities of Greece and Asia Minor. All Ptolemaic and Seleukid kings had difficulties with the Phoenician cities which had similar traditions of independence and rebellion [64]. In many cases the new cities founded in and since Alexander's time might have acquired those same aspirations, for, after all, the colonists came from such places and will have brought their political ideas with them. In the Seleukid state the new cities never did aspire to independence, and this was due, in all probability, to the governmental system which was set up by Seleukos Nikator himself.

There is some doubt about ascribing the system of Nikator rather than to a later Seleukid because the details of the system are attested only in later sources. Yet Seleukos needed a reasonably efficient government system for controlling his enormous kingdom. Even before Ipsos, it stretched for a good 2,000 kilometres from west to east and Ipsos expanded that by another 500. He had seen the eastern satrapies slide into effective if unacknowledged independence twice already, first at the time of Perdikkas and Eumenes, and then by his own actions in defying Antigonos. As he moved back to the west, the danger of a further repetition of this separation was obvious. So he had to organize an effective provincial government. Then there was the problem of his new cities, which had to be prevented from behaving like real Greek cities, but which would scarcely submit to being treated as subjects by the governors. They had to be controlled, and they must not be allowed any real independence, but this had to be done delicately.

The large Persian-type satrapies were a great temptation to men who wished to emulate the career of, say, the young Seleukos. One solution was to split them up into smaller units. Some sign of these smaller governorships, called hyparchies, had already appeared much earlier. There are references to local governors during the campaigns of Antigonos [65]. It will have been Seleukos who put the matter into clearer and more regular practice by making these local officials the top rank of governors in some areas, and by thus eliminating the satrapies which came between the hyparchs and the king. These smaller units often have the suffix *-ene* added to their name – Kommagene,

Adiabene, and so on. Yet it was not always possible to get rid of the great satrapies, since in some parts of the state it was clearly more dangerous to get rid of a governor with wide authority than to keep one and risk rebellion. A satrap in Baktria, for instance, was a necessity in order to discourage or ward off nomad attacks. But Babylonia and Media were two areas where the satraps had great power and temptation and where the danger of invasion was much less.

The stages of this process are to a large degree uncertain, even guesswork. It is very noticeable, however, that there was never a satrap for Syria in the Seleukid empire. Instead there are signs of a division of Syria into four smaller parts, also called satrapies, but named after cities, implying that the areas around those cities were their provinces. Two of the names are early, Chalkidene and Kyrrhestike, the latter known from the time of Seleukos himself [66]. The other two names are Antiochene and Apamene, and they can only have existed *after* 300, when their name cities were founded. Thus the whole set of names dates from the 290s. This may, therefore, help to date the other names of the type. In Babylonia, for instance, there are such names as Charakene and Mesene, and in Mesopotamia there are Gordyene, Adiabene, Osrhoene [67].

At the same time, it has to be admitted that the state of our knowledge is such that it is quite possible that the satrapies existed but no record of them survives. All that can be said is that the sources at our disposal suggest strongly that the centre of the Seleukid state, the economic heartland of the Fertile Crescent, was subdivided into a large number of relatively small provinces of which we have names for about a dozen. The example of Syria suggests that it was Seleukos himself who was responsible for this new provincial governmental system.

The frontier areas, on the other hand, were much too sensitive to be left to small and weak governors. Hence Baktria (which always seems to have included Sogdiana) had a satrap (Stasanor) until the Seleukid conquest in, say, 306. By c. 250, under a satrap, it broke away [68]. That satrap, Diodotos, had clearly been in power for some time, for he had gathered sufficient local support to make his bid for independence successful. This leaves no more than a generation (c. 306 to, say, c. 265) without the record of any satrap. Part of that period is filled by the rule of Antiochos I, who was given authority over a vague area called the 'Upper Satrapies' in 292 [69], which he retained until 281 when he moved west. Considering the state of our sources, this record amounts almost to proof of the continued existence of the office of satrap in Baktria.

The 'Upper Satrapies' is an office which recurs later in Seleukid administrative history, too often when its holder rebels. In this first instance, it is a sign, in effect, of a joint-kingship, with Antiochos controlling the east and Seleukos the west. In this case it worked because these two made it work [70]. Later, others failed to make it work. The point here is to emphasize that Seleukos, whose responsibility it clearly was, adapted the system he found to the needs of the new state. The large provinces of Persian and Alexandrine times were too large, while the personal control which Antigonos seems to have exercised was too difficult. Seleukos tried smaller satrapies or hyparchies in some areas, but had to accept huge satrapies on the frontiers. Given the slow communications of the time this governmental problem was insoluble. If he had lieutenants he could trust, the king could appoint them to the great satrapies. But Greeks and Macedonians could not be trusted. The temptations were too great. Everyone would remember that every single king in the Hellenistic world was descended from a man who had made himself king by seizing power or territory by force. The process was repeated often enough for ambitions to be inflamed regularly. And Seleukos himself was the most conspicuous example of the rewards of this rise to kingship.

The cities presented an analogous problem. It was the political theory of the day that cities were sovereign. They passed decrees in the name of the council and the people of the city. There was no room in the theory for a king of a large territorial state to rule over a city, nor for a satrap either. But, as so often, people managed well enough without paying too much attention to the theory. The practice, at least in Syria, was that both king and cities faced the same problem – how to control and exploit the indigenous Syrian population. The answer was an alliance. In this alliance the king, by virtue of his military power and his economic wealth, was clearly the predominant partner, but this disparity could cause resentment. Seleukos instituted a system which allowed him to control, gently but firmly, the cities. The instrument was an official called *epistates*, often translated 'governor', but this is too authoritarian a term. For the *epistates* gave advice, and passed on messages from the king, which were not phrased as orders [71]. The cities then did as the king and his representative suggested. The cities could also appoint their own representatives at the king's court, by honouring one of the 'King's Friends' [72], though the key to the system was the *epistates*. In addition, every city had a great acropolis, large enough to hold a big garrison. That at Beroia, for instance, was a fifth of the area of the city. The garrisons were there in two capacities: to protect the cities and to dominate them. The emphasis, no doubt, was on protection, but the domination was equally clear. The system only worked because of the unspoken and probably largely unacknowledged fear of Syrian disobedience and rebellion, but it did work [73].

So the cities were operating in conjunction with the king to dominate and exploit the countryside, just as the garrisons dominated the cities. The alliance of king and cities was so overwhelmingly powerful that there was no native Syrian rebellion for a century and a half. This city-control was not needed throughout the kingdom. It certainly operated in Media, where the local social relations were similar to those in Syria – Greek cities allied with the king against the local Median population – with the added complication that half of Media was independent of Seleukos' kingdom. This was the northern half of the old satrapy, called Atropatene after the satrap Atropates, who had been appointed by Alexander [74]. In Seleukos' eyes he must have been a great nuisance, all the more so since he could claim an even greater legitimacy than Seleukos' himself – if anyone noticed such subtleties by then.

Once again, our sources are exiguous. It may be that the *epistates* system was not needed in Babylonia, at least at first, since the local population was basically friendly to the king, nor perhaps in Baktria, where the external nomad threat would provide an effective social cement. So it is possible that, like the subdivision of the unwieldy satrapies, it was a system which was implemented only where needed. Indeed it could not operate without the existence of Greek cities. Where the system did exist, it can only have been the work of Seleukos, since it was clearly required very early in the lifetime of the cities. Seleukos will have needed the assurance of control from the start. His position as founder, his prestige as victor, and his alliance with the gods were all part of the system of control, along with his appointments of *epistatai*, hyparchs, and satraps.

It seems possible that all this administrative organization took place more or less simultaneously with the foundation of the Syrian cities and the carefully calculated diplomacy which resulted in Seleukos' alliance with Demetrios. If it was not quite simultaneous, the new administration seems to have been installed soon after as part of the remarkable innovation and creativity which Seleukos displayed in the period after the Ipsos battle. In that time Seleukos constructed a state which in its main outline lasted almost two centuries, organized its administration, and founded cities to hold it together. Above all, he converted Syria from a land which had been trampled on and over by every army in the Middle East for the past century into a bastion of urban life which lasted in the form he gave it for a thousand years, and bears clear evidence of his work to this day. From a source of weakness it became a seat of power. It is for this that his family became known later as kings of Syria, since that land became their final home and refuge in the last disastrous century of their rule. Yet all was not smooth and serene. Syria was still a salient rather than the heart of the state, and Seleukos needed to be active and alert in its defence.

8
DIPLOMAT AND RULER (298–293)

Seleukos' portraits on his coins show little to distinguish him from other men. One authority detects a martial look to him; paradoxically, this is in reference to a coin-portrait which shows him without armour, and put out by his son, after Seleukos' death [1]. A bust which has been attributed to Seleukos, now in Naples, shows a head which seems to be smaller than the ideal, with a thick neck, and bulging eyes set too closely together. A mop of unruly hair probably owes more to sculptural fashion than reality [2]. An investigator has detected in his portraits signs of physical fitness [3], not an unexpected trait in a Macedonian aristocrat, trained to war, who fought many battles and lived to be murdered in his late 70s while out riding. His appearance is not at all like that of his son, Antiochos, who seems more careworn with inturned lips which might only be due to bad teeth [4]. Of other members of the family – Apama or Stratonike or Phila – no known likenesses exist.

The marriage of Seleukos and Stratonike was intended to symbolize the alliance of Seleukos and Demetrios, but this alliance was no more sincere than any other agreement of its type. The interests of both men had indicated that the alliance was to their individual advantage at that particular moment, since each was isolated and each felt under threat from the alliance of Ptolemy with Lysimachos and Kassandros. This temporary identity of interest did not, of course, prevent them from seeking advantage in each other's sphere. Seleukos used the alliance to contact at least two cities of Asia Minor: Ephesos received an envoy, Nikagoras of Rhodes, who spoke in the name of both kings and brought the news of the alliance [5];

Miletos had already received two embassies from Seleukos and his first wife Apama and his son Antiochos promising rich gifts for the Apollo temple at Didyma [6]. These cities were in Demetrios' area, and so these embassies are examples of Seleukos' active diplomacy opening up areas hitherto closed to him.

The arrival of Demetrios in the east raised a major problem. Before he arrived Demetrios had controlled Cyprus and Tyre and Sidon, all of which were in Ptolemy's sphere, the island being an old Ptolemaic obsession, the cities being surrounded by Ptolemy's lands. Then Demetrios conquered Kilikia on his way to the wedding at Rhosos. This had radically altered the political position, for Demetrios now appeared to be very threatening indeed, but to Seleukos as well, not just to Ptolemy. Demetrios' eastern possessions – Kilikia, Cyprus, Tyre, Sidon – now enclosed Seleukos' Syria on the north, west, and south; furthermore, Demetrios now held a large part of the Asian mainland, and he had a common boundary with Seleukos along the Amanus range.

It was fortunate for Seleukos, then, that Demetrios, in his usual fashion, missed the point. He was beguiled by the friendly meeting with Seleukos at Rhosos and does not seem to have appreciated the true precariousness of Seleukos' internal situation. In this context the choice of Rhosos as the meeting place assumes a certain significance. It may well have been convenient as an anchorage for a sea-king, as suggested earlier, but it was also very much out-of-the-way. It is cut off from the rest of Syria by the rugged Amanus mountains. Geographically it is in a narrow plain blocked off from access to anywhere else. Seleukos had conspicuously not established a city in this plain, and similarly he conspicuously did not choose the obvious anchorage for the meeting, which was Myriandros, a few miles north, which had been the normal trading place for Phoenicians in the previous century [7]. The choice of Rhosos, therefore, has the appearance of being designed to prevent Demetrios from getting any information about internal Syria, and to avoid his contacting any of his old comrades and subjects. News from the meeting was controlled by Seleukos, and his propaganda probably lies behind our accounts of the two kings being nice to each other [8].

Demetrios was certainly ambitious to expand in the east. He

conquered Kilikia and raided into Ptolemy's territory as far as Samaria. This was prelude and cause of the next shift of the diplomatic kaleidoscope whereby Seleukos is credited with reconciling Demetrios and Ptolemy [9]. The only occasion for this is after the raid on Samaria and before Demetrios returned westwards. Seleukos' motives here have not usually been considered, for, after all, it was the others who made peace, but if he really did take the initiative, as our source says explicitly, his reasons will have been cogent. One can discount the wish to reconcile his new father-in-law to his old friend; such feelings may have existed, but diplomatically they are irrelevant. By contrast the raid by Demetrios on Samaria may well have looked like the beginning of a major conflict, and Seleukos was not ready for a new war. His organization of Syria was still in its early stages; none of his new cities was built as yet; none of his new harbours was operational; and a war on his borders could not fail to involve him sooner or later.

If they went to war seriously, Demetrios and Ptolemy would fight in Palestine, in Phoenicia, and on the sea, perhaps in Cyprus and Kilikia. Whoever won would then inevitably pose a threat to Seleukos' lands, though the real danger to him would arise if the winner was Demetrios. Ptolemy would probably not be able to prevent Demetrios from conquering Palestine at the least, though he would probably be able to hold on to Egypt. If past conduct was anything to go by, in fact, Ptolemy would not even try to defend Palestine, but would withdraw his forces to stand on guard at Gaza or Raphia or Pelusion, and wait for Demetrios to go away. At that point Demetrios would be in control of Palestine, Phoenicia, Cyprus, and Kilikia, and the sea between them, everything from the River of Egypt to the Taurus – except for Seleukos' Syria. He would remember his father's kingdom, and his father's dismantled city of Antigoneia, and his and his father's former subjects. He might well attack Syria. He might not be able to help himself.

If Ptolemy won, on the other hand, an eventuality which was unlikely, given past form, the situation would be only marginally better from Seleukos' point of view. Ptolemy would then hold Palestine still, and perhaps all of Phoenicia except Arados, while Demetrios, whose control of the sea was unlikely to be impaired, would hold on to Cyprus and Kilikia. Rebuffed in the south, Demetrios might well turn upon Seleukos' Syria for compensation.

Demetrios was the real danger, partly because he was unpredictable, partly because of his charm and charisma, but mostly because he had a claim on the allegiance of large numbers of Seleukos' new subjects. Seleukos was on his way towards neutralizing this: by the marriage with Stratonike, by diluting the old Antigoneians with the new settlers, by sheer elapsing time; but Demetrios must not be able to get at his old subjects. There is always an adventurousness about old soldiers, a hankering to win lost battles, to follow a leader such as Demetrios. If Seleukos was to hold on to the fruits of victory, Demetrios had to be fended off.

The continuance of the war between Demetrios and Ptolemy, which had more or less begun with Demetrios' raid on Samaria, was thus as much a danger to Seleukos as to Ptolemy. It was therefore not difficult to persuade Ptolemy to make peace. The pleasure of the meeting with his new ally made the susceptible Demetrios similarly amenable. Peace was concluded, presumably on the basis that each would hold what he had. Certainly Tyre, Sidon, Cyprus, and Kilikia remained under Demetrios' control.

Demetrios was all the more inclined to establish peace in the east because another opportunity was opening up in the west. His wife Phila had gone to visit her brother Kassandros when her other brother Pleistarchos had been ejected from Kilikia by Demetrios [10]. (An excellent example of the insignificance of such relationships in diplomacy; Seleukos' relationship with Demetrios was no closer.) Phila returned to her husband later in 298, having missed the wedding at Rhosos and all the negotiations with Ptolemy, bringing the news that Kassandros was dying. This prospect at once stimulated Demetrios' ever-active imagination and his erratic ambitions.

Phila also brought news of the situation in Kassandros' family. His wife, Thessalonike, favoured one son, the youngest, above the other two. The eldest of these sons, Philip, was ill with the same disease which was killing Kassandros. This family imbroglio was likely to sap Macedonian strength [11], and meanwhile Kassandros was effectively powerless. Demetrios went back to Greece to meddle in these muddy waters.

His various enemies watched the developing situation with their usual anxiety. Were he to gain control of all Greece and possibly Macedonia while holding on to his eastern outposts, none of them would be safe. Whether they actually concerted measures or whether they simply followed one another's lead we do not know, but they all acted. Demetrios became involved in a siege of Athens, held until then by Kassandros. The fighting took longer than he expected, as it always did [12]. While thus fully occupied, Demetrios was stripped of most of his overseas possessions. Lysimachos campaigned along the Aegean coast, mopping up the Greek cities there [13]. Ptolemy moved into Cyprus, ignoring Tyre and Sidon, and took the whole island except for Salamis, which he besieged [14]. Seleukos crossed the Amanus and took over Kilikia [15].

A story is told about this series of events. Seleukos, it is said, sent a message to Demetrios demanding that he hand over Tyre and Sidon. When Demetrios refused, Seleukos took Kilikia. An alternative has Seleukos offering to buy Tyre and Sidon, to which Demetrios replied with indignation [16]. Both versions seem unlikely. The purchase-version sounds very much like a propaganda-story, similar to the later exchange between Seleukos and Lysimachos, when Seleukos became indignant at the suggestion of selling the captured Demetrios. The basic truth, however, is surely correct, for Seleukos ceetainly regarded Tyre and Sidon as of greater value than Kilikia, and would surely have wanted them first if he could get them. Kilikia, after all, was indefensible if he chose to attack it, for all he had to do was send a force over the Amanus. Possession of Tyre and Sidon, on the other hand, would give him control of all Phoenicia and thus provide access (as Demetrios had recently demonstrated) to Palestine. Hence possession of Tyre and Sidon would, in effect, give Seleukos Palestine as well, and Kilikia would fall into his lap easily. Thus Seleukos may well have tried to persuade Demetrios to hand over the two cities to him.

The basic problem is that we do not know the actual sequence of events. A possible reconstruction might go like this: Ptolemy sent an army to Cyprus which overran the whole island except for Salamis, where he became involved in a siege. Demetrios could not send help, being fully stretched in Greece (which was why Ptolemy had chosen that moment to attack). Seleukos communicated with Demetrios, offering to take over Tyre and Sidon on the assumption that they were next on Ptolemy's agenda. Demetrios easily saw through this transparent move and refused Seleukos' 'help'. Seleukos will have realized that Ptolemy would not necessarily go for Tyre and Sidon next; he might go for Kilikia. Demetrios might not have seen that, and might not have appreciated Seleukos' difficulty. Demetrios' rejection of Seleukos 'help' was thus the effective end of their alliance, for Seleukos must now look out for himself – not that he had ever done otherwise. Seleukos' move into Kilikia, therefore, was made partly in order to forestall Ptolemy. Ptolemy, who may or may not have intended a further move, had, in the event, to be content with Cyprus. Tyre and Sidon were still too strong to be attacked, and so, once Salamis was taken, peace returned. Meanwhile, Lysimachos' campaign along the Ionian coast will not necessarily have coincided with these events other than by the existence of an opportunity to despoil Demetrios which all of them had seized more or less simultaneously.

It will have been a considerable relief to Seleukos to have removed much of the power of Demetrios from his doorstep. The longer Demetrios kept away from Syria the less likely it would be that he would be able to command the loyalty of any of Seleukos' subjects. Vigilance, however, was constantly required, and Ptolemy was an ever-present threat; while, in Asia Minor, the morose Lysimachos was steadily consolidating his power and adding small conquests and Demetrios still possessed a fleet in the Aegean.

By the time Seleukos took Kilikia, in 294, the new cities of Syria will have become walled and thriving settlements, raw, dusty, unfinished, but recognizable as Greek cities. The combined power of the cities and their citizens, the citadels and their garrisons dominated the countryside. That countryside was partly owned by the city and its citizens, and partly owned by the king, but wholly inhabited by Syrians. They paid rents and taxes to whichever of these was their master and in addition the cities paid their tribute to the king [17]. Seleukos was thus enormously wealthy, and this wealth, of course, enabled him to employ a large army.

The native population of the kingdom was thus effectively dominated by the royal army and by the cities, both of which were overwhelmingly Greek and Macedonian in composition. Yet there is also evidence that Seleukos was sensitive to the resentment this could cause. In effect he had to deal with three different peoples, identified by their languages and by their distinctive cultural and political traditions: Syrians, Babylonians, and Iranians. His first extended contact had been with the Babylonians, ever since his first appointment as satrap there in 320. Then, from 312, Seleukos had ruled over Iranians, though his contacts there had also gone back to his marriage to Apama. Similarly Seleukos was scarcely ignorant of Syrians, for he had campaigned through their land under Alexander and under Perdikkas before he acquired the direct rule over them.

Given the long period during which Seleukos ruled these various peoples, it is not surprising that his policies towards them varied and changed over time. In 320–315, as satrap of Babylon, he had been at his most conciliatory. In 312–308, in the war against Antigonos, that policy had continued. In the eastern campaigns, it seems likely that he had been fighting against the locally settled Greeks and Macedonians, and the Iranian population had perhaps stood aside from the conflict. The conciliation of Chandragupta Maurya may have been part of the same policy, though it is more likely to have been due to the Indian ruler's overwhelming power. When he returned to the west, Seleukos' large cavalry force was presumably mostly Iranian in personnel, though their actual origin is unknown. After the final campaign against Antigonos, and the victory at Ipsos, Seleukos had less need to conciliate the native peoples. Now his main need was to attract the Greeks and Macedonians to his side. The only way his lands could be made attractive to western immigrants was by offering those immigrants the chance to become wealthy, which in effect meant offering them the ownership of land. Thus the immigrant Greeks and Macedonians were settled in the new cities and given plots of land to live off, but those plots continued to be farmed by the peasantry of the native populations [18]. No Greek would go to the trouble of moving from Greece to Syria simply to be a peasant again. Thus the old policy of conciliation had to change.

This is not to say that the policy was abandoned. Seleukos knew full well that the native peoples could make a lot of trouble if they were antagonized – after all, that was what his original policy of conciliation had been intended to avoid. But after Ipsos it was more necessary to favour the Greeks and Macedonians, and so the Babylonians and the Syrians and the Iranians became much more obviously less important. In Babylonia there was a greater emphasis on the Greek cities. The new city of Seleukeia-on-the-Tigris was given conspicuous favours, so that Babylon began visibly to fail. The priests did their best, putting out the stories of bad omens for the foundation of Seleukeia, but Seleukos was prepared, and the story of its spontaneous foundation began to circulate. The decline of old Babylon could not be arrested, and this quite evidently meant that the gods favoured the new city. Also memories of Seleukos' old conciliation policy were strong, and perhaps there were local resentments at the priests as well.

Syrians had never benefited from Seleukos' conciliation policy, and now they suffered from his determination to establish the new cities in their land. In one sense this might have been a welcome move, for the cities would mean increased wealth, though in the short term it was likely enough a disaster for the local population. Yet Seleukos' part of Syria was not totally devoid of political authorities, although its treatment at the hands of its successive conquerors had left it overwhelmingly a peasant society. There were two native political powers still potent in 301: off the coast, and very close to the Ptolemaic boundary, was the city and kingdom of Arados; inland was the town and ex-kingdom of Bambyke.

Apart from these two places there had been no settlements in northern Syria which could be described as urban when Alexander passed through. The Syrian cavalry which had fought on with the Persians until the battle of Gaugamela was presumably part of a chieftain class; the Persian defeat would also mean their destruction, both as a class and probably as individuals too. Aradus, however, had survived Alexander's conquest by a timely submission [19]. It was a Phoenician city, built on an offshore island, and it dominated a stretch of the nearby coastline, its *peraea*. It may have been under Demetrios' control for a time after Ipsos, but with Seleukos in control of the coast, the island had to come to terms with him. The kingship was retained, and control of the coast remained with the city; that is, Aradus and its *peraea* became a sub-kingdom of the Seleukid state [20]. This was delicate handling indeed by Seleukos, far more delicate than any Greek or Macedonian ever received. It might be possible to explain it away as a Seleukid reaction to the awkward situation of Phoenicia with Demetrios and Ptolemy and Seleukos all competing for control over the cities. But there is also the treatment of Bambyke to be considered.

Bambyke is in northern Syria also, but is well away from the coast, not far, in fact, from the Euphrates. It had a notable temple to Atargatis, and this, and possibly some industry, was the basis of its wealth. When Alexander was in Egypt, a local ruler, called Abd-Hadad, had coined in silver at Bambyke, thus making a pretence at independence [21]. He did not survive, at least not as an independent ruler; but his town did. Sometime between 298 and 293, Seleukos' wife Stratonike became patroness of the temple [22], and Seleukos promoted the town to the status of a city, giving it the wholly suitable new name of Hierapolis [23]. No doubt there was some Greek settlement at the place, but it was always the temple, aggressively Syrian and feminine, which was the main power in the city [24]. This promotion of a native temple-town deep in Syria to the status of a Greek city is not just a most unusual event; it is unique.

When these two events – the conciliation of Aradus and the promotion of Bambyke to be Hierapolis – are taken together, then it is possible to discern a definite royal policy towards the Syrians. These two were the only native Syrian political entities above the village level in Seleukos' time. The king did not eliminate them. There was no sack of Arados as Alexander and Antigonos had sacked Tyre, no destruction at Bambyke. Instead, both places were nurtured and cosseted, promoted and recognized, and conciliated. In the midst of the great new cities of Syria, dependent as they were on the labour of Syrian peasants, these Syrian cities continued. There was to be no careless alienation of those remnants of the old ruling group in Syria. It was, of course, a clear recognition on the part of Seleukos that these political entities had some real power, and that that real power was firmly rooted in the Syrian population. The realization that these cities had some political strength was also an implied recognition of the latent political strength of the peasantry as a whole. And Seleukos' recognition of it meant that this strength remained latent. To be even more Machiavellian about it, it may also have occurred to Seleukos that a standing threat from the Syrian peasantry was an admirable way of keeping the Greeks and Macedonians in the cities quietly and firmly on his side, for the alliance of king and cities clearly depended on the cities' perception that a threat to their well-being existed. To eliminate that threat would be to risk the dissolution of the alliance.

The Iranians were the most numerous of the non-Greek-speaking peoples in Seleukos' kingdom. They inhabited all the eastern part of the kingdom, from the Zagros mountains to the Jaxartes river, with more of them beyond that river. They were the former imperial people, whose ability to resist Alexander and Seleukos had been fatally weakened by their own divisions. These divisions were largely the product of the geographical disunity of their country. There were mountain tribes in the Zagros and the Elburz which separated off the major groups one from another. The Medes were perhaps the most numerous, living in northern Iran between the Elburz and the central deserts, with their major centre at Ekbatana. The Persians proper lived in the south, Peukestas' old satrapy, between the deserts and the Persian Gulf. The Baktrians were also Iranian, living in the Central Asian river valleys. These and other groups each had their own traditions, and were divided from one another by the usual tribal enmities. Potentially their power was very great, and it had been an alliance of Persians and Medes which had provided the power behind the construction of the original Akhaimenid empire.

Seleukos need not necessarily have known this, but his organization of Iran was designed, deliberately or not, to emphasize and perpetuate these divisions. In some ways he only had to take up where earlier Macedonians had left off, but he seems to have added certain details himself. Perhaps remembering Antigonos' experience with the outspoken Persian in Persis, Seleukos seems to have left that area to its own devices. By the end of his reign there was a local Persian ruler there, who presumed to mint coins in his own name [25]. This suggests that he was already well established, though one episode records the existence of a satrap of 'King Seleukos' called Cheiles [26]. A new centre to replace Persepolis was developing at Istakhr, where the architecture is clearly Iranian in inspiration [27]. Persepolis itself appears to have been abandoned by about 300 B.C., according to the evidence of coins [28]. A local ruler was an excellent way of developing a local patriotism, and so of perpetuating Iranian divisions. He cannot have become established without the permission, tacit or explicit, of Seleukos. One can, therefore, assume that Seleukos was well aware of, accepted, and even approved, this development.

Media and Susiana were the areas of Iran which it was essential for Seleukos to control. Media was wealthy in itself, it was populous, and through it ran the main high road to the east, to Baktria and India. It had been fought over repeatedly, for these very reasons, since Alexander passed through in 330. It had been the basis of the potential power of Peithon. After his elimination an Iranian had been made satrap by Antigonos, but it was a Macedonian called Nikanor whom Seleukos had dispossessed in 312. By then the northern part of Media had become detached from the main stem, ruled by Atropates, who was originally satrap but went on to establish a dynasty [29].

Seleukos accepted that situation, and concentrated his efforts at control in the main, southern, part of Media. There he established a series of cities, based in large measure on Median towns taken over and hellenized by establishing a Greek-speaking population, a garrison in each citadel, and a Greek constitution to ensure that the local governmental power remained in friendly hands, and of course an *epistates* to make certain the Greeks knew what was what. In this way, Ekbatana became a royal residence as it had been for the Akhaimenids, but may not have been renamed. It could not avoid having a garrison, however, and therefore, a Greek-speaking population. Nearby were Greek cities: at Nihavand, given the name Laodikeia, at Concobar (now Kangavar) and one, whose Seleukid name is not known, at Khurrha [30]. This group of four cities gripped the central part of Media tight and dominated the main pass through the Zagros towards Babylonia. Further to the east there were cities like Ray, called Europos, and Hekatompylos on the main route, and an Alexandria at Merv [31]. There may have been others in this area to watch the hills to the north, but enough are known to show that Seleukos had identified Media as a key area. It separated the semi-independent Iranian areas of the north and south – Atropatene and Persis – from one another. It provided a reservoir of military manpower in the central area, guarded the route farther to the east and thus connected the two major bases of Babylonia and Baktria.

Susiana had been an area associated with Seleukos since his brief period as satrap under Antigonos during the latter's campaign against Eumenes. On his recovery of Babylonia in 312, Seleukos had gone on to seize control in Susiana as well [32]. Susa was one of the old imperial cities and had been, and still was, a great citadel. It became an important mint for the Seleukid dynasty [33], and was, no doubt, strongly garrisoned. At some point it was re-founded as a city, with the name Seleukeia [34]. Susiana was thus a strongly held area between Persis and Babylonia, and between the mountains and the coast, where there were new cities east of the mouth of the Tigris-Euphrates at Charax and Antioch.

This suggests strongly that Seleukos was even less certain of the allegiance of the Iranians than of the Syrians. Given the recent imperial glory which the Iranians had enjoyed, this is hardly surprising. Seleukos employed the usual mixture of control and conciliation together with an added determination to enforce and perpetuate the divisions between the various Iranian groups. The Iranians themselves, by Seleukos' perception of them, seem to have only partly rejected the new political scheme of things. Those who benefited were the aristocracy, who kept control of much of the land, paying tribute to the king, or even became local rulers, like the lords of Persis or Atropatene. The quantity of land taken by the new cities was, given the huge area of Iran, relatively small. Further, the Iranian specialization as cavalry gave them an opening into the royal service. Thus the Seleukid settlement of Iran not only reinforced the geographical divisions but the social divisions as well, for an implicit alliance existed between the aristocracy and the dynasty, at the expense, of course, of the peasantry.

In the east, this order of things was presumably repeated. If they were to escape conquest by their wilder Iranian nomad cousins from beyond the Jaxartes, the settled Iranians of Baktria needed to support the government of the dynasty, and needed also the technical and organizational expertise of the Greeks and Macedonians. This meant cities. Baktria, with the usual Greek exaggeration of the partly-known, gained the reputation of having a thousand cities [35]. Certainly many towns grew in the area during the Seleukid period and after. Some had been founded by Alexander, others were encouraged by the Seleukids. Details, as so often, escape us, at least until excavation of the sites can be resumed and extended. Some certainties, however, do appear in the sea of conjecture. Kandahar had been an Alexandria and continued as a Greek city even under the rule of the Mauryas [36]. Baktra became the capital of the later Baktrian kingdom and can be presumed to have had a Greek civic organization [37]. The discovery of the Greek city at Ai-Khanum upstream from Baktra gives promise of other discoveries of an equally spectacular nature in the future [38]. The results of the Soviet excavations in Central Asia are becoming more available and some trustworthy conclusions are emerging [39].

One major conclusion has emerged as a result of an investigation of the development of fortification in Central Asia. It appears that a new type of city-wall, high and solid, replaced the hollow casemated type which was in use before the Hellenistic period. This is interpreted as a reaction to the greater besieging power of Hellenistic armies, equipped with the engines which Demetrios had used with such mixed fortunes. The hollow casemates are said to be more effective against nomad archers [40]. The chronological development is clear enough, but the interpretation is less certain. It may be an indication of the concerns of the Seleukid government, and could thus fit in well with the fortification of other cities in Media and Syria. In that case it suggests that the enemy to be feared in Baktria was not the nomads, for the casemated walls were quite sufficient protection against them, and they were revived later, after the Hellenistic period, but the local population, that is, the Baktrians.

This is difficult to credit. There is no hint of conflict between Greeks and Iranians other than these walls, and the continued existence of Baktria for two centuries after Alexander, first as a Seleukid province and then as an independent Greek-ruled kingdom, presupposes a working alliance between the Greeks (who provided the ruling dynasties) and the Iranians, who were the majority of the population. The available evidence is thus difficult to reconcile. What is quite certain is that when more evidence is available the conclusions are likely to be different from anything we say now. Nevertheless it is also very likely that it will become clear that the foundations of Hellenistic Baktria were laid partly by Stasanor and partly by Seleukos and Antiochos, and that the rule of these last during a quarter of a century set the pattern for the following two centuries, both as to the continuation of the province-cum-kingdom, and as to its ultimate destruction.

There is also the Apama-factor. One of the reasons why Seleukos was able to move confidently into Iran must have been the fact that he was married to an Iranian woman. Apama was the daughter of the Baktrian who had led the resistance to Alexander's conquest with energy, spirit, and resource [41]. The children of the marriage were thus half-Iranian, though we do not know if they were bilingual. Presumably Apama died in the period 300 to 298, between Seleukos' naming of cities after her and his marriage to Stratonike. Though it is possible that Apama was still alive at the date of Seleukos' second marriage, there is no hint of this in our sources — which are good for the second marriage. Apama was adult in 324 at her marriage, and would thus have been nearing fifty by 300, a good age for a woman at the time. There was no tradition of polygyny in the Seleukid house, and it was Seleukos who set the traditions. In addition, mistreatment or rejection of Apama seems unlikely for the very reason that her marriage to Seleukos was so valuable to him: it would alienate those Iranians, specifically the Baktrians, who had been conciliated at least in part by the existence of that marriage. Given Seleukos' life, it is the political considerations which probably weighed with him the most. Of their children we know only Antiochos by name. The treaty with Chandragupta in 303 had included a marriage clause, which may have involved Seleukos sending a daughter to India. If so, her name is lost. Antiochos was adult in 301 when he commanded the cavalry at Ipsos.

Seleukos and Stratonike had a daughter, Phila. Then, in 293 or 292, Seleukos handed over his wife to his son. This took place at a great public ceremony at which Antiochos was also appointed to be his father's viceroy in the east. The story was later elaborated that Antiochos fell in love with his stepmother and became ill with his desire. The story has a doctor, Erasistratos, diagnosing the problem and persuading Seleukos to surrender his wife to preserve his son's sanity. Since the son was a man of at least 30 years of age at this time it seems highly unlikely that he needed a doctor to diagnose his problem. But it does make an amusing story [42].

It is, of course, no more strange a marriage than many others among the rulers of the Hellenistic period. It is tempting to look for a political motive behind it, but there is nothing obvious to be discerned. Perhaps the personal is the only motive. Stratonike and Antiochos were only a few years apart in age, while Seleukos was at least 35 years older than his wife. That the marriage and the posting to the east occurred at the same time is perhaps also a personal reaction. But there can be no doubt that the east did require the full attention of a competent man with full authority, while it was also clear that Seleukos could not possibly leave the west. Transferring Stratonike to Antiochos prevented any possible hostile reaction from Demetrios out of outraged fatherly pride. Performing the whole thing at a public ceremony presumably also prevented too many sniggers and gossiping stories.

The result for the kingdom was a definite strengthening of the dynastic grip. Seleukos' conquests were so huge that, like Alexander, he had found that he could not govern them adequately. Once again he instituted a system which became normal in the Seleukid house, of using the eldest son of the king as viceroy in the east. The difficulty was, of course, that very few of the later eldest sons were capable of ruling. Seleukos' own son, however, was as capable as he was himself.

Antiochos had been virtually a full partner with his father since Ipsos, where he had been second-in-command of Seleukos' army. There are also a number of other men, known only vaguely, who were employed by Seleukos in high positions. Patrokles was left in command in Babylonia in 312 when Seleukos went off to conquer Media [43], and he reappears at intervals for the next thirty years. He was employed to investigate the Caspian Sea [44], perhaps during Seleukos' campaigns in the east, though perhaps more likely in the quieter 290s. Whatever he did, he failed to dispel the ancient notion that the Caspian was a bay of the encircling ocean. He reappears finally in the crisis of 286–285 [45] which will be dealt with in the next chapter. His role then was portrayed as putting backbone into an irresolute king. This might be true, but it might also indicate a king with a greater appreciation of political complications than his bluff soldierly lieutenant. A second general we know of in Seleukos' employ is Demodamas, who campaigned beyond the Jaxartes [46], possibly as satrap of Baktria, possibly on the orders of Seleukos or Antiochos or both, and who acted as royal agent in his home-city of Miletos [47]. Megasthenes was sent by Seleukos to India, and acted as an ambassador at the court of Chandragupta Maurya [48]. Megasthenes probably went on his own account, but became involved in diplomacy while in India, for a resident envoy seems quite unnecessary. It may also be, of course, that he exaggerated his own importance; that was hardly a trait unknown amongst the Greeks. A few other men are known from inscriptions [49], but they remain distressingly few. Seleukos ruled Babylonia for over thirty years, and the east for a quarter of a century, and Syria for twenty years, yet we know the names of no more than half-a-dozen of the men who acted as his officials.

These men, at least the first two, Patrokles and Demodamas, ranked as Friends of the king. During Seleukos' reign, this semi-formal rank was solidifying, like other procedures, into a formal position. Another of them was probably the doctor Erasistratos, if he really existed outside the story of Antiochos' love-sickness. These were men whom the king consulted, either alone or as a council, and, judging by the stories told of them, they were expected to be both blunt and frank. This is likely enough, when it is recalled that Seleukos was not born king, but retained a certain approachability and absence of aloofness from his soldierly days. Perhaps Antiochos did so, too, for his father was not a king until Antiochos was in his late teens. After these two, however, the dynasty became dignified and irresponsible.

9
DIPLOMACY AND DEFENCE
(293–286)

Seleukos' decision to appoint his son to be ruler of the eastern part of the kingdom is presented in our sources in connection with Antiochos' marriage to Stratonike. Seleukos is portrayed as sacrificing his wife and half his kingdom for his son's happiness. This is the stuff of fairy-tales and it has all the appearance of Seleukid propaganda. It is also so thoroughly unlikely as cause-and-effect that other reasons must be sought. Generally, giving in to the ignorance we are in as a result of the failure of our sources, the usual explanation is the vague one that the empire had grown too big to be ruled by one man [1]. But as an explanation of the specific act of making Antiochos king in the east, this is not good enough. The Akhaimenids had ruled an even bigger empire. Seleukos' kingdom before Ipsos was almost as big. Seleukos had ruled the whole empire for eight or nine years after Ipsos by himself. So a more specific, concrete, immediate reason is needed.

Only one historian seems to have essayed an explanation. W.W. Tarn put the appointment in the context of the rebuilding of three of the Macedonian colonies in the east. Alexandria-in-Margiane (Merv) was destroyed by barbarian attack, rebuilt by Antiochos, and renamed as Antiochia-in-Margiane; Antiochos equipped it with a wall of great length, 120 stades in Pliny, 1,500 in Strabo [2], which apparently surrounded the whole oasis. Alexandria-Eschate, the Farthest, on the south bank of the Jaxartes, was also rebuilt as Antioch-in-Scythia; according to Tarn, this implies its previous destruction. The crossing point of the Oxus at Termez was also refounded by Antiochos as Antiochia-Tarmita; this again presupposed an earlier destruction. These were Tarn's 'facts', upon which he based the theory of a great nomad incursion into Baktria in 293, during which the cities were destroyed, and which necessitated the despatch of Antiochos to the east [3].

This theory has not been widely accepted. Tarn restated it briefly in the second edition of his book on Baktria [4] and J. Wolski has used it [5]. The main problem is that modern historians in effect dismiss the east as cavalierly as did Diodoros. But it is important, and not only for itself. Antiochos was in the east when Seleukos died, and this imposed a hiatus in Seleukid history which allowed all sorts of mischief to be perpetrated in his absence. In addition, the Greek kingdoms in Baktria and India are both fascinating in themselves and crucial to a number of matters which are of greater significance. So what it was that took Antiochos to the east is thereby, both in itself and in its consequences, also important.

It is difficult to accept all Tarn's reasoning. In particular he strains every muscle to have three destroyed cities, but only in the case of Merv has he any serious ancient support, for Pliny does say it was destroyed by barbarians. The 'rebuilding' of the other two cities does not necessarily imply a previous physical destruction; it could be a matter of development. Certainly Antiochos did enough to justify renaming them, but it is possible that Alexander's original foundations had not been up to much in the first place. It is therefore even less possible to accept Tarn's hypothesis of a nomad invasion in 293 – partly because of the uncertainty about the cities, and partly because there are other barbarians in the area besides nomads.

And yet... And yet... *something* compelled Seleukos to hand over half of his hard-won kingdom to his son. Antiochos really did wall-in the oasis of Merv. Tarn's identification of Antioch-in-Scythia as the erstwhile Alexandria-Eschate seems good, as does, with less certainty, his Antioch-Tarmita with another Alexandria. All these Antiochs are clear evidence of much work being done in Baktria by Antiochos I. And the only possible reason for a wide-ranging fortification campaign, the only possible reason for walling in an entire oasis, is the nomad menace. Nothing else makes sense. It has to be assumed that, during Antiochos' rule in Baktria, the threat of a nomad invasion was perceived as being very real.

This is not to accept that the postulated invasion took place, nor the wholesale destruction of cities. The rebuilding does not necessarily imply an early destruction in all cases. The Baktrian Alexandrias were numerous, but perhaps none of them was ever large. Certainly Alexander had done little to ensure that they were actually built, and at least two rebellions by his colonists [6] imply that *they* did little or nothing to build up their new homes either. It is better to imagine that the Alexandrias needed *building* in the 280s, not *re*building. A series of re-foundations and re-namings does imply a major effort by Antiochos to justify discarding Alexander's name, though it is likely that Alexander's memory was not popular in Baktria, either with Baktrians or with Greeks.

The appearance through the dimness of our sources of this information, small though it is, makes it clear that Antiochos was fully occupied from 293 onwards in the east. The rebuilding, or building, of three cities, given the state of our sources, suggests that even more were fortified and built and organized and populated. It was probably as great a work as Seleukos was accomplishing in the west.

Seleukos should have been the man who attended to problems in the east, but his presence was required in the west of his kingdom because it was in the west that the greatest danger lay, a danger even greater than a nomad invasion. Only in Egypt, Asia Minor, and Macedonia were there political organizations sufficiently powerful to pose a credible threat to the continued existence of his entire kingdom. In the east, the Mauryan empire in India was certainly powerful, but it was not a threat, and the nomads of the steppes could be kept out of Baktria by a resolute defence, as the Akhaimenids had shown, and as Antiochos was to show. Internally the Iranians were divided and could be induced to remain quiet, the Syrians had been successfully dominated, and the Babylonians were conciliated. But in the west any one of the three great Macedonian kingdoms was capable of destroying the Seleukid state.

Of the three Ptolemy's Egypt was possibly marginally less dangerous than the other two. Ptolemy had never shown any serious interest in moving north of the Eleutheros river, and the continued possession of Tyre and Sidon by Demetrios was a further guard on any northward advance from Egypt. Nevertheless Ptolemy was the one king who maintained an ability to strike directly into Syria with little or no warning, for there was no geographical barrier forming the boundary. The boundary with Lysimachos' kingdom was the Taurus mountain range, with few and narrow passes, easily guarded and blocked. Demetrios was separated from Syria by almost a thousand miles of sea. In each of these cases a warning of attack was certain, but Ptolemy could come by sea or by one or all of three parallel land routes. From the road along the Phoenician coast, he could cross the small and shallow Eleutheros river, which formed no real barrier; inland, the Biqaa valley was an ideal corridor for invasion; beyond that, east of the Antilebanon range, there was another route, already used from north to south in Alexander's conquest, and Ptolemy could easily reverse that march.

The absence of a geographical barrier against invasion from the south was therefore made good by establishing an artificial barrier [7]. The city of Apamea became the military headquarters of Syria. Its situation, on the southern tip of a limestone plateau with pathless steppe to the east and a swampy valley to the west, allowed it to block the only inland route to the north. The coast route from south to north was also blocked, partly by the fact that it was a more difficult route, and partly by the well-fortified city of Laodikeia-ad-Mare, which controlled a large harbour, and stood behind (if you are from the south) an awkward river.

Apamea was not left to stand alone, however, in its task of controlling the inland route. To the south of the city, and thus between it and the source of the invasion in Ptolemaic Palestine, there were strings of fortified settlements. None of these places was large, and some were never more than villages, and there is some doubt about the precise location of some of them. Yet enough evidence exists to reconstruct the whole, and thus to discern the purpose of the system. One line of these forts controlled the route along the foot of the Bargylus mountains; the second line controlled a series of crossings of the Orontes river, and the route along that river. The northern half of the Biqaa valley was left unguarded, and seems also to have been virtually unpopulated [8]. Thus a Ptolemaic invasion would first have to pass through land which was a virtual desert, though no doubt it would be carefully watched by Seleukid scouts. After this difficult advance, the invader would need to overwhelm a series of fortified towns, and finally to capture a great city. It was impossible in the face of all that to mount any sort of surprise attack.

The siting of Apamea, well back from the land actually under Ptolemaic control, and with all its satellite forts spread before it, presupposes that this plan existed from the start, that is, from about the year 300, when Apamea was founded. It will have taken some years for the plans to be implemented as walls and forts and buildings, but by 294, it seems likely enough that the defence of the southern frontier was solid enough for Seleukos to make his move into Kilikia in safety. This in turn brought Seleukos' boundary to the line of the Taurus mountains, and for the first time into contact with the lands of Lysimachos.

It is sometimes thought, as a result of one of Appian's careless catalogues, that Seleukos controlled land north of the Taurus from the time of his march through Kappadokia in 302 [9]. Appian lists Seleukos' conquests at one point, and includes an area he called 'Seleukid Kappadokia' [10]. Appian's list here is in two parts, first three lands, then a group of peoples one of which is the Arabs, which Seleukos never ruled. In the previous sentence he says that Seleukos got 'inland Phrygia' after Ipsos along with Syria, which is not the case. This is a terrible hotch-potch, containing two certain mistakes (Arabs and 'inland Phrygia'), or rather, so it seems, three. If it means anything the term 'Seleukid Kappadokia' is that part of Kappadokia which was ruled by Seleukid kings, as opposed to that which they did not rule. This can only refer to the independent kingdom of Kappadokia; the Seleukid part is therefore the southern section which the Seleukid kings gripped tight, since it contained the main route connecting Syria with western Asia Minor. But there is no reason to believe that it was ever under Seleukid control before the conquest of western Asia Minor in 281. Geographically, it is highly unlikely that Seleukos would even try to hold any of Kappadokia before he had secure communications with it from the south, and that means Kilikia. Finally, in 286 Lysimachos' son Agathokles campaigned in Kappadokia without any Seleukid protests. It is best to see Seleukos' control of 'Seleukid Kappadokia' as dating from his campaign against Lysimachos in 281.

So Seleukos' north-western boundary was, first, the

Amanus, and then the Taurus. The advance through Kilikia had been due to a fear of Demetrios. It may have brought Seleukos and Lysimachos into direct contact, but this was not the intention behind Seleukos' move. His aim was essentially defensive, to remove Demetrios' power from his doorstep. This was all the more necessary in that, at the same time, Demetrios made himself master of Macedon [11].

Demetrios was a poor king, and steadily antagonized his subjects by his erratic behaviour, and his laziness and negligence, but while he ruled, his fellow kings needed to be most vigilant. This may be another factor in Seleukos' domestic and imperial rearrangements in 294 and 293: at least the notoriously strong family loyalty of the Antigonids would not cause a rebellion in his own household. For, after all, Demetrios, given his past life, could never be content with Macedon alone. He was compelled by his pride and his ancestry to aim at the empire which his father had ruled, which in turn was that of Alexander. He devoted much of his energy to building up a land force as powerful as his navy [12].

Demetrios' first target would be Lysimachos, who was not only his immediate neighbour in Thrace and Asia Minor, but seems also to have excited his personal dislike. It was this obvious threat which persuaded Lysimachos to remain on good terms with Ptolemy and Seleukos. It is a measure of the threat posed by Demetrios that these three should be allies. They brought the wild and unpredictable King of Epeiros, Pyrrhos, into their network, but he proved to be uncontrollable. This alliance-network, of course, concealed much mutual antipathy. Syria divided Seleukos and Ptolemy. Seleukos and Lysimachos, whose relationship previously seems to have been more or less cordial, based on their mutual success at Ipsos and their geographical separation, now had a common boundary, and there are hints in what developed with Demetrios that strains were developing in their relations.

Lysimachos had been one of Alexander's personal bodyguards, and had started his career as a ruler as satrap of Thrace. For a long time he had concentrated on maintaining and solidifying his power in that difficult land. Ipsos had allowed him to expand into Asia Minor, though just how far east and south his authority extended is unclear. Certainly he ruled in the western interior, Phrygia, and around the

Hellespont, and he had a strong alliance with the Black Sea city of Herakleia-on-Pontos. The old royal road through Gordion and the southern route through the Anatolian lake district were lines along which power inevitably flowed inland and east. The Taurus seems to have been his boundary to the south east. In Kappadokia the power vacuum left by the Macedonian civil wars had been filled by local dynasts, the chief of whom was probably a son or grandson of the man killed by Perdikkas, though no-one seems to have predominated [13]. There is no clear indication of the extent to which Lysimachos' power spread into Kappadokia, but it is reasonable to suppose that he held control of the main routes. To the north, where the great central Anatolian plateau is cut by rivers into valleys and hills and then breaks down to the coast, there was plenty of scope for independence and defiance. The central fortress of the later Kappadokian kings was at Gaziura in the Iris valley, and along the coast were Greek cities – Sinope, Amisos, Trapezos – which were usually independent, and whose history was largely controlled by events in the interior and south of Anatolia. The real guarantee of independence for Kappadokians and cities alike was the continued enmity between the great Macedonian rulers. So long as they were preoccupied by each other, they would leave others alone.

Lysimachos' conquest of Ionia in 294 introduced a new source of tension into his relationship with Seleukos. Authority in the Ionian area had never been one and indivisible, even under the Akhaimenids or Alexander. There were too many cities, too many corners and bays and valleys and islands in which a *de facto* independence could be maintained. The Macedonian civil wars had accentuated these divisions, particularly after the proclamation of freedom for the Greek cities by Antigonos in 314. This inevitably meant a loosening of central control, even if 'freedom' can only be understood in its most exiguous sense. After Ipsos this fragmentation went further, for Demetrios held on to several cities for some years, while Lysimachos expanded his authority. Lysimachos did not even pay lip-service to the notion of civil freedom. He instituted, for example, the office of *strategos* of the Ionian League [14] which until then had been little more than a religious friendly society. Then there were some cities which were actually independent, but usually frightened. Inevitably there were also those which changed hands and altered their status repeatedly.

In Lysimachos' original campaign against Antigonos in 302, for instance, the responses of the Greek cities had varied. Beside the Hellespont, Lysimachos had been welcomed by Lampsakos and by Parion, but had been resisted by Sigeion, which he captured, and by Abydos, which succeeded for the time being in keeping him at bay [15]. The Ionian cities had similarly reacted variously to the arrival of the general Prepelaos, acting for Lysimachos and Kassandros, whose conquests were reversed later by Demetrios [16]. The result was that, after Ipsos, Lysimachos was faced by a complex variety of relationships, which took ten or more years to sort out. Some cities had to be captured, some were left alone. Gradually he wore most of them down to some semblance of obedience. The Ionian cities were eventually placed collectively under the authority of the new *strategos*, Hippostratos of Miletos [17]. He rewarded some of the cities: Ephesos and Smyrna were given new defensive walls [18]; Priene was made free; a judgement was given in Priene's favour over some land nearby [19]; Skepsis was rehabilitated and permitted to withdraw from the synoecism which made Antigoneia [20]; but Antigoneia continued in existence, renamed as Alexandreia Troas and walled [21]; its near-neighbour, Ilion, was enlarged by being allowed to incorporate some small and failing cities nearby [22].

In the interior of Asia Minor, the local political unit was not so much the city as the small principality. There were some urban centres, Sardis for example, which were usually under close supervision by one of Lysimachos' officials [23]. Other urban centres were more in the nature of local strongholds, which later developed civic constitutions. Dokimos, the old Macedonian turn-coat, was the founder of Dokimeion, which was his principality. Another was founded by Themison, perhaps the former Antigonid admiral, whence Themisonion [24]. Both of these are situated near to, but not within, the older settled areas. Dokimeion, for example, is 100 kilometres from Kelainai, Antigonos' old centre, and rather less from Synnada, known to have been one of Antigonos' forts, but it was away from the main centres, as though Dokimos had seized control of borderlands. Themisonion is situated between the old southern highway and Karia and Lykia, again a borderland area. Somewhere in that area was also the principality of Akhaios, one of whose estates is later attested near the Ionian coast [25]. Pergamon was a Lysimachean stronghold under the command of Philetairos [26], who was later to have the idea that he might convert his official position into one nearer to that of his semi-independent neighbours. There will have been other men like these, hovering on the edge of independence, yet deterred from making the final break by Lysimachos' brooding and formidable presence.

For an outsider to the area such as Seleukos, there was plenty of scope in this for interference and intrigue. From Syria he could scarcely hope to establish an actual physical presence in the sense of gaining control of a city or receiving the allegiance of a people or a faction or a local lord. He could, though, establish a spiritual presence. All cities enjoyed receiving benefactions, as did all temples, and any king who was rich in resources could give gifts and have his name inscribed, and thus gain an influence far from his base.

Seleukos had begun extending his influence during his alliance with Demetrios. About 299 the two kings Demetrios and Seleukos, now in-laws and allies, sent a Rhodian, Nikagoras, as their ambassador to Ephesos to announce the marriage of Seleukos and Stratonike to the city, which having changed hands twice in the Ipsos war, was for the moment under Demetrios' control. The city replied to Nikagoras' embassy by passing a decree honouring the ambassador, and through him his kings, and by conferring honorary citizenship on him [27]. To be sure, this would scarcely create a faction for Seleukos among the citizens, but it kept his name before their eyes, and reputation was his main purpose.

One of the better ways to establish a reputation in one area, and hence a presence, was by paying attention to a shrine. The oracle of Apollo at Didyma near Miletos was at once a centre of religious worship for Ionia, and an oracle whose own reputation was fast expanding. It had predicted divinity for Alexander, who in return had been generous to it [28]. Hence association with Didyma was, if one was a king, association with Alexander. But Seleukos had gone further. Three of the stories which clustered around him concerned Apollo, specifically Apollo at Didyma. The story of his mother Laodike dreaming of Seleukos' conception, had one version in which Apollo was named as Seleukos' father [29]. This version became well known in Ionia, and it is referred to at Ilion, in two inscriptions, and at Erythrai, in a stanza of a festival hymn [30]. Another story circulated that Seleukos stopped at Didyma back in 334 when he was an officer of Alexander's, and the oracle called him 'king'. This is a particularly suspect story since Seleukos himself is said to be the source, for he is quoted as raising his followers' spirits with it on the ride to Babylon after the battle of Gaza [31]. It is unacceptable both because of the source and because of the prediction, for no-one was predicting kingship for the Macedonian generals even in 312, and Seleukos said the prediction occurred in 334. A second version of this story sounds more plausible. Seleukos' question to the oracle is said to have been whether he should return to Macedon, and this gives the context, in the first winter of Alexander's conquest, when some of the young men were sent home. The answer was that Seleukos should not return and that he would do better to stay in Asia [32]. The vagueness is very oracular. This story may well be approximately accurate [33].

The precise origins of these stories are less important, perhaps, than their purpose. It seems likely that they became known only when Seleukos began to show an interest in the political situation in Ionia – after Ipsos, that is. He returned to Didyma the statue of Apollo which had been looted by Dareios the Great back in 494 at the end of the Ionian revolt [34]. Statues of Seleukos and Apama were put up at the temple [35]. Demodamas, Seleukos' general, visited Miletos, the city within whose boundaries Didyma lay, and presented a stoa and shops to the city in the name of the king's son Antiochos [36]. The rents from the shops were to be devoted to Apollo's welfare at Didyma. All this may well have been quite sincere in the sense that Seleukos does seem to have been devoted to the god, but there can be no doubt that he was also reaping a clear political benefit as a result of his devotion.

The marriage to Stratonike thus opened a route of influence for Seleukos into Ionia, for Demetrios continued to control much of it for some years after the marriage. The process had begun at Miletos, as is shown by the presentation of statues of Seleukos and Apama, which must have taken place before the Stratonike marriage, whether Apama was dead by the time of the marriage or not. This is the area which Lysimachos took over from Demetrios in 294, capturing Ephesos by a ruse, and which he then controlled though his *strategos*. By that time, however, the Seleukid myth-machine had been at work, and had begun to legitimize Seleukos' interest in the area. It is surely no accident that, later, it is in this very area, at Priene, that we have records of his gifts, and that it was at Erythrai that he was celebrated as the son of Apollo [37]. The ground had been well prepared at Didyma for these plantings-out of the seeds of influence. It all suggests that the royal competitors had made Ionia into a very sensitive area. It is clearly also no accident that it was precisely here that Demetrios landed later on, in his last campaign [38].

This inscriptional evidence is sufficient to show that Seleukos was interested in this sensitive and unstable area from the immediate aftermath of Ipsos. On the other hand it is not until the late 280s that there is evidence of his hostility to Lysimachos, yet it is a reasonable assumption that hostility was latent. All these lords were suspicious of each other, and with good reason. After all, the ambition of each of them was likely to be insatiable. There are cases where it is now clear that this ambition was not present. Kassandros, for instance, or Ptolemy, were seemingly content with just a fragment of Alexander's empire. But this only became clear afterwards. At the time it was only safe to assume the worst. For there had been clear cases of overwhelming ambition: Alexander, of course, and Antigonos. And now Demetrios, in control of Macedonia. And Seleukos. Ptolemy knew of Seleukos' ambition, and it is one of the obvious reasons for his determination to build defences. Probably Lysimachos knew it. Probably Lysimachos shared it.

Further, there were plenty of possibilities for acquiring more lands. None of the kingdoms of these Macedonian lords was stable; all were composed of bits and fragments of territories stitched together with no common centre other than the person of the king. None of them was likely, on the evidence of earlier attempts at building kingdoms, to survive beyond the death of the founder. Alexander's empire had collapsed. So had Antigonos'. So had Kassandros'. Even Seleukos' kingdom could be thought of as breaking up already, with the installation of Antiochos in the east. This appointment now appears to be a masterstroke, in that it enabled Antiochos to establish his own power-base from which to claim the rest of his father's inheritance when Seleukos died, but even so it only held the east into the kingdom for another generation.

All possible methods had, therefore, to be employed in holding the heterogeneous empire together. If conciliation of a particular group would serve, then they were conciliated, as the Babylonians; if force would work, then force was used; if administrators were needed, then they were best recruited from outside, so that they depended wholly on the king; if propaganda would help, then stories of the king's devotion to the gods could be circulated. Stratonike was promoted as patroness of the Atargatis temple at Bambyke [39]; Apama had joined in dedications to Apollo at Didyma [40]. The king was said to be descended from Apollo himself [41]; a fake genealogy was concocted to put Seleukos into the same family as Alexander, and hence an Argead and a Heraklid [42].

Coinage could be used to spread the propaganda message, though just how effective this was is unclear. Herakles, Zeus, Apollo, and Athene were popular types, but nothing here necessarily distinguishes Seleukos from anyone else [43]. These, after all, were the main deities of the Greco-Macedonian peoples; not to put them on the coins would be more surprising than to portray them. Certain devices, however, are more characteristically Seleukid. An anchor is used, recalling the birthmark said to connect Seleukos with Apollo. An elephant or a chariot drawn by elephants recalls Seleukos' Indian campaign, and the use of elephants at Ipsos. Nike, victory, appears sufficiently often to help explain Seleukos' title of Nikator, even though he suffered his share of defeats. Many of the early coins were issued in the name of Alexander, so it seems unlikely that Seleukos was seriously using them as propaganda vehicles. As historical sources there is also doubt. Dating these coins is difficult and precise dates are disputed. It is not therefore useful to interpret the coins in the light of historical events, nor to derive historical events from the coins. In the nature of things the coins were produced when and where the king's treasury required them. The coin hoards always show a great mixture. Any message the king wished to convey on his coins was therefore unlikely to be heeded unless it was repeated regularly. Hence the very general, even bland, coinage types. The one certainty is that they were designed to reinforce the other messages of stability and longevity and divine favour, which Seleukos desired for his kingdom. By invoking the deities so often, and insistently referring to victory, Seleukos was in fact revealing the basic instability of his short-lived kingdom, and the precariousness of his victories.

Ptolemaic Egypt tends to look more stable. Yet its boundaries fluctuated almost as often, if not quite so wildly, as did those of Seleukos. Kyrene, Palestine, Cyprus, even the Upper Nile, all proved to have fissiparous qualities in the century after the death of Ptolemy I, and even before his death in the cases of Kyrene and Cyprus. It is not surprising, therefore, that Lysimachos' kingdom, which only existed from the aftermath of Ipsos, was just as fragile as the rest. At times it looked like a re-appearance of the old Phrygian or perhaps the Lydian kingdom, and at others it seemed to be an anticipation of the later Byzantine state, but none of these moments is at all relevant. The continuation of the Seleukid and Ptolemaic states was due to the ability of Ptolemy II and Antiochos I, not to some divine law of geography or of history. The success of the family of Antigonos in holding on to the throne of Macedon was due mainly to the ability of Antigonos Gonatas, but also in part to the exhaustion of Macedon. In the same way, Lysimachos' realm could have survived the death of its founder if he had left a capable heir. He did not, and so his kingdom collapsed.

Thus, hostility between the various Macedonian lords was a normal state of affairs, just as mutual suspicion had been the normal condition at Alexander's court, of which they were all graduates. Only the behaviour of Demetrios, whose ambition to recreate his father's kingdom was all too evident, could supersede this mutual animosity. Had he displayed a spark of diplomatic ability, Demetrios might well have created the conditions in which he could have gained territory here and there, though in the end, he would have provoked a coalition against him. But diplomacy was never his preferred activity. He steadily built up his armed force in Macedon, while simultaneously profoundly annoying his Macedonian subjects. His fall was inevitable. Once he had provoked the formation of a hostile coalition and an invasion of Macedon had begun, the Macedonian army took the first opportunity to desert him. Literally, they went home, and Demetrios went on the run again [44]. Lysimachos took first half and later all of Macedonia. At sea, Demetrios' fleet seems to have become Ptolemy's, since the latter was suddenly able to intervene actively in mainland Greece for the first time for twenty years or more, and the Island League came under his protection as well. In Phoenicia, Tyre and Sidon fell to Ptolemy as well. A little later Philokles, King of Sidon, was in command of the Ptolemaic fleet [45]. Ptolemy had done even less to gain this prize than he had to gain Palestine at the time of Ipsos.

Once again Seleukos gained little or nothing. Only those with territory contiguous with that of Demetrios' were able to seize fragments as they flew free from the self-destruction. Seleukos' lack of success was not only annoying; it was positively dangerous. If Ptolemy's ambition were to grow, he now had the power to go with it. His possession of Tyre and Sidon removed a major block on a northward move from Palestine. His possession of Demetrios' fleet gave him control of all the Eastern Mediterranean from the Peloponnese to Cyrenaica. No fleet in that area could approach it in strength. He could land troops on any coast from Messenia to Syria, if he chose (and, in fact, Ptolemaic troops were soon landed in Attika, a feat which had been quite out of the question before Demetrios' fall). Ptolemy already controlled some of the cities of Karia and Lykia, and these were now much more firmly in his grasp. Furthermore Seleukos now no longer had to face old, conservative Ptolemy I, whose territorial ambitions were well known and clear. From 285 onwards, if not before, a son of the old man, Ptolemy II, shared power in Egypt and his ambitions were unclear [46]. It was yet another element of instability.

Lysimachos' accession of strength was equally ominous. He gained eastern Macedon in 287, on Demetrios' fall [47]. This was a significant gain of power and territory in itself, but it was even more important in that it was accompanied by the removal of a hostile neighbour from Lysimachos' western frontier. It had been the threat posed by Demetrios which had concentrated Lysimachos' attention on the west. Now it seemed as though he would be able to look elsewhere, eastward possibly. And he and Ptolemy were long-time allies, linked by marriages. Seleukos was surely nervous, and looked to his defences.

For the moment all attention was concentrated on the upheaval in Greece and the Aegean. Demetrios was still alive and kicking. Fighting was continuing in Attika and central Greece; Ptolemy's fleet was only in partial control of the seas. Demetrios had recovered from worse positions in the past, after Ipsos, for example, or, even earlier, after Gaza. He still had some thousands of troops and several bases in Greece, including the fortified ports of Piraeus and Corinth. All the kings were watching, stabbing ineffectually at him – Ptolemy in Attika, Pyrrhos from his (western) half of Macedonia [48] – though Demetrios identified Lysimachos as his prime target. In this he was probably correct, for once, in that Lysimachos was undoubtedly the most formidable of the three kings in a personal, and even in a military sense. He may also have been correct in that Lysimachos' lands were ripe for disaffection. As usual, however, Demetrios' calculations missed out one factor, and that was the vital one.

Despairing of a sufficiently spectacular success in old Greece, Demetrios gathered his forces to attack Lysimachos. He landed at Miletos, the soft spot which Seleukos had already identified. Gathering opportunistic allegiances from cities and local potentates, he moved about Karia and Ionia, then into Lydia, where he captured Sardis, apparently without difficulty [49]. Then the miscalculated factor appeared, in the person of Agathokles, Lysimachos' highly competent son. Chivvying and nudging, he shoved Demetrios ever deeper into the interior of Asia Minor, along the road to the east, and at the same time retook all Demetrios' conquests in the west. Demetrios' force steadily dwindled in the face of failure. Agathokles, just as steadily, refused to fight him and simply blocked his way west. Demetrios reached the Taurus, crossed the pass, and appeared in Kilikia, his old territory, now ruled by his ex son-in-law, Seleukos [50].

Agathokles had refused to fight Demetrios for the same

reason that Seleukos now also refused to fight him: he could not rely on the loyalty of his men. Before Agathokles had arrived to face Demetrios, the latter had won over several of Lysimachos' officers – and cities and men and money. Many of the men in Lysimachos' army were former soldiers of Demetrios and his father, either from Macedon or from before Ipsos. Agathokles could not risk losing his whole army by a sudden desertion. This failure to stand and fight must have been immensely frustrating to Demetrios, who was surely relying on such defections to provide him with a sufficiently large force with which his new empire was to be conquered. Instead he was gradually moved east, until he made the best of it and put it about, so it seems, that he was going to recruit his strength in Armenia and Media [51]. If he was serious in this, he was actually talking of reclaiming the allegiance of the colonists established by Seleukos and Antiochos in Media, men who had presumably been part of Antigonos' pre-Ipsos army. No doubt this prospect simultaneously chilled the hearts of Seleukos and of Demetrios' own men.

The danger to Seleukos was manifest, but he could not simply deflect Demetrios somewhere else. For a start, there was nowhere else, for Agathokles blocked the Taurus passes. Second, Seleukos was diplomatically isolated, and feeling very threatened. A revival of the old alliance with Demetrios against Lysimachos and Ptolemy was clearly a possibility, but it would still leave the problem of Demetrios unsolved. The alternative was a fight between the armies of Seleukos and Demetrios, in which Seleukos might well lose, and from which only Ptolemy and Lysimachos could benefit. It was clear by this time (winter 286–285) that Ptolemy I had fallen under the influence of his wife Berenike, and that his son by her was likely to have a major say in affairs. It must have been clear also by this time that the situation in Macedon was very unstable, and that Lysimachos was likely to have the edge over the erratic Pyrrhos, if only because he was a Macedonian, whereas Pyrrhos was an Epirote. With Lysimachos in control of all Macedon and all Asia Minor, and Ptolemy II wishing to establish his new authority with a victory, Seleukos was clearly facing serious trouble. Once more, as in 300–298, he had only a short time to escape the trap.

He tried negotiations with Demetrios first, offering to

establish him in Kataonia, that is, north of the Taurus [52]. This was technically Lysimachos' territory, if anyone's, so the implication is that Demetrios would have to continue the fight against Agathokles, being supplied, presumably, by Seleukos. For Seleukos this would re-establish the old alliance with him in control. It would also provide a distraction for Lysimachos from his grasp at Macedon. But the idea does not appear to have appealed to Demetrios – winter in Kataonia is not a pleasant prospect – and so Seleukos had to settle for Demetrios wintering in Kilikia. This in turn implies that Seleukos withdrew all his forces from that province, which he had ruled for the past ten years. Demetrios clearly camped there with Seleukos' permission. It might be thought from this that the old alliance had been re-activated, but it seems to have been merely a convenient and temporary arrangement. For Seleukos, Demetrios' only value was as a threat to Lysimachos. For Demetrios, on the other hand, Seleukos was a potential source of supply and at the same time a very tempting target. Perhaps Demetrios' men, who seem to have been both loyal to him and somewhat distrustful of him, made plain their preference for fighting Seleukos rather than the alarmingly efficient Agathokles backed by the stolid and determined Lysimachos. Seleukos did not yet have much of a reputation for victory. He had won at Ipsos, but only with Lysimachos; he had won at Gaza, but only in partnership with Ptolemy; whatever had happened in Baktria and India, Seleukos had actually ended by giving territory away. To Demetrios' battle-hardened men, Seleukos may well have looked the softer option. In this, like their master, they miscalculated.

The real danger to Seleukos was that Demetrios would make an appeal to the loyalties of his old soldiers. They were now settled in all Seleukos' new cities, seventeen years older than at Ipsos, but all the more romantically-minded for the passing of the years. Even if they did not actively join him in arms, they might refuse to fight against him, or they might seize power in their cities. The possibilities were numerous and quite sufficient to unnerve Seleukos.

Demetrios, if he calculated in this way, had missed the point, for, while Seleukos might well have been unnerved, he did have other resources. In the spring of 285, Demetrios brought his force east, over the Amanus, an event which clearly marks the end of any actual or potential alliance. Demetrios had decided to reject whatever offer Seleukos made. At first he had some successes against Seleukos' forces, which can only have confirmed Seleukos' reluctance to face him in full battle. It is said that Patrokles argued for fighting, but Seleukos would not [53]. It is a scene which might even have taken place. Its clear suggestion of a greater political insight on Seleukos' part is rather obvious, but this was why he was the king and Patrokles the general.

Then the campaign suffered an enforced delay while Demetrios recovered from an illness. This allowed some of his troops to reflect on the odds facing them, and they began to desert to Seleukos. From them Seleukos will have got a clearer idea of the size and state of morale of Demetrios' force. When Demetrios recovered, he found that Seleukos was clearly more determined to block him, the more so, since the disturbances to his rear that he had feared had not in fact occurred. No doubt he also had agents in Demetrios' camp, spreading sedative messages. When he crossed the Amanus again, therefore, Demetrios moved into a trap. He was blocked in all directions, and could not advance. He could reach no city, for he was stuck in the narrow valley of the Kara Su, which was overlooked by Kyrrhos, high on its hill, solidly fortified, and no doubt held by a specially picked Seleukid garrison. Demetrios moved back into the Amanus: his retreat had begun again. Seleukos followed him, as Agathokles had, and now he hemmed Demetrios' forces in, a fact driven home to Demetrios' men by the sight of the camp fires on all the hills around them, night after night. When Demetrios drew up his remaining men for a last fight, Seleukos knew he had them. He took off his helmet and walked towards Demetrios' line. He appealed to them to give up the hopeless fight and to surrender. It worked with most of them, and Demetrios himself was captured soon after [54]. The factor which had been miscalculated in this attack on Seleukos was the fact that the best generals do not win victories often because they win without having to fight at all.

10
VICTOR AND VICTIM
(286–281)

The capture of Demetrios triggered a series of events in all the kingdoms. Seleukos had to decide what to do with him. At first, so the story goes, Demetrios was treated as a king. Reassuring messages were carried to him from Seleukos. The messengers, members of Seleukos' court, were honoured to meet the famous adventurer, and gradually more and more of them attended on him. Seleukos grew alarmed and suspicious, and arrested Demetrios. He ringed him with armed guards and then put him in gilded captivity in Apamea [1]. This sounds likely enough, and suggests nicely the atmosphere of a royal court where courtiers are at first uncertain how to act, then interpret a royal hint in a way which earns a royal rebuke. But it is not simply a matter of reactions inside Seleukos' court.

There was also the question of relations within Seleukos' family. Demetrios was, after all, the father of Seleukos' daughter-in-law; he had been Seleukos' own father-in-law for a time. Antiochos and Stratonike watched the contest in Kilikia from a distance, but it cannot have been anything less than painful. Seleukos made certain that he was the source of news, and consulted his son (and so Stratonike as well) by letter. A corrupt fragment of Diodoros shows that these consultations involved all the possible solutions including the restoration of Demetrios as king [2] – but king of what? There was no territory still holding out for him except that under the control of his son Antigonos Gonatas in Greece. If Seleukos seriously considered that possibility, it means he was considering a war in Greece, which in turn would involve conflict with both Ptolemy, who had Demetrios' fleet, and Lysimachos, who had Macedonia.

Seleukos' international policy, in fact, was not fundamentally altered by Demetrios' capture. He was still threatened by the alliance of Ptolemy and Lysimachos. Demetrios, even as a prisoner, was still a card in the game, and might be played at the right moment. The report of his possible restoration was no doubt circulated as a means of keeping Ptolemy and Lysimachos unsettled. Demetrios' personal attractiveness had been demonstrated by the dazzled reaction of Seleukos' courtiers. His final campaign, though it had ended in failure, was one where none of his enemies had dared to fight him directly. He still had a territorial base, though it was small, which was controlled by his son in central and southern Greece; the members of the family were notoriously loyal to one another. Demetrios was still thirty years younger than Seleukos, Lysimachos, and Ptolemy. If Seleukos was directly attacked, or even directly threatened, by either of the other kings, Demetrios could be released, and, rumour will have said, would be released. No doubt it was the knowledge of his position which so gnawed at Demetrios' pride as to drive him to the drink of which he is said to have died two years later [3]. The real cause was his powerlessness and humiliation.

Lysimachos' reaction to the news of Demetrios' capture was twofold. In the first place, it meant that the immediate threat to his south-eastern frontier no longer existed. So, at the other end of his kingdom, in Macedonia, he was able to move west into the half of the kingdom which had been Pyrrhos' share two years before [4]. There was no resistance to this move, and Pyrrhos faded from the scene for some years. Lysimachos' power was now very great indeed. Or, rather, it appeared to be great. He controlled all Macedon, regarded by all as the great source of military manpower. He also had access to the main sources of mercenary troops in old Greece and the Asia Minor coast. Yet appearances deceived. Demetrios had already discovered that the Macedonians were by no means eager to repeat the conquests of Alexander [5]. When he tried to lead them overseas they simply went home. Lysimachos' apparent accession of strength was therefore less decisive than it appeared, though by eliminating a possible front in the west, he was necessarily strengthened elsewhere.

Lysimachos' other reaction was to try to persuade Seleukos to eliminate Demetrios, by offering him 2,000 talents to ensure

Demetrios' death. Naturally Seleukos refused. His real reason was that Demetrios was far too valuable a diplomatic counter to be thrown away, but, equally naturally, he did not say so. Instead, he publicly rebuked Lysimachos, putting about his feelings of revulsion at the very suggestion and pointing out that he would incur religious pollution if he so broke his pledged word [6]. Lysimachos' eminently intelligent suggestion – for he and his subjects could argue forcibly that they had suffered quite enough at Demetrios' hands – was seen to rebound on him, and he was portrayed as a vindictive and underhand plotter and assassin. No doubt he was all of that, but to be branded as such publicly was a distinct loss of face. Seleukos' conduct of this exchange is very similar to his reaction to Ptolemy's seizure of Palestine after Ipsos.

The immediate reaction in Egypt to the capture of Demetrios is not known, but it is perhaps no coincidence that within nine months Ptolemy's son Ptolemy II had been made joint-king. No doubt this was partly due to the old man's great age, but it was also the result of a long intrigue in the court by Berenike, the wife of Ptolemy's dotage, in favour of her own son [7]. The choice, as it happened, turned out to be a fairly good one as Ptolemy II's rival for the kingship, his half-brother Ptolemy Keraunos, proved to be a thoroughly erratic type. Ptolemy II, on the other hand, was as careful and calculating as his father had been. For the kingdom this transition from one king to another was smooth. And it was a transition. The joint-kingship, which lasted from 285 to the old king's death in 283, meant that the old policy continued while he lived. That policy now was to maintain control of the sea and to hold to the alliance with Lysimachos, but not to push Seleukos too far; the policy was, as it had been for over thirty years, essentially defensive [8].

However, the defensive was not necessarily going to be the preferred policy of Ptolemy II, once he was free to make his own decisions. For a start, it would help if he could demonstrate a victory early in his personal rule; and he had the instrument for this purpose in the newly acquired fleet. While Demetrios lived, this might turn out to be a dangerous instrument to use, but once he was dead (an event which occurred in the same year as that of the elder Ptolemy) that fleet could be put to use.

In the short term, then, Seleukos could use the threat of Demetrios' release to deter any attack on his territory. It was only a short-term deterrent, though, for soon the others would realize that his threat was a mere bluff. As it happened, the bluff worked just long enough for Lysimachos to embark on the path to self-destruction.

Ptolemy Keraunos, excluded from the kingship in Egypt, went off to see if he could drum up support elsewhere. What he actually wanted is not clear now, though one would guess that his first choice would be Egypt. Probably at the time he was willing to accept anything which would give him power. He first went to Seleukos [9], it seems, which does suggest that he was looking for support for an attempt to seize power in Egypt. Had he had a real understanding of the international situation he would not have bothered. The existence of a pretender to the Ptolemaic kingship would not make Seleukos attack Egypt so long as the possibility of an attack from the north also existed. Keraunos' first move is therefore a clear sign that the old king was not just the victim of a marital intrigue in his choice of successor. Seleukos put Keraunos off, and let him go on to Lysimachos.

Lysimachos could no more afford to give him support than Seleukos, though for different reasons. He was Ptolemy's ally, and to break that alliance could well expose his own kingdom to attack. At the same time, however, Keraunos found a welcome at Lysimachos' court, for his own sister Lysandra was married to Lysimachos' able eldest son Agathokles. These relationships were not necessarily very potent, but in most circumstances familial affection could be allowed to operate.

There may be yet another aspect to Keraunos' welcome. The Egyptian kings presumably woke up to the danger posed by Keraunos as his wanderings continued. His appearance at Seleukos' court would have been sufficiently alarming, after all. By the time he reached Lysimachos, there would have been time to establish communications, and to ensure that Keraunos was made welcome and to make certain that he stayed there. Actually what Ptolemy II surely wanted was the death of his rival, a presumption supported by the speed with which Keraunos left Egypt when the succession was arranged. But Lysimachos was shrewd enough to appreciate Keraunos' potential as a threat, just as Seleukos had been with Demetrios. At any rate Lysimachos did not kill his guest, though he did not give him any help either.

For a year or so, then, the three kings were held in balance by a web of suspicions and threats. Seleukos threatened to release Demetrios onto Lysimachos, who held Keraunos as a threat against Ptolemy, whose mastery of the sea gave him the ability to threaten everyone. It was a situation of such delicacy that it was bound to be upset soon, and, once upset, the instability inherent in the whole situation would precipitate a major conflict, leading to another shaking of the kaleidoscope. Other players in the game – Pyrrhos, Antigonos Gonatas, Antiochos, the Greek states – were waiting to seize their chances. The history of the past fifty years, since Philip II attacked Persia, was full enough of rapid changes of fortune to give everyone involved the hope of wealth, power, and fame.

The precarious situation was upset by Lysimachos. In all three of the kingdoms the royal court was the only element of power which counted. It was where policy was made and whence decisions emanated. It was also highly personal: within the court, the king was the only source of power. None of the kingdoms had as yet any serious pretensions to a governmental infrastructure. Indeed, only Ptolemaic Egypt developed a bureaucratic machine for government in the whole Hellenistic period. Getting things done, therefore, depended on gaining access to the person of the king. Delegation of authority was minimal, because it was dangerous. Any man with an independent source of power was liable to become independent in fact. Seleukos had devolved power to Antiochos, but had made sure it was a clear division, and had publicized the division in such a way that it was not possible to play off one king against the other. Ptolemy I had, from 285, devolved some power to Ptolemy II, but he appears to have done so in a way which invited problems. He had created antagonism between Ptolemy II and Keraunos, and had continued to reign and rule alongside Ptolemy II. It is a reasonable supposition that, had he lived longer, there would have been more trouble at the court of Alexandria.

Lysimachos operated a different system. At least after his acquisition of part of Macedon in 287 he used his eldest son Agathokles as his strong right arm. It was Agathokles who had skilfully shepherded the dangerous Demetrios out of Asia

Minor. No doubt it was also Agathokles who had regained the allegiance of those of Lysimachos' officers who realized that their switch of sides when Demetrios arrived had been too hasty. It was Agathokles who re-established Lysimachos' rule in Sardis and in those cities of Ionia which Demetrios had temporarily held. This could well have occupied Agathokles during all of 286, and the continued menace of Demetrios in Kilikia will also have required Agathokles' attention and presence in the eastern part of Asia Minor for the next year.

In all this Lysimachos' own absence will have been noted. By all accounts Agathokles was a capable and likeable man. He clearly had a wide authority, of perhaps viceregal scope, to deal with the emergency. This was a perfect situation for intrigue at Lysimachos' court. Undoubtedly Agathokles had enemies; no heir apparent could avoid them. The arrival of Ptolemy Keraunos at Lysimachos' court was the catalyst for further trouble.

It was perhaps not necessary for Keraunos to actually do anything. His mere presence was provocative enough. He was the son of a king who had rejected him for another son by a different mother. Exactly the same situation obtained with Lysimachos. Agathokles was Lysimachos' son by Nikaia, a daughter of Antipatros. But Lysimachos had married again, and by this wife, Arsinoe, a daughter of Ptolemy I, he had other children, including a son. To complicate matters even more, he had yet another son, Alexander, by an unknown Thracian woman. The absence of any accepted rule of succession left the situation ripe for trouble. It was absolutely necessary for Arsinoe to put forward the claims of her own children, and the arrival of Keraunos was a blatant reminder to everyone that the eldest son of a king was not the automatic heir. Agathokles' absence allowed his rivals to become more prominent in the royal court, the one place which counted. Agathokles' semi-independence and his achievements in Asia Minor were no doubt also put forward as evidence of his ambition, his dangerous ambition.

Now this was all quite normal, and Lysimachos will have been putting up with it ever since he could remember. The absence of Agathokles and the presence of Keraunos no doubt added a certain spice of viciousness to the rumour and innuendo. One rumour had it that Arsinoe's spite against

Agathokles was that of a rejected lover. All quite normal. Except that this time Lysimachos was temporarily persuaded. Arsinoe's arguments were powerful enough for Lysimachos to order Agathokles to be put to death. Rumour added that the knife was wielded by Keraunos [10].

In this Lysimachos had gone further than had become customary. Ptolemy Keraunos had been allowed to leave the Egyptian court; Antiochos had been allowed to leave the court of Seleukos; even Pyrrhos had lived, despite hair-raising adventures. Executing one's own son had been avoided, though most other crimes could be laid at the feet of every king, from murder and betrayal to incest and bigamy. Worse, Lysimachos soon realized – no doubt through the agency of a sincere friend – that the accusations against Agathokles had not been true. By then it was too late.

Lysimachos was a ruler who had never gained much popularity. He had a reputation for toughness, and he had never bothered with the Hellenic civic freedom cant of Antigonos or Demetrios, or even Ptolemy. He had imposed his rule on the Greek cities in his kingdom, and he had encouraged the synoecism of others, without too nice a concern for the wishes or feelings of the inhabitants. He had maintained peace and order, but that was never enough, and the 'order' chafed the longer the peace lasted. It seems likely that Demetrios' adventure in Asia Minor, and Agathokles' success against him, had persuaded many cities that the peace of Lysimachos really was a good thing after all, especially as mediated through the acceptable Agathokles. But there was no fundamental reservoir of loyalty towards Lysimachos.

The Greek cities of Asia Minor, strung along the coast, ancient and well-practised at bending with the political wind, were not the only element in the political configuration of Lysimachos' kingdom. It had been constructed fragment by fragment: Thrace, Phrygia, two parts of Macedonia, Ionia, were all added one at a time over a period of forty years. In the absence of a bureaucratic governmental structure, the integration of these pieces of territory into a coherent state was minimal. Once the court which was presided over by Lysimachos began to disintegrate, and Lysimachos' own authority thereby decreased, the fragments began to separate off of their own volition.

The killing of Agathokles was a clear signal to others of Lysimachos' children that Arsinoe had triumphed. Even when he knew the false nature of the intrigue to which he had fallen fallen a victim, Lysimachos did not repudiate Arsinoe and her children. Lysimachos' other son, Alexander, was clearly in peril of his life, and he and Lysandra, Agathokles' widow, with Lysandra's children, fled to Seleukos [11]. Ptolemy Keraunos went with them, his second appeal to Seleukos.

The destination of the royal refugees shows clearly enough that the ultimate beneficiary of the court strife was Seleukos. By this time the old Ptolemy was dead, and the reins of power were in the hands of Ptolemy II. At first his grip was uncertain, and it is possible that the events at Lysimachos' court had strained the alliance. Certainly the attention of Lysimachos would be directed well away from foreign affairs at the time. Keraunos could have only one of two ambitions – to succeed Ptolemy I or to succeed Lysimachos (perhaps as guardian for Lysandra's children). Ptolemy II had to assume that the first of these ambitions was operative, and take his precautions accordingly. In addition it is likely enough that Ptolemy II was beginning to develop his own foreign policy, based on his overwhelming naval strength. Something along these lines is a necessary element in the situation, in order to explain why it was that Ptolemy took no part in the war between Seleukos and Lysimachos which began in 282, a year after the death of Agathokles. The existence of Keraunos at Seleukos' court was sufficient to neutralize Egyptian diplomacy.

It was not just the court of Lysimachos which broke up; that part of his kingdom which was in Asia Minor fragmented as well. The governor of the town and castle of Pergamon, Philetairos, sent secret messages to Seleukos promising to join him if war came [12]; Philetairos can scarcely have been the only one. Asia Minor was a complex mosaic of cities and principalities which could easily break up, and most of the elements had a hankering for independence. There were native peoples who had similarly taken advantage of the disturbed conditions to establish powerful local positions – the Pisidians, for example, or the lord of Bithynia, Zipoetes. Not one of these political fragments was capable of challenging the might of any one of the kings, but all of them were adept at the necessary political intrigue and footwork. That they had survived so far indicated as much. Some of them at least will have had lines laid to Seleukos even while protesting loyalty to Lysimachos. Miletos, Ephesos, and Erythrai, for example, had had contacts with him going back twenty years or even more. The more cautious will have maintained contact with Antigonos Gonatas and with Ptolemy as well, especially those on the coast and within reach of Ptolemy's fleet. The fact that we only hear of one, Philetairos, is partly chance, partly intelligent secrecy, and partly due to the fact that he was the founder of the later Attalid kingdom, so that his story became the founding myth of the dynasty.

There can be no doubt that the war which began during 282 began as a result of aggression by Seleukos. He saw his chance to expand again and took it. He was a wily politician, cautious in the way that Demetrios could never be, but adventurous in the way that Ptolemy never was. In fact, among the successors of Alexander, the one he most closely resembles is, ironically, Lysimachos, in his ability to add province to province to make a kingdom and then province to kingdom to produce an empire. Before embarking on this new campaign, Seleukos must have been quite confident that Ptolemy II would not interfere, for he was able to campaign for a year and more in Asia Minor without so much as looking over his shoulder.

Why Ptolemy II allowed Seleukos to do so is difficult to understand. It is possible that he was simply too inexperienced to react, but this seems unlikely: he had had two years of his father's tutoring, and the situation must have been considered. Perhaps Lysimachos' association with Keraunos finally soured the alliance. Perhaps Seleukos threatened to loose Keraunos on Egypt. Possibly Ptolemy II had decided he could pursue a different policy from that of his father, in reaction to the recent domination of the old man. Maybe he calculated he could pick up plenty of loot from the wreckage of whichever kingdom was destroyed in the war. All of these reasons may have entered into Ptolemy's calculations. What does seem to be certain, and very surprising, is that Seleukos knew full well that he had nothing to fear from Egypt, that he could take the full strength of his army into Asia Minor and leave Syria with no more than a police-guard. That confidence suggests more than mere assurances from Ptolemy, which he would never trust in any case. Perhaps there was trouble in Egypt which prevented Ptolemy from intervening. The lack of ancient information is revealed by this long set of speculations. The net result is that Ptolemy did not intervene, and Seleukos knew he would not.

The refugees from Lysimachos who went to Seleukos' court must have gone there as a result of promises they had already received that they would be welcome. They could have gone to other courts – Antigonos Gonatas, Ptolemy, or even to one of the cities. But they could only go where they were assured of asylum. That is, Seleukos had made it clear that he would welcome them, though it is not clear just what other promises he had made. Lysandra must have wished the succession to Lysimachos for her own children; Alexander may not have thought of himself as in line while Agathokles lived, but the possibility must surely have occurred to him since. A parallel may have been thought of with Antiochos; each was the son of the king by a woman of the 'native' peoples – Alexander of a Thracian woman, Antiochos of a Persian. If Antiochos could become king in the Greek Far East, so could Alexander in Thrace or Asia Minor. But Seleukos had his own ambitions, to conquer Lysimachos' territory for himself. He would scarcely have embarked on such a hazardous campaign for someone else's benefit. On the other hand, the fragmented nature of the political geography of Asia Minor would certainly allow him to promise rewards, if not the kingship. It is quite certain that both Alexander and Lysandra were with Seleukos all the time, as was Keraunos, and Alexander was given an independent command in the war. Whatever Seleukos had promised, it held them to his side for a year and more.

We have almost no information on the campaign between the two wily old commanders. Alexander's separate command resulted in his capture of Kotyaion [13], but whether this was part of the main campaign or a mopping-up operation is not known. Similarly we know that Seleukos captured Sardis [14], but not when. He invaded Lysimachos' territory by an unknown route, but perhaps by the quickest way, along the southern road by the Kilikian Gates and the Anatolian Lake

Country. The battle, in Lydia not far from Sardis [15], took place in the middle of Lysimachos' territory, where quick switches of side could take place. Lysimachos was in a trap. Seleukos won. Lysimachos died. Lysandra gloated and wanted to leave Lysimachos' body unburied; Alexander insisted, however, on proper burial rites being celebrated [16].

Arsinoe and her children were in Ephesos when the battle took place, and only escaped in disguise from the exultant mob which formed when the news of the king's death arrived [17]. But she was not finished yet. She went across to Macedon and established herself in Kassandreia [18]. This could only be a temporary refuge, for Seleukos was on his way. There can be no doubt that Seleukos always intended to occupy Macedon. This was what the war with Lysimachos had been all about. He did not hurry [19], perhaps reckoning that a period of confusion and hardship for the Macedonians would made his arrival all the more welcome. And Asia Minor had to be settled: leaving it in disorder behind him would be unwise.

Asia Minor certainly presented sufficient problems for any conqueror. Those who had stuck by Lysimachos for too long needed to be punished; those who had turned coat in time had to be rewarded; those who had bolted for independence had to be curbed or conquered or let go. As usual most of the details have vanished, and all we have are occasional items. Herakleia on the Black Sea escaped into independence by bribing the Lysimachean garrison and jailing his governor [20]. Philetairos of Pergamon was confirmed in the possession of his city and castle, which was one of the places which minted coins in the name of Seleukos [21]. The main mint was probably at Sardis [22], which was and remained the main governmental centre for the whole area; it was probably the most productive of the Asia Minor mints, which in turn suggests an important garrison stationed in the citadel – a fact which could have been deduced anyway. Magnesia on the Maeander minted for Seleukos in the Ionian area [23], and Seleukos' generous interest in Apollo at Didyma in the past no doubt ensured him a welcome at Miletos, as would his removal of Lysimachos' recent heavy-handed rule.

Cities which did not become the sites of mints cannot always be located within Seleukos' kingdom. He spent seven months in Asia Minor between the victory at Korupedion and his departure for Europe, and it is likely that quite a lot was still left undone at the end of that time. One of his methods can be seen in operation in the north. Heraklea-on-Pontos was visited by an envoy of his called Aphrodisios [24], who appears to have paid visits to other places in the area as well. Heraklea had its own grievances at its treatment by Lysimachos, and it was long remembered that it was an exiled citizen of Heraklea who gave the old king his death-blow [25]. But Heraklea was not so aggrieved at Lysimachos that it was prepared to fall into Seleukos' arms without more ado. What the citizens wanted was independence, and as it happened, they were in a position to enforce their intentions. Aphrodisios fell into an argument with the citizens, not surprisingly, since his mission was obviously diametrically opposed to their wishes. He referred the problem upwards and Heraklea sent a delegation to Seleukos.

Again the meeting was unsuccessful [26]. We catch a brief glimpse of Seleukos in action, seated in his audience chamber, listening without much patience to the arguments of the city's envoys. They spoke with such a thick Doric accent that he could barely understand them, and finally he deliberately turned away from them, dismissing them unsatisfied. The envoys went home, reported, and their city sent out other envoys to form an alliance for mutual defence with Byzantion, Calchedon, and Teos. These northern cities were later joined, in what present-day historians call the 'Northern League', by a chieftain called Mithridates [27]. He had escaped from an episode of liberation by Antigonos twenty years before [28], and had established himself with a group of followers in one of the inland valleys of northern Asia Minor as a local potentate. His centres were a fort called Kimiata and a city called Amaseia, a suitably dual kingdom for a man who was probably of mixed Greek and Persian ancestry [29]. Seleukos sent one of his generals, Diodoros, into Kappadokia, probably to bring Mithridates to heel, but Diodoros failed [30]. Mithridates, then or later, began calling himself king, and was invited to join the Northern League. Another chieftain who was most interested, no doubt, was the Kappadokian ruler who was Mithridates' neighbour to the east, for Mithridates' victory protected him. In the face of Seleukos' power, therefore, all the northern cities and kings drew together. This, as it happened, was sufficient to safeguard their collective independence in the long run, but only because of the extraordinary series of events in the area during the next decade.

The cities of the coast clearly felt that, by the death of Lysimachos, they had escaped from an ordeal. The inscriptions from several of them attest the welcome they gave to Seleukos. Ephesos went through the revolution which forced Arsinoe to flee for her life [31]; Miletos elected Seleukos' son Antiochos as its honorary chief magistrate, the *stephanophoros* [32]; Priene put up statues to both kings [33]; at Erythrai a festival called the Seleukeia was instituted, and the festival hymn included a reference to Seleukos' father Apollo [34]; two cities, Magnesia-on-Maeander and Kolophon, named one of their tribes 'Seleukis' [35]; at Ilion an altar was put up to Seleukos, a month was named for him, and a festival instituted [36]. Perhaps not all of these were voted at once, but had they waited even three or four years, it would have been Antiochos who would have received all these honours. The fact that Seleukos was named strongly suggests that all this was at least in part a reaction to the removal of Lysimachos' rule.

Inland there is less evidence, largely because there were fewer cities. Sardis has been noted already; Magnesia-by-Sipylos, in a strategic position in the Hermes valley, was always a garrison point for the Seleukid state, and this is likely to have been started by Seleukos [37]; exemption from taxation was granted to a shrine of Pluto and Persephone at a village called Acharaea, near Nysa [38]. Many other measures were taken either by Seleukos or by his son later; in this case it is likely to have been Antiochos' work, reconstructing after the damage caused by the Galatian invasions.

Sardis was to be firmly held by a garrison, as all conquerors did, but to Seleukos it was not merely the centre of administration after his conquest, but the beginning of the old Royal Road which led to his other lands in the east. Each end of the road was firmly held by cities and garrisons, and now he began the process of fastening his grip on the route itself.

There were in fact two routes to the east. One swung north through Gordion and Ankyra – the route taken by Alexander. The second was shorter, and ran along the base of the Pisidian hills, and through the Anatolian lakes. This was the route chosen for development, though the northern route may have figured in his plans as well. Its interruption by the Galatians prevents us seeing what Seleukos might have begun. The key to the southern route was to block attempts at cutting it which might be made by the mountain peoples to the south, the Pisidians and the Isaurians. All conquerors had tangled with these peoples and all had returned with little success to show for their efforts [39]. Seleukos would have done so as well, no doubt, if he had had the time. His initial measures were characteristically defensive: he organized the foundation of garrisoned cities close to the hills.

The precise date of these foundations is not always clear, but there is a group of six whose names are highly suggestive. Due south of Sardis, on the Lykos river, was founded Laodikeia; to the east, along the road, were Apamea, at the site of Kelainai, Antigonos' old base, then Apollonia, and an Antioch, and finally another Laodikeia, called Katakekaumene, 'the Burnt', from mines nearby. South of this line, thrust forward up aginst the mountains was a Seleukeia, called Sidera 'the Iron' [40]. This set of names is exactly the set used by Seleukos in Syria, with the addition of Apollonia, a most suitable name for the road towards Didyma. Geographically five of them enclose the Pisidians in a crescent of forts. (The southern edge of Pisidia was clearly left for Ptolemy, establishing himself in Pamphylia, to control [41].) It cannot have escaped Seleukos' notice that if the Pisidians were successfully blockaded on the north, their raids would perforce be directed south, and would therefore be Ptolemy's problem. The one city of the six which does not actually face the mountains is Laodikeia-by-Lykos, and this may well be a later foundation, possibly by Antiochos II [42]. It is separated somewhat from the rest, and is the only one with a repeated name. The other group of five, however, are all named distinctively and as a group, are so reminiscent of the similar groups of four – twice, in Syria and in Media – that instructions for their foundation surely came from Seleukos, even if direct evidence is lacking.

There are certain areas of Asia Minor where Seleukos either did not care to exert his authority or did not have time to do so, and some of these were becoming subject to Ptolemy II. Several islands which had been subject to Lysimachos were seized by Ptolemy's fleet. Samos, for example, was the scene of a delegate meeting of the League of the Islanders held in

280 under the presidency of Philokles, King of Sidon, who was Ptolemy's viceroy in the north [43]. Chios was under Ptolemaic control during the 270s, and was likely enough snapped up in 281 [44]. These complemented the control of the Island League – to which was added Thera and Itanos in east Crete by the 260s [45], and which ensured Ptolemy's control of the southern Aegean for the foreseeable future.

On the mainland also, Ptolemy's forces seized numerous cities, but only those within convenient reach of his fleet. He had inherited a few places in Karia from his father, and now he added to his inheritance. To Kaunos was added Halikarnassos and Myndos [46], and by the 270s there is evidence of Ptolemy's control of Iasos and Amyzon as well [47]. Along the southern coast in the 270s he controlled Lissa and Arnaia and probably Patara [48]. At Telmessos Ptolemy son of Lysimachos, no doubt one of Arsinoe's children, was lord of the town in the 260s and was probably emplaced by Ptolemy II soon after his expulsion from his father's inheritance [49]. He founded a dynasty which lasted over a century, adding one more to the principalities of Asia Minor. Pamphylia had been in and out of Ptolemaic control for thirty or more years; Ptolemy II posted a governor there (the 'Pamphyliarch') who controlled Termessos inland and may have been responsible for founding two towns called Arsinoe [50].

These areas are conspicuously not areas of Seleukid activity. Karia, Lykia, and Pamphylia had all been ignored by both Lysimachos and Seleukos in their fighting and organizing. In snapping up these trifles, Ptolemy was not in any danger of falling into a dispute with Seleukos. Indeed Seleukos seems to have ignored Ptolemy totally. This made sense, for if Ptolemy's attention, and his fleet, and perforce part of his army, were all busy with cities on the coast of Asia Minor, Syria remained safe. The possibility surely exists that an agreement to partition Lysimachos' lands had been made beforehand, though this seems less likely than that the two kings simply left each other alone.

After seven months spent arranging matters in interior and northern Asia Minor, with some success, and presumably in watching Ptolemaic activity in the south, Seleukos was ready to move on. The timing suggests that he was prepared to allow things to settle down after the recent upheavals, and to allow his lieutenants to deal with detailed problems. It was, of course, one way to run his empire, but his treatment of Heraklea, when he was apparently bored and rude to the citizens [51], also suggests that he was weary of ruling and that it required a major crisis to rouse his interest. Certainly he left a lot of detail unattended to, and one of those details was still present at his court.

Seleukos moved across the Hellespont into the Gallipoli peninsula. This has been assumed to be more of a symbolic than a purposeful move, from Asia to Europe, an earnest of Seleukos' intention of returning to Macedon but no more than that. It is assumed to be a 'homecoming', and he is thought to have longed to return to his ancestral home [52]. A story circulated that the hearth of his home spontaneously burst into flame [53]; perhaps the story began circulating at about this time. It would fit this mood and time very well if the story was invented to coincide with this move. For this attitude of 'home-longing', however, there is no contemporary evidence. And to set against Pausanias' comment that he 'pressed into Macedonia', Appian says he crossed the Hellespont to possess himself of Lysimacheia [54] – one late source cancelling out another. If we knew more about Seleukos' movements in the seven months since Korupedion, it might appear that the movement across the Hellespont was no more symbolic than a move from Sardis to, say, Didyma.

If it can be assumed that he regularly shifted his base of operations, then the move to Gallipoli was no more than a move to another area in which he intended to enforce his authority. His agent Aphrodisios may have been sent to an out-of-the-way corner like Heraklea-on-Pontos, but a vital artery of trade and power like the Hellespont will have required the king's personal attention. This is not to say that the symbolism of the move escaped either Seleukos or his contemporaries, as the hearth story may indicate, but it was a move which he would have made eventually. It was not a move which took him to Macedonia; even across the Hellespont, he was not really any nearer to Macedon than he had been at, say, Ilion. The division of Europe and Asia is more than usually meaningless just here. The move did, however, put him close to Lysimachos' foundation city of Lysimacheia, a place which it was absolutely necessary for him to gain and hold, and whose treatment would be a signal to others of Lysimachos' friends in Europe. Objectively, a journey by the king to the Gallipoli peninsula was clearly necessary, whether or not he intended to go on to Macedon. As a journey it must not be invested with too much significance.

As if all this organizing activity was not enough, Seleukos had an even worse problem to face after his victory over Lysimachos – what to do about Lysimachos' army. Those soldiers who had survived the battle had the same sort of options as those who had survived Ipsos – they could join the victor, they could fight on for Lysimachos' heirs, they could go off to enlist with someone else, or they could fade away into civilian life, possibly helped in this by Seleukos or by cities needing larger populations (as at Herakleia). If we knew what each man did, no doubt examples could be found of all these options and more. From Seleukos' point of view the important options were the first two – joining him or fighting on for Lysimachos' family. Some men went off with Arsinoe and her children to Kassandreia, and others who had homes in Macedon will have returned there. Both of these might be counted by Seleukos as his enemies. But most of the troops probably enlisted under Seleukos. He was present, the victor, rich, and was probably regarded as the more-or-less rightful king by many, especially when Lysandra, her children, and Alexander were with him [55]. For professionals, indeed, there was little alternative, unless they were to hawk their services round the market. Which is not to say that they were all willing recruits to Seleukos' army. Given time, Seleukos could have weeded out the discontented and reconciled the rest. But he did not have time.

Seleukos probably dismissed much of his own army home. They had come to Asia Minor from Syria and points east, and were now domiciled there. He no doubt kept some men with him, the mercenaries and selected corps, in order to leaven the Lysimacheian mass, but it is likely that the majority of the troops in his immediate service when he crossed the Hellespont were ex-Lysimacheians.

Also with him, if not in his actual service, was Ptolemy Keraunos. Contact between the discontented troops and the ambitious prince was fatal. Seleukos' itinerary was presumably known in advance, and his visit to Lysimacheia was no doubt planned and signalled well beforehand. It may well have excited some apprehension in the city. Seleukos was a man for symbolic gestures, as the various stories in circulation about him already showed. It could be that he would order the destruction of their city as a symbol of the end of Lysimachos' rule. He had, after all, destroyed Antigoneia, and he was allowing Babylon to fall down. In each case he had replaced the previous political centre with a city of his own, named for himself. Lysimacheia itself had recently suffered severe damage from an earthquake [56], and a completion of this destruction was something the citizens must have feared.

Lysimacheia was in fact already a replacement city, for destroyed Kardia [57]. Seleukos might have been expected to reverse matters. We do not know, nor perhaps did the citizens, but there were plenty of possibilities. After all, in international affairs, control of the Hellespont was a most vital matter, and Lysimacheia was sited where it was with the intention of exercising that control. It had become even more important in the light of the hostility of the Northern League, and the advances in the Aegean being made by the Ptolemaic fleet. Thus, the more the position of Lysimacheia is considered, the more likely it seems that Seleukos would have been conciliatory. Another enemy, just here, perhaps going independent and joining the Northern League, would be very dangerous. It would block his advance to Macedon for a start. And he was not the sort of ruler who created enemies carelessly, as Antigonos had been. At the same time Seleukos will not have been pleased at the prospect of his dead rival's city carrying that rival's name and populated by his dead rival's partisans, situated right across Greece's food supply line. The population had made their feelings clear by receiving the ashes of Lysimachos, and giving them honourable burial [58]. Destruction was thus, at least in the minds of the citizens, a definite possibility.

Presumably Seleukos crossed the Hellespont at its narrows and then travelled north towards Lysimacheia. Ptolemy Keraunos was with him. Afterwards oracles warning Seleukos not to cross into Europe, and to avoid 'Argos' were produced. One was even said to be from Apollo of Didyma [59]. Even if it had been given, no doubt Seleukos would have ignored it, just as he ignored and manipulated similar warnings from the

Babylonian priests. He had manipulated and invented so many stories of this type that he can have had no credulity left. Both of the oracles are far too convenient to be believed.

Keraunos had scented the rottenness in Seleukos' present situation – an apprehensive city, a discontented army, an overconfident king. During the previous month, he had prepared the ground for his *coup*, but there seem to have been no precise plans, just a knowledge on his part that a blow struck now would be fully acceptable to many of those around the king. He chose a moment when Seleukos and he were more or less separated from the others of the king's entourage, when Seleukos turned aside to inspect an altar he had spotted. This clearly indicates the impromptu nature of the *coup*, though, as subsequent events showed, a plot was clearly afoot. Keraunos stabbed Seleukos to death, and then rode to Lysimacheia on a horse kept ready for this very eventuality. In the city there was an escort waiting for him, and a diadem, which he immediately put on. With this escort he presented himself to the ex-Lysimacheian soldiers who were present and was at once hailed as king [60].

Now, the escort was clearly ready and waiting, and knew what he intended. This suggests a deep-laid plot. On the other hand, Ptolemy could not have relied on being able to get Seleukos alone. It must have been most unusual for a king to be alone at any time, especially in potentially hostile territory. Thus the assassination looks like a brilliant improvisation. Perhaps the plot itself was due to be sprung when Seleukos reached the city. The troops by whom Keraunos was hailed king were not numerous, for they were no more than the garrison of a single city, and his escort will have been relatively few as well. Only the escort knew that something was due to happen, and even they cannot have expected the leader of their plot to dash in amongst them with the news of the death of Seleukos. As for Seleukos, he had clearly become careless. He should have known better than to allow himself to be alone with a Ptolemy.

11
RECONQUEROR
(281–271)

Seleukos had been the Successor who had combined Alexander's insatiable ambition with Philip's political sense. In all the others, various failings had prevented their final success. Antigonos' arrogance, Demetrios' restlessness, Ptolemy's caution, Kassandros' ruthlessness, were all fatal to any enduring achievement comparable with that of Alexander and Philip. Seleukos alone shared Alexander's ambition *and* had displayed Philip's political sense. And he had lived a long time.

These qualities had been devoted to building up a great empire. When he died he ruled, in effect, the same empire which the last great Persian king had had, in about 350, that is, the full Akhaimenid empire, less Thrace and Egypt – and he was about to occupy Thrace. Further, anyone with any imagination could see that, after Macedon and Greece, he would turn on Egypt. It is perhaps no accident that he died at the hands of a Ptolemy. His elimination must have been a topic for discussion in the Ptolemaic household for twenty years.

Seleukos' long life is important. He had been around so long, and had ruled some of his lands for such a long time, that his rule had been accepted and institutionalized. He had been able to split his empire with his son, and still keep it whole. He had been able to leave Babylonia and Syria without his presence for years at a stretch, and still be their king. He had developed a governmental system which functioned in his absence. In this he owed much to his Akhaimenid predecessors, whose system had survived the Macedonian Wars more or less intact.

He had also added something. The cities he founded throughout his empire were the links in the imperial chains. The Persians had done something similar, by planting settlers in various parts to provide a local military reservoir. Alexander's settlements, though often called cities, were in fact not much different from the practice of the Akhaimenids. Seleukos systematized this idea into the city-colonization he promoted. It was this which formed the bony structure of his kingdom. It was the cities which were the most solid basis upon which the state he founded rested for the next two centuries.

This, essentially, is Seleukos' achievement: a city-strewn kingdom, which lasted for two centuries, until reduced to a local state by the Roman and Parthian and Jewish conquests between 189 and 130. Not a bad achievement for a man who had begun as an ordinary junior officer in Alexander's army, and was reduced to a fugitive at one point in his career. Yet it is not just Seleukos' achievement. It is also his son's. Without Antiochos' abilities and determination, this kingdom would have collapsed, as Alexander's did, and as did those of Kassandros and Antigonos and Lysimachos. This is Seleukos' other achievement: to leave an able and adult successor, something Alexander failed to do.

As the news of the killing of Seleukos spread, the empire he had built up over thirty years did progressively collapse. The news was spread most busily, it seems, by Ptolemy Keraunos himself, who sent letters to Egypt, Macedon, Epiros, Bithynia, and Heraklea. To Egypt he pointed out that now he had a kingdom of his own, he was no longer any threat to his half-brother Ptolemy II [1]. It is possible that someone may even have believed him. Keraunos seems to have had the gift of short-term plausibility, the attribute of the confidence trickster at all times and places. He wrote to the Bithynian ruler, Zipoetes [2], an old enemy of Lysimachos and an ally of Seleukos [3], but a man who was actually suspicious of anyone nearby who had any power. Keraunos made contact with Lysimachos' widow Arsinoe in Kassandreia [4], who was probably the nearest thing to a Macedonian ruler there was at the time; he suggested marriage as a means of providing protection for her children, a traditional Macedonian arrangement which had brought Philip II to the throne. Keraunos made contact also with the city of Heraklea-on-Pontos, Seleukos' enemy, which was so pleased to see the end of Seleukos that the city's fleet was made available to assist the assassin [5]. Presumably he did not mention his simultaneous contact with Zipoetes, with whom Heraklea had been fighting [6]. No doubt Heraklea and its partners in the Northern League were also pleased to be able to establish a powerful naval presence in the Hellespont, and equally glad to assist Keraunos to go elsewhere: he was a dangerous fellow to have either as a friend or as a neighbour. There is no need to assume sincerity on either side in this relationship. Keraunos also contacted Pyrrhos of Epiros, who had some splendid ideas for an alliance which would give him the services of some of Keraunos' soldiers in a new adventure [7].

In Asia Minor, the news would not require Keraunos' aid in being spread. Philetairos of Pergamon, sitting in his castle on a heap of treasure that no-one now owned, at once began negotiations to recover Seleukos' body [8]. Keraunos sold it to him, for he needed money to pay his army. So Philetairos was able to cremate the body, thus gaining credit with both Keraunos and Antiochos, the dead king's son. He also made it well known just what he was doing, gaining further credit with Greek and Macedonian opinion. He was clearly an apt pupil of Seleukos in the matter of publicity. Keraunos showed little or no interest in Asia Minor, other than to neutralize Philetairos and Zipoetes, and form the naval alliance with Heraklea. Collectively this formed a screen against any interference from the east. Thus the actions of Philetairos take on an added significance. He was at once in a strong position, but one which might become very vulnerable at any moment. His control of the cash in his vaults gave him the power that great wealth always provides, but it also made him a target for attack by anyone – specifically in this case Keraunos or Antiochos – who wished to establish contol in Asia Minor.

Philetairos' intervention had to be carefully timed. He had to allow the first euphoria to evaporate, so that Keraunos would see the need for cash, but if he waited too long Keraunos might become desperate or greedy. The same sort of timing might well have guided the actions of whoever masterminded Heraklea's diplomacy. In fact, a coalition of Heraklea and Philetairos is surely not unthinkable. Philetairos was already allied with Kyzikos [9], and Heraklea's fleet in the

Hellespont protected Philetairos as effectively as it protected Heraklea or Keraunos; shifting Keraunos' army to Macedon was in the interests of both. Philetairos' offer of money was also cunningly disguised by the purchase of Seleukos' body: Keraunos might have thought that no-one would consider it to be a bribe.

By his acquisition of the body, Philetairos declared his political choice in the new circumstances. He paid honour to the dead man, and the only reasons – personal ones aside – were to gain favour with the dead king's son, Antiochos, and to gain credit with public opinion. Once Philetairos had done this, it was a clear signal to the other princes and the cities of western Asia Minor that Antiochos had potent local support, that Philetairos' wealth was at his disposal, and that Keraunos was not on his way. The influence Philetairos wielded would thus be decisive for other lords, and it helps explain the very delicate handling he got from Antiochos later.

On the coast, however, there was a choice for many cities, though independence does not seem to have been available as a serious option. It may well be in this period, after Seleukos' death, that many of the places known to be in Ptolemy II's control in the 270s were taken over. We know that Miletos was taken in 280 or early 279 [10], for example. But it is also noticeable that no attempt was made to establish a Ptolemaic presence in the north Aegean. Chios was the Ptolemaic farthest north for the present. An estate at Methymna in Lesbos was owned by Arsinoe [11], but this does not denote political control. The dominance of the Ptolemaic fleet was such that it would have permitted more extensive acquisitions, so this self-limitation was clearly deliberate, partly to allow a concentration in southern Asia Minor, and partly, surely, to keep out of the way of Keraunos. Those coastal cities which Ptolemy II did not want were thus left to be snapped up by Antiochos. At the same time it was clearly accepted that interior Asia Minor was Antiochos' area. Antiochos' immediate problem, however, was that he was a long way off.

Seleukos was killed in the fourth Babylonian month, that is late August to late September, of 281 [12]. The news would move as fast as any news of the day, but it seems that it was still unknown in Uruk in Babylonia in December [13], though it is likely that it was known in Seleukeia earlier. Nevertheless it is very unlikely that the news was heard in the city in less than six weeks. This makes it possible that Antiochos – assuming he was in Seleukeia – heard the news in the middle of October at the earliest, or perhaps not until the middle of November, assuming the killing took place late in September. Either date would mean that Antiochos – again assuming he was in Seleukeia – could scarcely set out for the west before late October, and perhaps not for another month, and even that does not allow time for gathering troops and supplies. By the time he reached Syria the Taurus passes would be blocked by snow. He could not possibly reach Asia Minor in force until the spring (April? May?) of 280. If he was further east on receiving the news, in Media or Baktria, he would not be much later in reaching the west, for the winter might permit travel as far as the Taurus, but the Taurus would still block him until the spring.

The cities and provinces of Asia Minor, therefore, had a good nine months (September to May) during which to consider their responses and their attitudes to Antiochos. They could have no doubt that Antiochos would arrive, sooner or later, for he was most unlikely to forego any part of the inheritance of his father. This would mean, at the least, all of Asia Minor and the Hellespont as far as and including Lysimacheia, but it could also mean Macedon as well. Hence the alliance of Keraunos, Bithynia, and the Northern League of cities would be expected to hold together, and in the winter of 281–280 no doubt the expectation was of a war between that alliance and Antiochos during the campaigning season of 280. That still left a considerable area of uncertainty, since there were plenty of others who might or might not join in the fight. Ptolemy II, for one, or Antigonos Gonatas, or Athens, or Pyrrhos.

In fact, it seems unlikely that Antiochos actually reached Asia Minor even by the spring of 280, for he found he had trouble along the way. The news will have reached Syria on its way to Babylonia, and the arrival of the news there sparked off a brief rebellion, which may or may not have been followed by an invasion from Egypt. This whole episode is shrouded in impenetrable mystery, and is known by no more than a phrase in an inscription from Ilion [14]. Upon this and one or two episodes in the Aegean, considerable conjecture has been built. That there was trouble for Antiochos in Syria is certain. That Ptolemy II's forces captured Miletos in late 280 or early 279 is equally certain. That these events are connected is, however, by no means obvious. The episode at Miletos appears to suggest that Ptolemy seized the city from Seleukid control. Certainly in the list of *stephanophoroi*, Ptolemy II had the power to make a gift of land to the city in the year after Antiochos held the office [15], thus implying a change of suzerain, but this may have been the result of an internal revolution. This is not enough evidence to prove a war between Ptolemy and Antiochos at the time (sometimes called the 'First Syrian' War) [16]. The evidence of Ptolemy's actions elsewhere in fact tends to suggest that he was being extremely careful not to quarrel with Antiochos, a policy which was merely a continuation of that he had observed towards Seleukos before his assassination. Ever since he took sole control of Egypt in 283, Ptolemy II had been consistently wary of becoming involved with the Seleukids, presumably due to his anxiety over the activities of Keraunos. He was still wary, even though an accommodation between Keraunos and Antiochos was clearly impossible now.

So the trouble in Syria was internal, and probably did not involve invasion by a Ptolemaic army. The inscription from Ilion refers to Antiochos recovering control of 'the cities of the Seleukis', which is taken to mean the Syrian cities. 'Seleukis' is a name applied, rather uncertainly, to all or part of northern Syria by later writers [17]. It is best taken to mean all the area within which Seleukos established his new cities, from the Ptolemaic frontier in the south to the Euphrates and the Taurus in the north. There were now no less than ten cities in this area, none more than twenty years old, containing a mixture of transplanted peoples whose primary loyalties might be to one of several kings, dead or alive, or to distant homelands. Seleukos had left them defenceless, for he would have taken as many soldiers as he could raise to fight Lysimachos, and a considerable proportion of them will have been still in Asia Minor. Ptolemy was near, possibly threatening; and now Seleukos was suddenly dead at the hand of another Ptolemy.

Antiochos, who now claimed to be their king, was a man they had not seen for twelve years. The impression may have gained ground that Antiochos' eastern kingdom was his alone, and that the western parts would go elsewhere. The shock of Seleukos' murder would be very great in these Syrian cities, of which he was the founder. Many of the troops stationed or living in those cities were absent. The situation for the people of the cities was full of uncertainty: who was king? where were their men? what protection did they have? This 'rebellion' may therefore have been no more than a time of confusion. The Ilian decree in fact ascribes the rebellion to the fact that the cities 'were hard pressed by harsh circumstances', and implies that they had been impoverished in the last years of Seleukos. This may well have been the case, the result of increased demands for men and money for the war in Asia Minor.

On the other hand, this rebellion does not seem to have been a really determined move against Antiochos. He never showed much anxiety for these cities once he had established his control over them, and there was no further movement against him. The Ilian decree says he re-established their prosperity, which sounds as though poverty had been the source of the trouble. Nor was the rebellion a serious move for independence, for no Syrian city (except, of course, Aradus) ever wanted independence or even autonomy [18].

Antiochos I, therefore, had to sort out the problems of Syria before he could move on to Asia Minor. Leaving the Seleukis till later would only increase the uncertainty and encourage more trouble to develop. The requisite assurances and friendly gestures were rendered during his enforced winter stay in Syria in 281–280. He will have assured the cities of his goodwill, and that the regime set up by his father would continue. He would collect what troops he could – not many, probably – and he would have seen off any Egyptian invasion, if there was one, though the more the situation is considered, the less likely it is that the invasion ever happened. All this need not have taken very long, and without the need for very much in the way of fighting, though since it is termed a 'rebellion', presumably some fighting was involved. However, it was not in the interests of either Antiochos or the Syrian cities to get involved in a civil war. Nevertheless the problem was serious enough to demand Antiochos' personal attention, and to detain him in Syria even after the army he had gathered was ready. He opted to stay in Syria to complete the process of pacification and reassurance, and to send the army ahead under Patrokles [19].

It may also be that Antiochos was delayed by the arrival of the ashes of his father. Philetairos had recovered Seleukos' body from Keraunos, then, after the cremation, ceremonial no doubt, the ashes were sent to Syria, where Antiochos interred them in a new temple whose precinct became called the Nikatoreion [20]. Assuming that the negotiations and cremation took some time, it is possible that the ashes only reached Syria in the spring of 280. The words of Appian cannot usually be pressed far, but the terms he uses to describe Antiochos' actions do suggest that there were many things to do in Syria in connection with the interment. So the army was given to old Patrokles, a large enough force to allow him to employ subordinate generals. He marched to Sardis and began the task of reimposing the authority of his king on the area. It was probably not very difficult in most cases; Philetairos, for one, had already given ample signs of his loyalty. On the other hand, there were distinctly delicate and difficult areas. Ptolemy's creeping annexation of the south coast had to be both watched and avoided. Patrokles could not risk getting involved in a war with Egypt at such a difficult time. The situation in the north also needed attention, and one of Patrokles' generals, Hermogenes, was sent with a detachment to the area [21].

Hermogenes had already contacted the city of Heraklea, and his force was formidable enough to induce that city to submit to generous terms. The city was all the more ready to do so when it became clear that Hermogenes was also charged with suppressing the independence of Zipoetes of Bithynia. Heraklea and Bithynia were old enemies. Hermogenes, originally from Aspendos, and so no doubt familiar with the political rivalries of Asia Minor, was thus operating successfully. But perhaps he was not as good a soldier as he was a diplomat, for his attack on Zipoetes was a disaster. His army was caught in an ambush and fled in panic; Hermogenes died [22]. Zipoetes was now well on his way to enforcing his independence, but this would mean that he would now become the object of an even more serious attack. No king could afford to let such a defeat go unavenged.

This setback clearly required the personal attention of the

king, and perhaps by this time Antiochos was at Sardis. Certainly Patrokles is no longer in evidence. Yet there were many other problems to be dealt with as well as Bithynia. The Egyptian successes along the south and west coasts were continuing, the activity of Keraunos and Antigonos Gonatas drew his attention to Greece and Macedon. The success of Zipoetes was annoying but not immediately threatening. Amid all this, some barbarian troubles in the Balkan interior probably went unnoticed.

Keraunos had sailed from Lysimacheia to Kassandreia. His troops were part of Lysimachos' old army and may well have wished to go home, though Keraunos will have had Macedon in his sights from the start. He had made no attempt on Asia Minor, and Heraklea's ships were needed to move his men quickly westwards. For he was not the only one aiming at the throne of Macedon. From Corinth came Antigonos Gonatas, son of the king before Lysimachos, Demetrios. The two fleets met and fought, and Heraklea's ships tipped the balance to Keraunos. This battle allowed Keraunos to reach Macedon, and he soon persuaded Arsinoe to marry him, though he killed some of her children almost at once. Gonatas meanwhile retired to Corinth, licking his wounds [23].

Antiochos was clearly concerned in this. On a personal level, no doubt he wanted revenge on Keraunos for the murder of his father. The hurt was partly assuaged by Philetairos' performance of the funeral rites, but the death of Keraunos would have provided a good deal more satisfaction. In addition, the soldiers used by Keraunos to establish himself in Macedon had been Seleukos' soldiers, even if they had previously been Lysimachos', and the ships which gave Keraunos the naval victory were from a city which soon acknowledged Antiochos' supremacy. Also, and politically more important than any of these matters, Antiochos presumably wished to become king in Macedon, as his father had been.

There were, however, considerable difficulties in Antiochos' way. Heraklea was perhaps the key. Whatever terms Hermogenes had extracted scarcely still operated after his defeat and death in Bithynia. Heraklea's ships, and those of the Northern League, controlled the Straits and the Sea of Marmora, thus blocking Antiochos' route west. He did not have the ships with which to cross the Hellespont, and until he gained control of these seas he did not dare risk crossing. He found he needed a fleet with him as well as his army.

This brought in his relationship with Ptolemy II. Once Keraunos was established at Kassandreia, it seems that the rule of one Ptolemy in Macedon was approved by the other Ptolemy in Egypt. Keraunos' promise to abjure any claim on Egypt was sufficient for Ptolemy II. Through his naval commanders in the Aegean, Philokles of Sidon and Kallikrates of Samos [24], Ptolemy II concentrated on maintaining and extending his command of the southern Aegean islands and the south and south-western coast of Asia Minor, from Chios to Pamphylia. In all this the only place which had been Seleukos' and which was now in Ptolemy's hands was Miletos, and that change, for all we know, may have been the result of internal upheavals, just as the Seleukid control of Ephesos had come about by a pro-Seleukid riot [25]. No other Ptolemaic acquisition was ever in Seleukid control. The two kings had carefully kept apart from each other.

Now that Antiochos intended to bring his ships to the Aegean, however, there was an increased danger of a clash. Antiochos for one had enough problems without a Ptolemaic war as well, so some contact between Antiochos and Ptolemy is required at this point, to arrange for the Seleukid fleet to be brought round from Syria, past all those Ptolemaic coasts and up to the Hellespont. The safest way was to warn Ptolemy and Philokles and Kallikrates in advance. In the process Antiochos will have indicated that he did not intend to dispute Ptolemy's hold on the coastal towns, including Miletos.

So the fleet sailed west [26]. At the same time, Antiochos made a peace with Keraunos [27], thereby shelving for the moment the problem of Macedon. This does not mean that he had given up his intention of ruling there, since there is no reason to believe that either ruler intended the peace to last very long. In this case, given the apparent nature of Keraunos' ambitions, it may be that he at least was serious in making the peace, but given the nature of the man, it seems likely that he would do something in the relatively near future which would give Antiochos a colourable pretext for reopening hostilities. For the moment, however, Antiochos could not do anything about Macedon, except acquiesce in Keraunos' control there. He may also have had a reasonably shrewd notion as to what would happen to Keraunos once the Macedonians realized what he was like. There would be time to deal with him later, if he survived. Meanwhile the real problem was the Northern League, lying along his flank and controlling the Straits. Until this menace was removed, he would not be able to get at Keraunos anyway.

There had been changes in the north since the defeat of Hermogenes. Zipoetes had died, and two of his sons now disputed the inheritance. One of these, Nikomedes, had allied himself with Heraklea, which thereupon fought against the other son, another Zipoetes, claiming success but failing to eliminate him [28]. Meanwhile Heraklea's ambitions were revealed elsewhere in attempts to enforce its control over Teos, Kieros, and Amastris, all of which had been part of the original alliance the year before. The nature of powerful Greek cities clearly did not change. The ruler of Amastris preferred to hand over the city to the control of Mithridates of Pontos rather than allow it to fall into the hands of Heraklea. Mithridates himself was also a member of the League [29].

There were thus plenty of gaps and cracks and strains in this alliance to allow a subtle operator to insert divisive wedges. The adhesion of Antigonos Gonatas to the League added yet more, and linked this war with others being fought simultaneously in Macedonia and Greece. Antigonos had been attacked by a combination of Peloponnesian powers headed by Sparta [30]. King Areus thereof had acquired wealth, the origin of which might be either Ptolemy or Antiochos [31], for both were interested in preoccupying Antigonos. The coalition began to break up after only one campaign, however, when Areus manifested the usual ambition to reduce his allies to submission [32]. Thus Antigonos, not without some difficulty, survived. He had retained control of a series of forts and cities in central Greece – Corinth, Piraeos, and others – and he also had a useful fleet [33]. This had been beaten by Keraunos' fleet with that of Heraklea, but it was not destroyed.

In Macedonia Keraunos had enjoyed his triumph for only a brief time. His murder of Arsinoe's children caused the lady to flee [34], but to the Macedonians all this was quite normal royal behaviour. Keraunos then went off to confront a barbarian invasion, and was killed [35]. No doubt by this time no-one was very sorry, but the invasion was much more serious than earlier ones, for Macedon was now all but exhausted. The invaders, Galatians under a variety of leaders, swamped the kingdom [36].

There were claimants to the now-empty Macedonian kingship, but the powerful ones were absent, and those who were present were weak. Kassandreia, under a popular tyrant called Apollodoros, detached itself [37]. Antigonos came north, fishing for power. Antiochos was stuck in Asia with his war with the Bithynians and the Northern League. Antigonos and the League had a mutual interest in blocking Antiochos, the first to prevent him from reaching Macedon, the second to keep his power at a distance. The alliance is quite logical in the short term, but each was using the other.

Here is the significance of the arrival of Antiochos' fleet. Its presence in the Straits gave Antiochos access to Thrace and thence to Macedon, if he wanted it. His power by land was such that it would be relatively straightforward for him to beat the Northern League, all of whom, except Byzantion, were vulnerable to his attack by land. If Antigonos wanted to maintain a credible claim to Macedon he had to prevent Antiochos from crossing the Straits, hence his adhesion to the alliance. Some fighting between Antiochos and Antigonos took place, which seems to have included a victory for Antiochos' forces, but neither was serious about the war. For one thing, while they fought each other, Macedon was escaping from them both, and suffering. So the war did not last long, and a peace was patched up very soon [38].

Antiochos' fleet met that of the Northern League in the Bosporos, but there was no battle [39]. Heraklea made an attempt to crush Zipoetes on behalf of Nikomedes [40]. Kyzikos became involved, and suffered [41]. Antigonos' withdrawal left the League open to conquest by Antiochos. Possibly he had already contacted Zipoetes the younger, for both were enemies of Nikomedes and Heraklea. Possibly Mithridates of Pontos, now in possession of Amastris, had been detached from the alliance as well; this would be a typical example of Antiochos' methods. If these contacts had not yet been made, they must have been under consideration, and they were obvious moves to both sides. The League was losing, and to survive it would need a new ally.

The Galatians who had killed Keraunos had now reached

the Straits. One band reached the Bosporos, where Byzantion saw its lands ravaged by a band under a chieftain called Leonnorios [42]. He then turned his people south against the city of Lysimacheia, still partly wrecked after the earthquake, and they captured and sacked it. Then they roamed the Gallipoli peninsula. Both at the Bosporos and at the Hellespont they tried to cross into Asia, and in both cases failed. At the Hellespont the Seleukid governor of Hellespontine Phrygia, Antipatros – presumably appointed by Antiochos during the last year – abandoned any pretence of assistance to the communities around Lysimacheia, and stood on the defensive in the Troad [43].

The Northern War was Antiochos' immediate concern, but now Leonnorios' band at the Straits was just as urgent. And it was the Straits which both separated and linked the two crises. Inevitably the two coalesced. Leonnorios led most of his people back to the Bosporos, after their ravaging of the Gallipoli peninsula. By now he will have become acquainted with the political situation in the area: across the Straits was Bithynia, a fractured kingdom under threat – perfect prey. A small band stayed behind in the Gallipoli peninsula under another chief called Loutourios [44], perhaps in dispute with Leonnorios, perhaps in expectation of help, perhaps just hoping to settle.

Inevitably, given the situation, they got across. Leonnorios and his band were hired by Nikomedes to squash his brother, by a treaty with the whole Northern League [45]. Loutourios' men got across to the Troad by capturing some boats used by the envoys of Antipatros [46]. Having sacked Zipoetes' half of Bithynia, Leonnorios' men then joined up with Loutourios' [47] and, true to their alliance with the Northern League, the whole band turned south to loot the rest of Asia Minor [48].

No continuous account can be written of the subsequent events, though stories were later told which indicate that most of the cities of the western coast were threatened at one time or another. The Galatians specialized in surprise attacks and fast movement and stayed nowhere for long. They could be defied from behind strong walls, if the will of the defenders held out. Few cities seem to have been physically captured, but many had their lands ravaged, and blackmail was often paid.

Kyzikos was one of the earliest sufferers, caught in the pincer of the two bands approaching from both sides, and had its lands ravaged [49]. Ilion, still unwalled, was occupied briefly [50], and no doubt looted and damaged. At Thyateira a man called Hyperberelaos set up an inscription to give thanks for the rescue of his son from the invaders [51]. Pergamon survived, and Philetairos used his wealth to help in the defence of selected politically useful friends [52]. Erythrai paid the raiders to go away [53], which would only mean that they would return later. Apollo of Didyma was robbed [54], as was only to be expected, and Miletos preserved a story that the women of the city were captured outside the city during the annual feast: numbers committed suicide at their treatment [55]. An Ephesian woman did the same [56]. At Priene, it is heartening to learn, the raiders met some resistance: when engaged in ravaging the city's lands, they were attacked and driven off by a sortie of the citizens; Sotas, son of Lykos, was honoured by his fellow citizens for heading this counter-attack [57]. Other places relied more on divine aid than self-help: Themisonion saved its citizens by hiding them in a divinely-revealed cave until the danger passed [58]. At Apamea-Kelainai the city was saved when the river rose in a sudden flood, which was ascribed to the intervention of the river-god Marsyas [59].

The quantity of sensible resistance which is recorded is meagre. Priene is the only place which saw to its own defence. All other places relied on someone else. Even Pergamon was relying on Philetairos to organize matters. There is also, again at Priene, a hint that the Galatians were not always unwelcome. They seem to have been assisted by a downtrodden social group in Priene's territory, called the Pedieis, who showed the Galatians where the loot was best [60]. Their attitude is precisely the same as that of Nikomedes of Bithynia who used the invaders' power to his own benefit.

In the face of this widespread paralysis, the responsibility for organizing resistance was Antiochos'. He was the king in these lands, and he had to show that he earned the title. It was a difficult problem, with vaguely organized bands of Galatians unexpectedly appearing almost anywhere. The story of the women of Miletos, surprised in the middle of a festival, demonstrates the difficulty. In such circumstances the traditional Greek fighting methods had to be revived. Instead of large Hellenistic armies, the old civic phalanx could be most effectively used, as at Priene, but the utility of cavalry was also obvious. Fortifications were required, and were required to be stoutly defended. Eventually the cities of the coast were protected by a string of Seleukid forts and cities, blocking access to them from inland. Above all, the need was to defeat the raiders. This could not be done in detail, but had to be accomplished in a great battle. Isolated defeats of raiding parties would not carry enough weight. Then, if they could not actually be exterminated or driven out, they had to be forced to settle down.

The precise dates of all these events are not easy to sort out, and, because of the variety of events and sources and places involved, even the precise order of events is unclear. Antiochos arrived in Sardis in the early summer of 280 and, in broad terms, there followed the war with the Northern League, the Galatian invasion, and Antiochos' fight back. Ptolemy Keraunos was killed, it seems, in spring 279. Antigonos Gonatas' war with Antiochos took place in the same year. But the various details are impossible to pin down more closely, and even if it were possible to be precise, there are so many unknown details that any precision gained might be thoroughly misleading. It is, in the state of our knowledge, perhaps best to have an impressionistic portrait.

During the years 278 to 276, then, Antiochos was fully occupied in salving as much as possible from the wreckage of Asia Minor, while Antigonos was attempting to insinuate himself on to the throne of Macedon, during which he ambushed and destroyed one band of Galatians [61]. The Northern League, perhaps somewhat shamefaced at what they had done, by proxy, to the rest of Asia Minor, was quiet, and in any case Antiochos' preoccupation guaranteed its members' independence. But there was also Ptolemy II.

Ptolemy II now had nothing to fear from his half-brother Keraunos, whose adventures had ended, as was always likely, in a violent death. Arsinoe had survived her marriage to him by fleeing for her life, and now she went to Egypt, where her brother was king. They were soon married and she thus became queen for the third time [62]. Ptolemy had been cautiously developing his strategic position in Asia Minor and the

RECONQUEROR

Aegean; now his forceful new wife turned his attention elsewhere. At least this is how it might appear. Certainly Ptolemy's foreign policy, from being apparently indifferent to the actions of Seleukos and Antiochos, became hostile. And this coincided with the marriage to Arsinoe.

To anyone else, it must have been obvious for some time that Antiochos' troubles were Ptolemy's opportunity. But this was not how it had seemed to Ptolemy. He was apparently content to see Antiochos preoccupied with the Galatians. The poet Kallimachos claimed a share in this for him, by magnifying his suppression of a mutiny by some of his Galatian mercenaries [63] – though this may be the opposite, a denigration of Antiochos' work. Quite possibly Ptolemy regarded Antiochos' fight against the barbarians as one on behalf of civilization as a whole and deliberately did not interfere.

Arsinoe was Ptolemy's wife by 275, and probably before. She will have arrived in Egypt before that, perhaps as early as 278. Certainly she will have been influencing Ptolemy's foreign policy from, say, 277. Of all this Antiochos was presumably well informed. The possibility of conflict with Ptolemy was always there, and anything which made it more likely will have come to his attention. Amidst his Galatian preoccupations, he made arrangements to deal with any intervention should it come.

Arsinoe had been ambitious to rule in Macedon, either personally or through her sons, and now Antigonos gained that throne, being more or less firmly seated by 276. At this point Antiochos finally wrote off Macedon and accepted Antigonos' occupation. The signal for this was the marriage of Antigonos to the daughter of Seleukos and Stratonike, Phila [64]. She was, in fact, Antigonos' niece, for he and Stratonike were siblings. Already, after only a single generation, these royal families seemed to be able only to marry each other. Politically the marriage aligned the two kings together against the Galatians, which was not so important, and the Ptolemies, which was decisive. The marriage took place as soon as Antigonos was firmly established, in the spring of 276, and the negotiations will have taken place earlier, probably beginning as soon as Antigonos had won his battle.

This alliance was by no means one between equals,

for Antigonos was, at the start and for years after, clearly the lesser partner. Therefore, he had to put more into the partnership. His control of Macedon provided a shield against further attacks from the Galatians, a group of whom had settled in Thrace. The Macedonian fleet helped balance that of the Northern League and that of Ptolemy II. In other words, for the initial period of the alliance at least, Antigonos was Antiochos' client. Given the presence of the Galatians in Asia, this was an eminently satisfactory recovery on Antiochos' part.

This may have been the trigger for war between Ptolemy II and Antiochos. The marriage of Ptolemy and Arsinoe, in political terms, might be considered to be aimed at Antigonos, for Arsinoe's son Ptolemaios had a claim to Macedon as the son of Lysimachos. The marriage, therefore, might be seen as a reply to the marriage of Antigonos and Phila. Without greater chronological precision than the sources permit, the question must remain open. War began, it seems, in 276, and it is as certain as anything can be that Antiochos would not have started it. It placed great strain on the kingdom. The Galatians were still very active in interior Asia Minor. The Ptolemaic army launched an attack, or at least prepared to do so, in Syria. Babylonia was taxed to the limit, according to a groaning clay tablet, to pay for the war [65]. And Antiochos deliberately widened the conflict by involving the ruler of Kyrene, Magas. This was another son of Ptolemy I, who had been placed as governor of Kyrene for thirty years. Perhaps Arsinoe's arrival worried him. At any rate, he now married Apama, a daughter of Antiochos and Stratonike, and thus Ptolemy II suddenly found himself attacked unexpectedly from the rear [66], just as Ptolemy I had been more than once.

So far, so good, if still somewhat vague. The difficulties over this war are immense. Nothing seems certain. The Magas-Ptolemy war is one event. Since the Antiochos-Ptolemy war certainly existed, something must have happened in Syria. A passage in Polyainos dealing with the capture of Damascus from a Ptolemaic governor called Dion by 'Antiochos son of Seleukos' has often been allocated to this war, but it is more likely an exploit of Antiochos III [67]. The likely events of the war are not so much full-scale attacks as probes into weak spots. Thus Antiochos encouraged Magas, which distracted Ptolemy II. Ptolemy sent his fleet, or part of it, through the

Straits to contact the Northern League [68]. Ptolemy hired Galatians [69]; perhaps he was in contact with those in Asia.

Antiochos was thus threatened on all his western borders, from Syria through Asia Minor to the Straits. He performed with his usual competence. While Magas' threat to Egypt prevented Ptolemaic action in Syria, Antiochos concentrated on Asia, and on the most important enemy, the Galatians. He visited Syria and then countermarched to Asia Minor, bringing with him a squad of elephants, which had been sent on by the governor of Baktria, having been especially collected by him from India [70]. (Presumably Seleukos' original 500 were now dead or too old for battle.) Possibly his absence had encouraged the Galatians to band together in a larger attack than usual, for Antiochos' return was followed by a great battle. The elephants, sixteen of the original twenty, made the victory decisive [71], and the Galatians retired into the interior of Asia Minor, no doubt shocked at civilization's willingness to use such monsters in its own defence.

The raids diminished after the Elephant Victory, helped by the practice of recruiting Galatians into Hellenistic armies [72], but they did not stop altogether. It was always a possibility that a Galatian chief would organize an expedition. But after the great victory, the Galatians could be seen as ordinary, if fierce, warriors. Eventually they were familiar enough and grudgingly admired enough to be portrayed sympathetically by the sculptor of the great altar at Pergamon. Probably also the raiders were wearied, and had developed a desire to settle – in fact, that is presumably why they were wandering in the first place. The absence of loot in areas which had been raided too often will have helped to diminish the appetite for raiding.

The Galatians were allowed – or so the Seleukids said – to settle in the Phrygian interior [73]. They split into three tribes. Presumably this was all done by a treaty arrangement with Antiochos, once he had shown his military superiority in the Elephant Victory. The essential weakness of the Galatians is shown by the area they were permitted to hold, which is probably the least attractive part of Anatolia, very different from the rich west and south.

The war died down. Magas was pacified by Ptolemy's assurance that he could continue as governor of Kyrene, all the more easily since it seemed impossible for Ptolemy to attack him. If Antiochos in Syria really did capture Damascus in this war, it will have been now, after the Elephant Victory, when he could turn away from Asia Minor. It would be difficult for him to hold on to the city, but a Ptolemaic siege there would effectively immobilize the Ptolemaic army throughout Syria. The Ptolemaic fleet which sailed through the Straits to contact members of the Northern League failed to revive the old Northern War. The League was now protected by the settling Galatians. An old suggestion of a Ptolemaic raid into the Persian Gulf has been refuted [74]. None of these moves could be decisive. Neither king was capable of dealing a serious blow at the other, and neither perhaps was interested in doing so. Antiochos had already shown that he was willing to settle for less than his father's full ambitions, by recognizing Antigonos in Macedon. None of the kings had known what it was like to be with Alexander in the conquest of the world; all were content with less. A peace was made, probably in 271, by which Ptolemy seems to have gained a few places along the coast of Asia Minor: it was a draw. Antiochos had successfully held together almost all of his father's empire, but he will have been brought to realize, as Seleukos never had to, the limitations of his power. Any territorial advance was now out of the question without a war against Ptolemy, and that was a war he could not win.

12

SAVIOUR
(271–261)

Antiochos I lived on for another ten years after the peace which ended the war with Ptolemy, but no-one seriously challenged him again; the problems he had to face in his last ten years were internal. An obscure quarrel in the royal house led to the execution of his eldest son Seleukos in early 267 [1], but he had another adult son, who duly became Antiochos II when his father died, having been joint king since Seleukos' execution [2]. Equally obscure is the quarrel which developed in 263–262 between Antiochos I and the new lord of Pergamon, Eumenes, the nephew of Philetairos, who had recently died. This resulted in a defeat for a Seleukid army under the walls of Sardis [3]. Pergamon thus slipped from near-independence into actual independence, but the death of Antiochos I the next year, and the preoccupation of his successor with a new war with Ptolemy in his first years probably had more to do with Eumenes' actual freedom of manoeuvre.

There is the usual hopelessness about the sources for these years, perhaps even more so than earlier. It seems to reflect an actual political quiescence. The evidence of the 270s from Babylonia suggests that there, in the richest part of the kingdom, actual economic collapse had been not far off [4]. Antiochos I had ruled in Babylonia, and in the lands to the east; he had had to establish himself in Syria in the face of widespread discontent, so widespread it could be called a rebellion; he had had to face and beat the invasion of the Galatians, whose favourite tactic was to ravage the fields of their victims, and whose range covered all western and central Anatolia. The wars of the 270s in other words had produced such widespread economic damage that a pause for recovery was essential. The wars from Alexander onwards had been fought by using the accumulated treasure of the Persians, and this had now been used up. Philetairos seems to have had the last large *cache*, 9,000 talents. From now on, every king had to finance his wars out of current taxation, and this would inevitably reduce activity. In Egypt Ptolemy II began the process of fastening the huge bureaucratic regime on the land, in order to squeeze taxes out of it [5]. In the Seleukid realm the answer was a period of peace.

Antiochos I's achievements as king, therefore, are twofold. In his first ten years, he put back together the inheritance of his father; in the second ten years he gave those lands time to recover. He was given the title of *Soter*, 'saviour', by cities in Asia Minor for his work specifically in saving them from the Galatians [6]. In a larger sense, however, he deserves the title for another reason. He inherited a kingdom which was in a state of collapse and disintegration, and saved it for his successors. In that process of reconstitution he had to cut his losses, and the losses he was prepared to sacrifice included Macedon, Thrace and the Gallipoli peninsula, central Anatolia, which became Galatia, and the north coast of Asia Minor, the cities and kings of the old Northern League. He also had to forego the 'recovery' of southern Syria which remained one of the unfulfilled ambitions of his family for seventy more years. There were other areas to which an actual independence or a local autonomy was either given or allowed, perhaps tacitly. In Asia Minor, the Galatians, by interposing themselves between the Seleukid lands and the north and east, in effect gave protection to the Kappadokians and the kingdom of Pontos. They may not have thought of it as protection at the time, but in the long run, it was behind the savage shield of the tetrarchies of the Galatians that the Mithridatids of Pontos and the Ariarathids of Kappadokia maintained their independence. Both dynasties were of Iranian origin, and this origin became steadily more emphatic the longer they lasted. Both had fought for their independence, but neither of them had much hope of success if the Seleukids could once concentrate fully upon them. This concentration was no longer possible, after 278, hence their independence.

Parts of the homeland of the Iranians also slipped into a sort of independence. Persis had been one of Seleukos' satrapies, loyal to him perhaps because he had rescued it from Antigonos, and perhaps because he made few demands upon it. Unlike Media, it was not necessary for him to establish Greek settlers there, or perhaps it was thought to be undesirable. Yet it is surely likely that the Persians were always fundamentally hostile to Seleukos and to Antiochos. The knowledge that they had been displaced from the mastery of Asia was always there. A story in Polyainos may reflect this basic antagonism, where a satrap called Cheiles had to suppress a rising by 3,000 Persians [7]. It is dated by a reference to a King Seleukos, and though this is not very specific it is most likely to be Seleukos I. Coins of Istakhr, naming men who use the title of *fratakara*, depicted before a fire-altar, may record the development of a certain local autonomy [8]. The title is Old Persian for governor, so it seems, which may be a deliberate scaling-down of ambitions from the more provocative 'king'. It may suggest that the title had been awarded by the Seleukids. The men named on the coins as holding the office are all Iranians: *Bgdt* (Bagadat), *Wbrz* (Oborzes), and *Wtfrdt* (Autophradates). One possible solution is to assume that Iranians were deliberately made Seleukid governors in Persis (maybe in succession to Cheiles). There were precedents for such appointments.

The coins themselves show a clear development, or more truly a clear artistic degeneration. The earliest coin is in the manufacturing and artistic style of the coins of the immediate successors of Alexander. The later coins degenerate, artistically; that is, the earliest of the coins looks to have been manufactured early in Seleukid history [9]. The near collapse of the Seleukid kingdom in 281–280 could be an appropriate moment for a gesture of Iranian independence in Persis as well as in Bithynia and Pontos.

Persis, of course, was now strategically unimportant. Once Arachosia was under Indian control, as was the case from 303 onwards, Persis became a backwater. Antiochos retained friendly relations with the second Indian Emperor, Bindusara, who will have been the ruler from whom the satrap of Baktria obtained the elephants later used in the Elephant Victory over the Galatians. The area called Gedrosia and Karmania, desert land in the main, was of little use to either Greeks or Indians, and quickly reverted to the status of a no-man's-land. Thus

Persis was left out on a limb. The Seleukid concern was with Media and the high road to Baktria, and that was firmly gripped by cities and satraps. The city of Antioch-in-Persis was established by Antiochos I, but the name is inaccurate, for it was placed more or less on the border of Persis. Its function can best be understood as that of a border guard, as Alexandria Eschate guarded Baktria.

Antiochos, therefore, held on to the essentials, and let the periphery go. Here is the real effect of the invasion of the Galatians. Before they moved into Asia Minor, Antiochos had been about to deal with the Northern League. Pontos was also unfinished business, since Mithridates' defeat of Seleukos' general Diodoros. Both would probably have succumbed, as would Kappadokia, if Antiochos had had the time. Antiochos would then have been free to cross into Europe, where Macedon would scarcely be able to resist. But once the Galatians were ravaging Asia Minor, all Antiochos' strength had to be devoted to containing them, and by the time that was achieved, and Egypt's attack fended off, that strength was used up. Galatian raids continued for the next century, and the Attalid dynasty made its name by another victory over them [10]. Seleukid policy in Asia Minor was devoted to holding on, not expansion. And once such a policy was adopted, contraction, and ultimate defeat, was inevitable.

For, once the periphery is detached, other areas then become peripheral. Geographically, Antiochos' kingdom by 271 had become reduced to a string of narrow lands along the two great roads, the Royal Road from Babylon to Sardis, and the other Royal Road, which became the Silk Route, from Babylon to Baktria, all fringed by autonomous princes and peoples. The next stage of disintegration would inevitably be to detach sections of the road itself.

The pattern here displayed was the pattern which was followed for the rest of the history of the dynasty – periodic collapse, followed by a limited recovery when detached parts were reunited to the main body of the kingdom. The trouble was that, after each collapse, the restoration work was less successful, and so the main body kept getting smaller. Each collapse left some pieces floating free permanently.

Antiochos, of course, could do no other than he did. Faced with the breakdown of his father's kingdom, he had no choice but to attempt to put it back together again. It was not lack of ability or intelligence or determination which left him with a less-than-wholly-successful enterprise. It was, ultimately, lack of resources. In retrospect it becomes clear that the crucial difficulty was in the timing of Seleukos' death. If he had died in battle at Korupedion, Lysimachos would have retained control of both Macedon and Asia Minor, and no Galatian invasion would then have taken place. If Seleukos had lived on, for perhaps another year, he would have had time to reach Macedon, and to establish his authority there. There would then have been no Galatian invasion. It was the timing of Keraunos' knife-thrust as Seleukos was moving into Europe which caused the collapse of authority in Macedon and thus let the Galatians invade, and it was that Galatian War which exhausted the Seleukid kingdom. From then on Antiochos was fully stretched just to hold on to what he held. It was impossible for him to gather sufficient resources to scotch any one of the threats to his position, so all the threats continued, and the longer that situation obtained, the less likely was it that the Seleukid kingdom would survive.

This is not to say that history was necessarily changed by Seleukos' murder. The problem of over-extension already existed in Seleukos' last years, and the acquisition of exhausted Macedon would not have been an increment of strength. The Galatians were simply the instrument which revealed that over-extension. If they had not halted Seleukid progress, then something else would have, though perhaps not just at that point. Ptolemy II would most likely have become sufficiently alarmed to open up hostilities in Syria before 276, or the Galatians might have invaded anyway, and Seleukos would have been one of the Macedonian rulers killed in the invasion. The more the possibilities are examined, the greater the difficulties of conquering Macedon from Asia appear to have been. But it does seem that the precise nature of the ways in which the limitations of Seleukid power were revealed – the murder of Seleukos and then the Galatian invasion – aggravated the difficulties. Many people in Asia Minor suffered severely from this over-extension of Seleukid power. There would have been kinder ways of showing them this historic truth. The painful collapse and the equally painful reconstitution of the Seleukid kingdom was a process which was distinctly unpleasant.

Of course the kingdom survived, after a fashion, for another two centuries, though its last generation was an unpleasant exercise in futility. In that time its existence provided the framework in which the great cultural developments of the Hellenistic period were transmitted eastwards. And people moved east too. It was a man of Magnesia-on-Maeander in Asia Minor, Euthydemos, who became one of the most notable Baktrian kings, and one would not willingly sacrifice the numismatic art of Baktria, or the Greek influences on Buddhist sculpture. Seleukos had, in that sense, built well. The parts of his kingdom really did hold together, when there was a sufficient glue of ability at the top. The dynasty repeatedly produced men of outstanding talent – Antiochos I, Seleukos II, Antiochos III, Demetrios I, Antiochos VII – who saved the ship of state for another generation. But Seleukos I had not done enough nor done well enough, and here the reason for the incomplete success seems to lie in the character of the man himself. His rise, as we have seen, had been long and slow. He had been compelled to wait for long years before achieving full independence of action. Not till 308, when he had beaten off Antigonos' attack, could he be said to be an independent ruler in his own right, able to determine his own policy. And then it had taken nearly thirty years for him to stitch onto his original kingdom the other pieces, one by one – Syria, Kilikia, Asia Minor. This delay may have been due to a shortage of resources, and it is certain that at Ipsos he fielded the smallest of the various armies. But even then he waited twenty years before attacking Lysimachos. And he never did get round to attacking Ptolemy. Lack of resources could be a good and sufficient reason for all this delay.

Yet somehow this seems like an excuse rather than a reason. Somehow the delay looks more like hesitation than caution. It fits in with Seleukos' early career, in which he received high office early, but always as a subordinate (under Alexander and Perdikkas), as though he performed competently but lacked confidence. If he really did consult the oracle at Didyma in 334, it was to ask if he should go home to Macedon or go on with Alexander; perhaps this was another suggestion of lack of self-confidence in his youth.

Of course this caution had its useful side. He only moved when he was fully organized, quite prepared, and the enemy was half-beaten. Thus he only attacked Antigonos when he could do so along with all the rest, and he only attacked Lysimachos when the latter's kingdom was already collapsing. No doubt this rendered success all but certain, but it was slow. He was perhaps at his best when on the defensive – in Babylonia when attacked by Antigonos, above all in Syria between Ipsos and the marriage to Stratonike. His ambition probably grew with success, from satrap to independence to king to empire. In a sense any successful general in the years after Alexander was morally bound to aim at the restoration of Alexander's empire, and hence also that of the Akhaimenids. Seleukos was the man who came nearest to realizing that ambition, nearer certainly than Antigonos, but it was the Akhaimenid state, shorn of peripheral bits and pieces, which he restored, not Alexander's. He never had a hope of recovering the Indus valley. The two bits he left till last, Egypt and Macedon, were the crucial ones; without them, his empire was doomed to decay, and doomed to debilitating warfare which only speeded up the decaying process.

As a soldier he was less outstanding than his nickname of Nikator, the Victor, would suggest. If he shared the honours at Gaza and Ipsos, he was defeated in India, fought Antigonos to a standstill, and beat Lysimachos at Korupedion, a distinctly mixed record. Most important, though, his victories were productive, while his defeats were barren. It is in his military career that his character is perhaps best revealed, and it was in Seleukos' character to hesitate and delay until the moment was ripe, perhaps overripe. He did this because all his life he had had to operate on a shoe-string, with smaller forces than his opponent. He had had to rely on guile and intelligence and duplicity and diplomacy to gain his victories – and in this he is Alexander's nearest successor as a soldier, far more so than the flamboyant and hopeless Demetrios. But those qualities are not sufficient to build an empire on more than a personal basis. So, while Seleukos is rightly called the Victor, it was his son who had to work for thirty years, from his appointment to rule the east until his death, to save his inheritance from disintegration. The work of the Saviour was as essential as that of the Victor.

APPENDIX

The royal journals say that Peithon, Attalos, Demophon and Peukestas, with Kleomenes, Menidas and Seleukos, slept in the temple of Sarapis...

(Arrian, *Anabasis*, VII, 26, 2)

The following is my argument for placing this story in the collection of propaganda stories and associating it with Antigonos' enmity towards Seleukos. (References are to Berve, *Alexanderreich* and to *RE*.)

1 The meeting place is fictitious, since Sarapis was only developed as a god after Ptolemy took over Egypt.

2 The inclusion of Kleomenes demonstrates that the list of men attending was made up later, for Kleomenes never left Egypt.

3 The inclusion of Kleomenes and Sarapis directs attention at Egypt and Ptolemy.

4 All of the men named with Seleukos had unpleasant or evil reputations:

Peithon murderer of the Greek colonists, assassin of Perdikkas, executed by Antigonos. (Berve, 621; *RE* XIX, cols 220–2.)

Attalos Perdikkas' brother-in-law, disruptor of the meeting at Triparadisos, attempted to seize Rhodes, probably killed in fighting against Antigonos in Asia Minor. (Berve, 181; *RE* II, col. 2158.)

Demophon an obscure seer who warned Alexander not to attack the city of the Malli in India, and was rebuked by Alexander for interfering with the loyalty of the army. (Berve, 264.)

Peukestas satrap of Persis who became a *quasi*-Persian, deposed by Antigonos after leading the fight against him in the east. (Berve, 634; *RE* XIX, cols 1395–8.)

Kleomenes a Greek from Naukratis who rose to become satrap of Egypt, eliminating rivals along the way; notorious for cornering the corn supply and making a fortune from a famine in Greece. (Berve, 431 and 432; *RE* XI, cols 710–12.)

Menidas (also *Menoetas*) Greek mercenary captain prominent in the battle at Gaugamela, assassin of Parmenio, died in rebellion against Antigonos. (Berve, 508 (Menidas) and 510 (Menoetas); *RE* XV, 851 and XV, 919.)

5 Thus these men between them had reputations which collectively stank in the nostrils of the Greeks (Kleomenes, Peithon), the Macedonians (Attalos, Menidas), the army (Demophon, Menidas, Attalos), and Antigonos (Peithon, Attalos, Peukestas, Menidas, and, of course, Seleukos).

6 I therefore theorize that this story was originally developed, perhaps from a true incident, into a propaganda story designed to place Seleukos in the company of a set of blackguards and Ptolemy. The obvious occasion for this is the moment when Seleukos joined Ptolemy, that is, in 315. Thus the originator can only have been Antigonos.

ABBREVIATIONS

LITERARY

A. *Anab*	Arrian, *Anabasis of Alexander*
A. *Succ*	Arrian, *Successors of Alexander*
App. *Mith*	Appian, *Mithridatic Wars*
App. *Syr*	Appian, *Syrian Wars*
C.	Q. Curtius Rufus, *Life of Alexander the Great*
D.	Diodoros Sikulos, *Library of History*
FGH	F. Jacoby, *Die Fragmente der Griechischen Historiker*, Berlin and Leiden 1926–58.
Grayson	A.K. Grayson, *Assyrian and Babylonian Chronicles*, New York 1975.
J.	Justin – *Histories*
Mal.	John Malalas, *Chronographia*
P.	Plutarch
P. *Alex*	Plutarch, *Life of Alexander*
P. *Dem*	Plutarch, *Life of Demetrios*
P. *Eum*	Plutarch, *Life of Eumenes*
P. *Pyrr*	Plutarch, *Life of Pyrrhos*
Paus.	Pausanias
Pliny *NH*	Pliny the Elder, *Natural History*
Pol.	Polyainos, *Stratagems*
Str.	Strabo, *Geography*

INSCRIPTIONS

Austin	M.M. Austin, *The Hellenistic World from Alexander to the Roman Conquest*, Cambridge 1981.

ABBREVIATIONS

Burstein	S.M. Burstein, *The Hellenistic Age from the Battle of Ipsos to the Death of Kleopatra VII*, Cambridge 1985.
CAH	*Cambridge Ancient History*, vol. VI 'Macedon', 1928; vol. VII 'The Hellenistic Monarchies and the Rise of Rome', 2nd imp., 1983; vol. VII part I, 'The Hellenistic World', 2nd edn, 1984.
CIG	*Corpus Inscriptionum Graecarum*, Berlin 1839–71.
Ditt, *Syll* (3)	W. Dittenberger, *Sylloge Inscriptionum Graecarum*, 3rd edn, Berlin 1915–24.
Harding	P. Harding, *From the End of the Peloponnesian War to the Battle of Ipsus*, Cambridge 1985.
I. Didyma	A. Rehm, *Die Inschriften, Milet*, vol. 3, Berlin 1914.
I. Ephesos	H. Wankel *et al.*, *Die Inschriften aus Ephesos*, 7 vols, Bonn 1979–81.
IG	*Inscriptiones Graecae*.
IGLS	*Inscriptions Grecques et Latines de la Syrie*.
I. Magnesia	O. Kern, *Die Inschriften von Magnesia am Maeander*, Berlin 1900.
I. Priene	F. Hiller von Gärtringen, *Inschriften von Priene*, Berlin 1906.
Michel	C. Michel, *Receuil d'Inscriptions grecques*, Brussels 1900–27.
Milet	T. Wiegand and A. Rehm, *Milet: Ergebnisse des Ausgrabungen und Untersuchungen seit dem Jähre 1899*, Berlin 1906–36.
OGIS	W. Dittenberger, *Orientis Graeci Inscriptiones Selectae*, Berlin, 1902–5.
SEG	*Supplementum Epigraphicum Graecum*, Leiden, from 1923.
Welles	C.B. Welles, *Royal Correspondence in the Hellenistic Period*, New Haven, Conn., 1934.

JOURNALS

AJP	American Journal of Philology
ANSMN	American Numismatic Society, Museum Notes
AS	Ancient Society
BAR	British Archaeological Reports
CP	Classical Philology
CQ	Classical Quarterly
CR	Classical Review
JHS	Journal of Hellenic Studies
MUSJ	Mélanges de l'Université St Josephe
RE	Real-Encyclopadie der classischen Altertumswissenschaft
RN	Revue Numismatique

NOTES

For full titles and so on, see the Bibliography.

1 Child and soldier

1 J. XVII, 1, 10; App. *Syr*, 63; Eusebius, *Chronographia*, I, 249.
2 J. XV, 4, 3.
3 On the Royal Pages: Hammond and Griffith, *Hist. Macedonia*, II, 401.
4 Str. XVI, 750; Stephanus, s.v. 'Laodikeia'.
5 J. XV, 4, 3.
6 P. *Alex*, 3.
7 Hadley, 'Seleucid Mythology', lists these stories; I cannot accept his further conclusions, however, and 'mythology' is a tendentious term for them.
8 Mal, 198; *RE*, s.v. 'Didymeia'.
9 Parke, *Oracles of Apollo* 33–43; Fonterose, *Didyma*, 14–15.
10 Berve, *Alexanderreich*, II, 441.
11 A. *Anab*, I, 24, 1 and 29, 4; Berve, *Alexanderreich*, s.v.'Ptolemaios'.
12 Stephanus, s.v. 'Oropus'.
13 Mal, 203; Paus. I, 16, 1.
14 On the two Europoi see Hammond, *Hist. Macedonia*, I, 166–7 and Map 14.
15 The Paionian crisis: D. 16, 3, 4.
16 Cawkwell, *Philip of Macedon*, Ellis, *Philip II*, and Hammond and Griffith, *Hist. Macedonia*, II (by Griffith) are the most recent treatments of Philip II.
17 Green, *Alexander*, is especially attentive to this aspect; other Alexander-biographers include, most recently Bosworth, *Conquest*.
18 A. *Anab*, V, 13, 4. On the hypaspists see Anson, 'Alexander's hypaspists' (arguing against Lock, 'Origins of Argyraspids'), and Bosworth, *Conquest*, 268, 279.

2 Commander and betrayer

1. Bevan, *House of Seleucus*, 31.
2. A. *Anab*, V, 16, 3 and 17, 6.
3. A. *Anab*, V, 13, 1.
4. A. *Anab*, VI, 2, 2.
5. A. *Anab*, VI, 6, 1.
6. They did not go with Krateros (A. *Anab*, VI, 17, 3) so must have remained with Alexander.
7. P. *Alex*, 66, 3–67, 1; A. *Anab*, VI, 24–6.
8. Hypaspists in attendance at, e.g., A. *Anab*, VI, 21, 3 and 22, 1.
9. A. *Anab*, V, 25, 1–29, 1; P. *Alex*, 62; D. XVII, 93–4; C. IX, 2, 8–3, 19.
10. Marriages: A. *Anab*, VII, 4, 6; Spitamenes: A. *Anab*, III, 29, 6–30, 5 and IV, 3, 6–7, for example.
11. Mal, 198.
12. A. *Anab*, VII, 8, 1–3.
13. The two versions: A. *Anab*, VII, 22, 5 (Seleukos) and A. *Anab*, VII, 22, 2–4 (the sailor); the story is discussed from the point of view of the Babylonian setting by Eddy, *The King is Dead*, 108–9; its propaganda element is recognized by Hadley, 'Seleucid Mythology'.
14. Eddy, *The King is Dead*, 108.
15. A. *Anab*, VII, 26, 2; P. *Alex*, 76.
16. Accepted either explicitly or by implication by Burn, *Alexander*, 180, and by Hammond, *Alexander*, 247. Accepted as true with the alteration of 'Marduk' for 'Sarapis' by Wilcken, *Alexander*, 238, Tarn, *Alexander*, I, 120, Hamilton, *Alexander*, 152, and Green, *Alexander*, 475. The event is recounted, with doubts, by Fox, *Alexander*, 467, and with even stronger doubts by Bosworth, *Conquest*, 172.
17. Opinion is divided on this. See Samuel, 'Alexander's Royal Journal', Badian, 'King's Notebooks', and Bosworth, 'Death of Alexander'. Hammond, *Three Historians*, 5–11, restates the view that the 'journal' existed. This may be so, but the point here is that the episode of the temple-vigil is not authentic in the way it is recorded in P. and A.
18. Fraser, *Ptolemaic Alexandria*, I, 246–50.
19. Badian, 'Administration'; Bosworth, *Conquest*, 229–45.
20. Errington, 'Babylon to Triparadisos'.
21. A. *Succ*, 1a, 1–5; C. X, 6, 1–9, 21; D. XVIII, 2; J. XIII, 2–4.
22. A. *Succ*, 1a, 2.
23. Hornblower, *Hieronymus*, ch. 4.
24. A. *Succ*, 1a, 2.
25. *FHG*, III, 667, Dexippos, fr. 1. See Bevan, *House of Seleucus*, I, App B, 322.
26. D. XVIII, 7, 1–9.
27. D. XVIII, 16, 1–3.
28. D. XVIII, 23, 1–3; J. XIII, 6; A. *Succ*, 21–3; Errington, 'Babylon to Triparadisos', 59–64.

NOTES

29 D. XVIII, 23, 3–4; Wehrli, *Antigone et Demetrios*, 33.
30 D. XVIII, 21, 7–9; Bosworth, *Conquest*, Appd A, 291–2.
31 D. XVIII, 28, 2–6.
32 D. XVIII, 36, 2–5.
33 Cornelius Nepos, *Eumenes*, 5.
34 Hauben, 'First War'; Errington, 'Babylon to Triparadisos', 59–64; Seibert, *Ptolemaios I*, 91–120.

3 Satrap and fugitive

1 D. XVIII, 36, 6; A. *Succ*, frag. 9, 30; Delorme, *Monde Hellénistique*, 23–32; Errington, 'Babylon to Triparadisos', 64–77.
2 D. XVIII, 39, 1–7; A. *Succ*, frag. 9, 31–8; Pol. IV, 6, 4.
3 D. XVIII, 39, 2.
4 A. *Succ*, frag. 9, 33.
5 The distribution of satrapies is detailed in A. *Succ*, frag. 9, 34–8 and D. XVIII, 37–9; for discussion see Errington, 'Babylon to Triparadisos', above all.
6 A. *Succ*, frag. 2, 3.
7 A. *Succ*, frag. 24, 3–5.
8 Grayson 10 Obv, 4–9.
9 D. XIX, 14, 1.
10 D. XVIII, 40, 1–42, 5; P. *Eum*, 9–11.
11 A. *Anab*, VII, 17.
12 Rostovtzeff, 'Seleucid Babylonia'; Dandamayev, 'Achaemenid Babylonia', and Sarkisian, 'City Land'.
13 A. *Anab*, VII, 17.
14 Grayson 10 Obv, 6.
15 Grayson 10 Obv, 7.
16 Van der Spek, 'Babylonian City'; Sarkisian, 'City Land'.
17 Sherwin-White, 'Seleucid Babylonia'; Funck, 'Innenpolitik'.
18 D. XVIII, 48–58; J. XIII, 8 and XIX, 1; P. *Eum*, 13, 2–3; Engel, *Antigonos I Monophthalamos*, 41–8; Delorme, *Monde Hellénistique*, 33–6; Westlake, 'Eumenes of Cardia'; Briant, 'D'Alexandre aux Diadoques'; Seibert, *Diadochen*, 110–15.
19 Bevan, *House of Seleucus*, I, 40–3; Bosworth, 'Indian Satrapies'.
20 D. XIX, 14, 5–6.
21 D. XVIII, 58–63 and XIX, 12, 1; P. *Eum*, 13, 2–4.
22 A. *Succ*, frag. 2, 38.
23 Heckel, 'Career of Antigenes'.
24 Grayson 10 Obv, 14.
25 D. XVIII, 60, 4–61, 3; P. *Eum*, 13, 4–8; Pol. IV, 8, 2.
26 D. XIX, 12, 1–13, 7 and 15, 1–6.
27 Grayson 10 Obv, 14–17.
28 D. XIX, 12, 3–5.
29 D. XIX, 18, 1
30 ibid.
31 D. XIX, 18, 2–7.

32 D. XIX, 21, 1–2.
33 D. XIX, 48, 6.
34 D. XIX, 19, 1–34, 8 and 37, 1–43, 9; see note 18, plus Devine, 'Paraitacene' and Thompson, 'Eumenes vs the Phalanx'.
35 D. XIX, 44, 1–2.
36 D. XIX, 44, 4.
37 D. XIX, 46, 1–4.
38 D. XIX, 48, 5.
39 D. XIX, 48, 3–4.
40 D. XIX, 48, 1–2.
41 D. XIX, 47, 1–4.
42 D. XIX, 48, 7–8 and 55, 1.
43 Antigonos' settlement of the east is not usually given much attention, but see: Cloché, *Dislocation*, 135–7; Bevan, *House of Seleucus*, I, 46–8 and ch. XIII; Schober, *Geschichte Babyloniens*, 83–90.
44 App. *Syr*, 53.
45 D. XIX, 55, 2.
46 D. XIX, 55, 2–5. Modern considerations of the quarrel of Antigonos and Seleukos are few and brief: Bevan, *House of Seleucus*, I, 48–9; Engel, *Antiogonos Monophthalamos*, 50–4; Cloché, *Dislocation*, 137; Mehl, *Seleukos*, 52–5.
47 Grayson 10 Obv, 19.
48 Parker and Dubberstein, *Babylonian Chronology*; Joannes, 'Successeurs'. On the chronology of all this time see: Errington, 'Diodorus Siculus'; L.C. Smith, 'Chronology'; S. Smith, 'Philip Arrhidaeus'; Schober, *Geschichte Babyloniens*, 106–23. The chronological problems are by no means sorted out yet.
49 See especially, Cloché, *Dislocation*, 95–118 and Will, *Hist. Pol.*, 46–52.
50 D. XIX, 56, 4–5.

4 Admiral and satrap

1 D. XIX, 55, 5.
2 D. XIX, 91, 4.
3 D. XIX, 56, 1–2.
4 D. XVIII, 55–7, 1 and 64–75; Fortina, *Cassandro*, esp. 43–58.
5 D. XIX, 56, 3.
6 D. XIX, 46, 1–5; Pol. IV, 6, 14; see Griffith, *Mercenaries*, 51.
7 D. XIX, 56, 5.
8 D. XIX, 56, 4.
9 ibid.
10 D. XIX, 56, 5.
11 D. XIX, 57, 1.
12 J. XV, 1; D. XIX, 57, 1–2. The reading of Diodoros is disputed here, with the suggestion that 'Kasandros' (*sic*) should read 'Asandros' (satrap of Karia) and that Lykia should be Kilikia. The

NOTES

proposed distribution makes good sense without these changes. See, for modern comments: Cloché, *Dislocation*, 143–7; Aucello, 'Politica dei Diadochi'.
13 D. XIX, 57, 2.
14 ibid.
15 D. XIX, 57, 4.
16 D. XIX, 57, 5.
17 A. *Succ*, frag. 10, 2.
18 A. *Succ*, frag. 9, 36.
19 D. XIX, 57, 4.
20 D. XIX, 58, 1–5.
21 D. XIX, 57, 4.
22 Hauben, 'Rhodes, Alexander'.
23 D. XIX, 58, 5.
24 ibid.
25 D. XIX, 62, 3.
26 D. XIX, 60, 3–4.
27 D. XIX, 60, 2–4.
28 D. XIX, 60, 1.
29 D. XIX, 62, 3–4. For the Cypriot situation see: Hill, *Cyprus*, 158–61.
30 D. XIX, 57, 5 and 60, 1.
31 D. XVIII, 56.
32 D. XIX, 61, 1–3.
33 Delorme, *Monde Hellénistique*, 40–5; Tarn, *Hellénistic Civilisation*, 10 and 64; Simpson, 'Antigonus the One-Eyed'.
34 A. *Anab*, VII, 26, 2–3; P. *Alex*, 76.
35 Fraser, *Ptolemaic Alexandria*, 246–8; Bosworth, 'Death of Alexander'.
36 Pearson, *Lost Historians*, 20.
37 Hadley, 'Seleucid Mythology'; for Hadley's 'mythology' I use 'propaganda'.
38 Heckel, 'Testament'.
39 Explored as a serious notion by Green, *Alexander*, 475–7.
40 D. XIX, 62, 1.
41 D. XIX, 62, 5.
42 ibid.
43 D. XIX, 62, 8.
44 D. XIX, 62, 5–6.
45 Errington, 'Diodorus Siculus'; L.C. Smith, 'Chronology'; Hauben, 'Years 313–311 B.C.'.
46 D. XIX, 62, 7.
47 D. XIX, 62, 6–8. Tarn, *Military and Naval Developments*, 132, implicitly denies Diodoros' claims on these big ships, by putting the invention of sevens in 314.
48 D. XIX, 62, 9.
49 D. XIX, 64, 5–8.
50 D. XIX, 64, 8; *OGIS* 5 (= Austin 13, = Welles, 1); Simpson, 'The

Peace of 311'; Delorme, *Monde Hellénistique*, 46–57; Seibert, *Diadochen*, 123–7.
51 D. XIX, 68, 3–4.
52 ibid.
53 D. XIX, 68, 2 and 5–7 and 75, 1–7.
54 D. XIX, 79, 1–3; Morkholm, 'Cyrene and Ptolemy I'.
55 D. XIX, 79, 4–5; Hill, *Cyprus*, I, 158–60.
56 D. XIX, 79, 5–6.
57 D. XIX, 75, 6.
58 D. XIX, 80, 3–84, 8; P. *Dem*. 5; J. XV, 1. See, for modern accounts of these events: Cloché, *Dislocation*, 160– 5; Will, *Hist. Pol.*, 58–61; Wehrli, *Antigone et Demetrios*, 48–52; Kertesz, 'Ptolemy I and the Battle of Gaza'.
59 D. XIX, 83, 1 and 83, 4.
60 D. XIX, 85, 2.
61 D. XIX, 86, 5.
62 D. XIX, 91, 4.
63 D. XIX, 85, 5–86, 1.
64 D. XIX, 86, 1–2.
65 D. XIX, 90, 1; App. *Syr*, IX, 54.
66 D. XIX, 91, 1–4. See Bevan, *House of Seleucus*, I, 54–64; Cloché, *Dislocation*, 165–6.

5 General and victor

1   D. XIX, 93, 1–2 and 5–7.
2   D. XIX, 93, 3–4.
3   D. XIX, 94, 1.
4   D. XIX, 92, 1.
5   D. XIX, 92, 1–5.
6   D. XIX, 100, 3.
7   D. XIX, 92, 5.
8   D. XIX, 91, 1.
9   D. XIX, 90, 1.
10 D. XIX, 90, 4.
11 Hadley, 'Royal Propaganda'.
12 D. XIX, 92, 5; App. *Syr*, 55; P. *Dem*, 7, 2.
13 See Bevan, *House of Seleucus*, I, 54–5; Cloché, *Dislocation*, 165–6; Mehl, *Seleukos*, 107–11.
14 D. XIX, 100, 3.
15 D. XIX, 94, 1–100, 2.
16 D. XIX, 100, 4; P. *Dem*, 7, 3.
17 D. XIX, 100, 7.
18 D. XIX, 100, 5.
19 D. XIX, 100, 5–6; P. *Dem*, 7, 3.
20 App. *Syr*, 55.
21 P. *Dem*, 7.
22 D. XIX, 100, 7; P. *Dem*, 7, 3 (7,000 troops); Mehl, *Seleukos*, 111–20.

23 D. XIX, 105, 1; *OGIS* 5 (= Austin, 31 = Harding, 132 = Welles, 1).
24 Simpson, 'Peace of 311', 26–7. See also Delorme, *Monde Hellénistique*, 46–57; Cloché, *Dislocation*, 170–8; Will, *Hist. Pol.*, 61–5; Cary, *Hist. Greek World*, 28–9 and App 3; Mehl, *Seleukos*, 120–4.
25 D. XIX, 57, 1–2.
26 Bevan, *House of Seleucus*, I, 56–7; Cloché, *Dislocation*, 180–1; Mehl, *Seleukos*, 129–34; Schober, *Geschichte Babyloniens*, 105–39.
27 E.g., Corradi, *Studi Ellenistici*, 16–19.
28 Grayson 10 Rev, 7–10.
29 D. XIX, 92, 5.
30 A. *Indica*, 43, 4–5.
31 Griffith, *Mercenaries*, 51–2.
32 Grayson 10 Rev, 11–12.
33 D. XVIII, 2–8.
34 Grayson 10 Rev, 7–8.
35 Grayson 10 Rev, 14–25.
36 D. XX, 21, 1–3; Hill, *Cyprus*, 159–60.
37 D. XX, 19, 3–4.
38 D. XX, 27, 1–3.
39 P. *Dem*, 7.
40 D. XX, 19, 2 and 20, 5.
41 On this western war, see: Cloché, *Dislocation*, 179–80 and 181–3; Will, *Hist. Pol.*, 67–74; Seibert, *Ptolemaios I*, 183–9.
42 Grayson 10 Rev, 26–43.
43 Grayson 10 left edge, 2.
44 D. XX, 45, 1.
45 Paus. I, 9, 9.
46 D. XX, 29, 1.
47 D. XX, 37, 3–6.
48 D. XIX, 105, 2–3; Wacholder's attempt to re-date Alexander IV's death, in 'Beginning of the Seleucid Era', does not convince.
49 D. XX, 37, 2.

6 Conqueror and king

1 P. *Dem*, 17.
2 D. XIX, 91, 1.
3 Isidore of Charax, *Parthian Stations*, 1.
4 Pliny, *NH* VI, 117.
5 Pliny, *NH* V, 86.
6 App. *Syr*, 55; D. XIX, 92, 5 and 100, 3.
7 D. XIX, 100, 5.
8 P. *Dem*, 38; App. *Syr*, 59.
9 Dillemann, *Haute Mésopotamie*, 78, identifies Antiochia-Arabis with the later Constantia, modern Viranshehir, some 130 kilometres west of Nisibis. His argument is essentially linguistic,

and he ignores other factors – strategic, the city name, water supply, and so on – which seem to me to be decisive.
10 D. XIX, 90, 1. The origin for this whole section is Rostovtzeff, 'Foundation of Dura-Europus'.
11 Pliny, *NH* VI, 119; App. *Syr*, 57; Isidore of Charax, *Parthian Stations*, 1.
12 App. *Syr*, 53.
13 D. XX, 45, 1.
14 Hadley, 'Foundation Date of Seleuceia'; Hopkins, *Seleuceia*, 1–7; Waggoner, 'Alexander Coinage at Seleuceia'.
15 App. *Syr*, 58.
16 D. XIX, 48, 1.
17 P. *Dem*, 18, 2; Gruen, 'Coronation of the Diadochoi'.
18 Wacholder, 'Beginning of the Seleucid Era' bases his theory on this fact.
19 J. XV, 4.
20 Narain, *Indo-Greeks*, 4–5 and references there; the date of the coins is notoriously difficult (see Narain's note 5 on page 4); Holt, *Alexander and Bactria*, 96–8, puts them between Alexander and Seleukos.
21 Tarn, *Greeks in Bactria*, 101, suggested an Oxyartes-dynasty.
22 *OGIS*, 213 (= Harding, 2 = *I. Didyma*, 479).
23 On that problem see the various articles by Wolski, especially 'L'Iran dans la politique des Séleucides'.
24 Narain, 'Alexander and India'.
25 D. XIX, 14, 8; Bosworth, 'Indian Satrapies'.
26 D. XVII, 93, 2; C. IX, 2, 1; P. *Alex*, 62, 2.
27 Thapar, *Asoka*, ch. 1, and *Hist. India*, I, chs 3 and 4; V.A.Smith, *Ox. Hist. India*, chs 3 and 4.
28 P. *Alex*, 62.
29 App. *Syr*, 55.
30 See note 27.
31 Burstein 50; Fraser, 'Son of Aristonax'.
32 Mehl, 156–93 and his large bibliography. His argument that Seleukos penetrated deep into India and conquered extensively is unacceptable, for the two simple and connnected reasons that Seleukos did not have either the time or the military resources (i.e. soldiers) to do so. He had no more than a year or so between dealing with Baktria and returning west, and even at the battle of Ipsos he had no more than 50,000 soldiers, only 20,000 of which were infantry. India, especially under a single ruler, was simply too big.
33 Str. XV, 2, 9; Skurzak, 'Traité Syro-Indien'.
34 Tarn, 'Two Notes: 500 Elephants'.
35 D. XIX, 58, 6.
36 D. XVII, 93, 2.
37 A. *Anab*, V, 15, 4; though D. says 130 (XVII, 87, 2) and C. (VIII, 13, 6) a minimum of 85.
38 Pliny, *NH* VI, 68.

39 D. XIX, 27, 1 and 5 and 28, 2.
40 D. XIX, 40, 1 and 4.
41 D. XIX, 82, 3–4.
42 D. XX, 76, 7.
43 D. XX, 53, 4; P. *Dem*, 18.
44 Gruen, 'Coronation of the Diadochoi'; Muller, *Antigonos und 'Das Jahr des Könige'*, passim, but cf. 69–77 on Seleukos.
45 Sachs and Wiseman, 'Babylonian King list'.
46 Edson, 'Imperium Macedonicum'.

7 Victor and organizer

1 P. *Dem*, 25; D. XX, 106, 1; Schmitt, *Staatsverträge* III, 446 (= Austin, 42 = Harding, 138).
2 D. XX, 106, 2.
3 D. XX, 106, 3.
4 ibid. This sequence – Kassandros to Ptolemy to Seleukos – is required by the strategic situation. There is no evidence that Seleukos and Kassandros were in direct communication.
5 D. XX, 107, 1.
6 D. XX, 106, 5. This is usually called a 'coalition'; see *CAH*, VI, 502–4; Will, *Hist. Pol.*, I, 79–83; Cloché, *Dislocation*, 210–12.
7 D. XX, 107, 1 and 110, 1–6.
8 D. XX, 107, 2–5.
9 D. XX, 108, 1.
10 D. XX, 108, 3.
11 D. XX, 113, 1.
12 D. XX, 113, 4.
13 ibid. For the problem of logistics see Engels, *Alexander and Logistics*.
14 D. XX, 109, 6.
15 D. XX, 109, 4.
16 D. XX, 108, 5–109, 3.
17 D. XX, 113, 1–2.
18 D. XX, 109, 6–7.
19 D. XX, 112, 1–4.
20 P. *Dem*, 28 and D. XX, 113, 4.
21 D. XX, 109, 5 and 111, 1
22 D. XX, 111, 3.
23 P. *Dem*, 28.
24 P. *Dem*, 28–9; Antigonos is shown as indecisive and clumsy, though this is not attributed by Plutarch to his age, rather to a presentiment of defeat. If the incidents are genuine, age is perhaps the better explanation.
25 P. *Dem*, 28, reading 5,000 for 500 as the excess of the allies' cavalry over Antigonos'.
26 P. *Dem*, 28–9; App. *Syr*, 55; D. XXI, 1, 2; Bar-Kochva, *Seleucid Army*, 105–10.

27 D. XX, 113, 4, where Seleukos has 12,000 cavalry; at P. *Dem*, 28 the allies have 15,000 at the battle (but see note 25).
28 Of the allied infantry force of 64,000, only 20,000 were Seleukos' men (P. *Dem*, 28 and D. XX, 113, 4).
29 This timing and placing is required by the terms of the truce with the commander in Sidon the previous year (D. XX, 113, 1–2); Ptolemy would know, by the end of the four-month truce, that the story of the Antigonid victory was false, and he would therefore return to the siege as soon as the truce expired; he had left garrisons in Palestine all along.
30 D. XXI, 1, 5.
31 P. *Dem*, 30; App. *Syr*, 55.
32 P. *Dem*, 30–1; D. XX, 112, 1; P. *Pyrr*, 4.
33 D. XXI, 113, 2.
34 This is presumption, but the Eleuthros later formed the boundary between Ptolemaic and Seleukid Syria; it seems reasonable to assume it was so from the start.
35 P. *Dem*, 29.
36 P. *Dem*, 30.
37 P. *Dem*, 31; Griffith, *Mercenaries*, 57.
38 Mal. 201 says Antigoneia had 5,300 citizens, to which must be added garrisons and conscripts from every other Macedonian settlement in Syria.
39 Robert, 'Monnaies de Troade'; Cook, *The Troad*, 198.
40 Welles, *Alexander*, 3–4 (= Austin, 40 = Ditt. *Syll* (3), 344).
41 Str. XIV, 1, 37.
42 Erythrai: *OGIS*, 223 (= Welles, 15); Miletos: *Milet* I, 3, no. 123; Colophon: Merritt, 'Inscriptions of Colophon', 1.
43 Synnada: D. XX, 107, 2; Kelainai: D. XIX, 68, 2 and 93, 4; Sardis citadel: D. XX, 107, 5.
44 Sidon: D. XX, 113, 1; Tyre: P. *Dem*, 32.
45 D. XX, 72, 1.
46 Frézouls, 'Toponymie'.
47 D. XXI, 1.
48 Rey-Coquais, *Arados*, passim.
49 A. *Anab*, III, 11, 4.
50 P. *Dem*, 31.
51 Mal. 198–203; App. *Syr*, 53; I have discussed this aspect of Seleukos' policy in Grainger, *Cities*, ch. 2.
52 Wagner, *Zeugma*, esp. 92–106.
53 Pol. V, 61, 1.
54 Str. XVI, 2, 4.
55 P. *Dem*, 29, for example.
56 Mal. 201; D. XX, 47, 6.
57 Mal. 201.
58 P. *Dem*, 31; Paus. I, 10, 2.
59 P. *Dem*, 31; Memnon 224b–25a.
60 P. *Dem*, 31.
61 ibid.

NOTES

62 P. *Dem*, 32.
63 Eusebius, *Chronographia* II, 119, redating to 298 as suggested by Corradi, *Studi Ellenistici*, 40, n. 3.
64 Arados' behaviour as a Seleukid subject was exactly what one might have expected of a Greek city – repeated attempts, over a period of two centuries, to establish its independence and acquire territory. See Rey-Coquais, *Arados*, 154–6 and Grainger, *Cities*, ch. 5.
65 D. XIX, 58, 1–2.
66 P. *Dem*, 48.
67 Tarn, *Greeks in Bactria*, ch. 1 and App 2.
68 J. XLI, 4; Str. XI, 9, 2–3.
69 P. *Dem*, 38.
70 For example, Molon and Antiochos III: Polybios V, 40 sqq.
71 IGLS III, 1183; Welles, *Alexander*, 45 (= Austin, 176); Robert, *Hellenica*, 7, 5–22 (= Austin, 158).
72 IGLS III, 1183, lines 3–4 (= Austin, 176).
73 See Grainger, *Cities*, ch. 6 for the fully detailed argument on this.
74 A. *Anab*, IV, 18, 3.

8 Diplomat and ruler

1 Richter, *Portraits*, III, 270 and nos 1865–6.
2 ibid. nos 1867–8.
3 Hart, 'Diagnosis of Disease'.
4 Richter, *Portraits*, no. 1869.
5 OGIS, 10 (= Burstein, 1).
6 OGIS, 213 (= Burstein, 2 = *I. Didyma* II, 479) and *I. Didyma* II, 480.
7 The city of Alexandria-by-Issos, at the north end of this plain (modern Iskenderun) cannot be shown to exist before the mid-second century: Grainger, *Cities*, 36–7, 147.
8 P. *Dem*, 32.
9 ibid.
10 ibid.
11 J. XVI, 1; P. *Dem*, 36 and *Pyrr*, 6; D. XXI, 7; Paus. IX, 7, 2–3.
12 P. *Dem*, 33.
13 Ditt, *Syll* (3), 368.
14 P. *Dem*, 35.
15 ibid.
16 P. *Dem*, 35–6.
17 Préaux, *Monde Hellénistique*, 384–8.
18 Cohen, *Seleucid Colonies*, ch. 2, 'The Colonists'.
19 A. *Anab*, II, 13, 7–8.
20 Rey-Coquais, *Arados*, 154–6.
21 Ronzevalle, 'Monnaies de la Dynastie de Abd-Hadad'; Seyrig, 'Le Monnayage de Hierapolis'.
22 Lucian, *De Syria Dea*, 17 and 19–21.
23 Aelian, *De Natura Animali*, XII, 2.

24 Lucian, *De Syria Dea*, 32–3.
25 Chase, 'Three Hellenistic Coins'; Naster, 'Fire-Alter or Fire-Tower?' ibid. 'Fratakara, Frataraka ou Fratadara?'.
26 Pol. VII, 39.
27 Stronach, *Pasargadae*, 185–8; Houghton, 'Early Seleucid Victory Coinage', 14.
28 Ghirshman, *Iran*, 231.
29 Str. XI, 13, 1; Ekbatana: Str. XI, 13, 5; Pliny, *NH* VI, 17; Nihavand: Robert, *Hellenica*, 7, 5–22 (= Austin, 158).
30 Concobar: Fard, 'Kangavar'; Khurra: Matheson, *Persia*, 189.
31 Ray: Str. XI, 13, 6; Hekatompylos: App. *Syr*, 57; Pliny, *NH* VI, 44; Merv: Str. XI, 10, 1; Pliny *NH* VI, 18.
32 D. XIX, 92, 5.
33 E.T. Newell, *Eastern Seleucid Mints*; Houghton, 'Early Seleucid Victory Coinage', 5–9.
34 *SEG*, VII, 2.
35 Str. XV, 1, 3; J. XLI, 1 and 4.
36 Helms, 'Excavations at Kandahar', 18.
37 Tarn, *Greeks in Bactria*, 114–16.
38 Bernard, *Fouilles d'Ai Khanoum*.
39 E.g., Frumkin, *Archaeology in Soviet Central Asia*.
40 Francfort, *Fortifications en Asie Centrale*, 27–30.
41 A. *Anab*, III, 28–30.
42 P. *Dem*, 38; App. *Syr*, 59 -61; Broderson, 'Liebeskranke Konigssohn' is not very helpful in understanding the event itself.
43 D. XIX, 100, 5.
44 Str. XI, 7, 3.
45 P. *Dem*, 47.
46 Pliny, *NH* VI, 49.
47 *OGIS*, 10 and 213; Robert, 'Démodamas de Milet'.
48 Str. II, 70.
49 Olshausen, *Prosopographie*, nos 126–9.

9 Diplomacy and defence

1 E.g., Bivar in Hambly, *Central Asia*, 31; Will, *Hist. Pol.*, 1, 267, both by implication.
2 Pliny, *NH* VI, xviii, 47; Str. XI, 10, 2.
3 Tarn, 'Two Notes: Tarmita'.
4 Tarn, *Greeks in Bactria*, 525.
5 Wolski, 'Les Iraniens'.
6 D. XVII, 99, 6; Curt. IX, 7, 1–11; D. XVIII, 7, 2 and 9.
7 On what follows see Grainger, *Cities*, 159.
8 Kuschke, *Archäologischer Survey*.
9 E.g., Mehl, *Seleukos*, 212–14 and his map.
10 App. *Syr*, 55.
11 P. *Dem*, 36–7; J. XVI, 1.
12 P. *Dem*, 42–3.

NOTES

13 Will, *Hist. Pol*, I, 292; Cary, *Hist. Greek World*, 96.
14 *I. Didyma*, 1; Ditt, *Syll* (3), 189 (= Michel, 465); Burstein, 8.
15 D. XX, 107, 2.
16 D. XX, 107, 3 and 111, 3.
17 Ditt, *Syll* (3), 189.
18 Str. XIV, 1, 21 (Ephesos) and XIV, 1, 37 (Smyrna).
19 Burstein, 12 (= *OGIS*, 13 = Welles, 7); Burstein, 10 (= *OGIS*, 11 = *I. Priene* 14).
20 Str. XIII, 1, 33 and 52.
21 Str. XIII, 1, 26.
22 Str. XIII, 1, 26; Cook, *Troad*, 364.
23 Pol. IV, 9, 4.
24 Tarn, *Greeks in Bactria*, 11.
25 Austin, 142 (= Burstein, 19); Wörrle, 'Antiochos I'.
26 Str. XIII, 4, 1.
27 Burstein, 1 (= *OGIS*, 1 = *I. Ephesos*, 5, 1953).
28 Str. XVII, 1, 43.
29 J. XV, 4.
30 Ilion: *OGIS*, 212 and 219; Erythrai: Ditt, *Syll* (3), 412.
31 D. XIX, 90, 4.
32 App. *Syr*, 56.
33 Parke, *Oracles of Apollo*, 44–6, is inclined to accept the 'king' oracles but calls the earlier one 'implausible'; Fonterose, *Didyma*, 41–3, 93–4, calls both of them 'not genuine'. It is surely obvious that they were inventions, probably by Seleukos himself.
34 Paus. I, 8, 5, and I, 16, 3 and VIII, 46, 3.
35 *OGIS*, 744 and 745 (= *Milet*, I, 3, no. 123).
36 Burstein, 2 (= *OGIS*, 213 = *I. Didyma*, 479).
37 Priene: *I. Priene*, 18; Erythrai: *IG*, XII, I, 6, and Powell, *Collectanea Alexandria*, 140.
38 P. *Dem*, 46.
39 Lucian, *De Syria Dea*, 17.
40 *OGIS*, 744 and 745.
41 J. XV, 4.
42 Libanius, *Oration XI*, 91; see Errington, 'Alexander in the Hellenistic World', 157, note 1.
43 On all this see the two fundamental books of Newell, *Coinage of Eastern Seleucid Mints*, and *Coinage of Western Seleucid Mints*.
44 P. *Dem*, 46.
45 The fleet: Tarn, *Antigonos Gonatas*, 105–6; Island league: Merker, 'Ptolemaic Officials' and Seibert, 'Philokles'.
46 Skeat, 'Reigns of Ptolemies', 10 and 29–30.
47 P. *Dem*, 44.
48 P. *Dem*, 46; P. *Pyrr*, 11.
49 P. *Dem*, 46.
50 P. *Dem*, 46–7.
51 P. *Dem*, 46.
52 P. *Dem*, 48.
53 P. *Dem*, 47.

54 P. *Dem*, 48–9. On this campaign see Bar-Kochva, *Seleucid Army*, 111–16.

10 Victor and victim

1. P. *Dem*, 50.
2. D. XXI, 20.
3. P. *Dem*, 52.
4. P. *Pyrr*, 12; J. XVI, 3; Paus. I, 10, 2.
5. Bosworth, 'Decline of Macedon'.
6. P. *Dem*, 51; D. XXI, 20.
7. J. XVI, 2; Paus. I, 6, 8.
8. Will, *Hist. Pol.*, I, 153–99, an essay on Ptolemaic foreign policy.
9. No ancient source is specific on what Keraunos did, though Pausanias implies that he went to Seleukos. This has provoked rival theories: either that he stayed with Lysimachos (Tarn, *Antigonos Gonatas*, 124, note 24) or that he went to Seleukos (Heinen, *Geschichte des 3 Jahrhunderts*, 7–20 and accepted by Will, *Hist. Pol.*, I, 102–3). The arguments are very evenly balanced, but are tipped towards Seleukos by Pausanias' words.
10. J. XVII, 1; Paus. I, 10, 3–4; Memnon, 225b, 6–14.
11. Paus. I, 10, 4; Heinen, *Geschichte des 3 Jahrhunderts*, 7–8 and 13–14.
12. Paus. I, 9, 10; Str. XIII, 4, 1.
13. Pol. VI, 12.
14. Pol. IV, 9, 4.
15. App. *Syr*, 62; Keil, 'Korou Pedion'; Bevan, *House of Seleucus*, I, App C, 322–3.
16. Paus. I, 10, 5.
17. Pol. VIII, 57.
18. J. XXIV, 2.
19. Pausanias says (I, 16, 1) he pressed into Macedonia, with an implication of speed and immediacy, but consideration of the timing confutes this: Seleukos took his time, as always.
20. Memnon, 225b, 32–226a, 2.
21. Newell, *Western Seleucid Mints*, 316–17.
22. ibid., 242–4.
23. ibid., 283–4.
24. Memnon, 226a, 9–14.
25. Memnon, 226b, 21–4.
26. Memnon, 226a, 14–22.
27. ibid., 22–5.
28. P. *Dem*, 4.
29. App. *Mith*, 9; Str. XII, 41.
30. Trogus, *Prologue*, XVII.
31. Pol. VIII, 57.
32. *Milet*, I, 3, 123 (= Burstein, 25).
33. *I. Priene*, 18 (= *OGIS*, 215).
34. *I.G.* XII, I, 6; Powell, *Collectanea Alexandria*, 140.

NOTES

35 Magnesia: *I. Magnesia*, 5, 69 and 98; Kolophon: Merritt, 'Inscriptions of Colophon', no. 6.
36 *OGIS*, 212.
37 Austin, 182 (= *OGIS*, 229).
38 Str. XII.
39 Kyros the Younger had used them as the excuse to get his Greek mercenaries marching eastwards (Xenophon, *Anabasis* I, 1) and Alexander had moved through swiftly without causing or suffering serious damage (A. *Anab*, I, 27, 5–28, 2); Perdikkas had raided them (D. XVIII, 22, 1–8); Antigonos had fought them (D. XVIII, 46, 3–48, 2).
40 *SEG*, VI, 593; Levick, *Roman Colonies*, 7–20; but Magie, *Roman Rule*, 1315.
41 Theokritos, *Idylls*, XVII, 88; Bagnall, *Administration*, 169.
42 Stephanos, 'Laodikeia' and 'Antiocheia', contradicting himself; Cohen, *Seleucid Colonies*, 15, note 55.
43 Austin, 218 (= Burstein, 92 = Ditt, *Syll* (3), 390); Hauben, 'Philokles'; Bagnall, *Administration*, 80.
44 *SEG*, XIX, 569.
45 Itanos: Bagnall, *Administration*, 120–3 and Spyridakis, *Itanos*, 70–1; Thera: *OGIS*, 44.
46 Austin, 135 (= *SEG*, I, 363).
47 Bagnall, *Administration*, 101 and 104.
48 Bagnall, *Administration*, 106.
49 Austin, 271 (= *OGIS*, 55).
50 Bagnall, *Administration*, 110–14.
51 Memnon, 226a, 14–22.
52 Pausanias I, 16, 1; Bevan, *House of Seleucus* I, 72.
53 App. *Syr*, 56.
54 Paus. I, 16, 1; App. *Syr*, 62.
55 Unnecessary agonizing has gone on over Seleukos' 'legal title' to Macedonia. The previous forty years had seen the replacement of legality by force and possession. Seleukos had as much right to rule in Macedonia as anyone else – once he got there.
56 J. XVII, 1.
57 Paus. I, 9, 9; D. XX, 29, 1.
58 App. *Syr*, 64.
59 App. *Syr*, 56 and 63.
60 Memnon, 226b, 1–14.

11 Reconqueror

1 J. XVII, 2.
2 ibid.
3 Memnon, 226a, 2–5.
4 J. XVIII, 2; Memnon, 226b, 33–4.
5 Memnon, 226b, 14–33.
6 Memnon, 226a, 2–3.

7 J. XVII, 2.
8 App. *Syr*, 63.
9 *OGIS*, 748; McShane, *Attalids*, 37.
10 Burstein, 25 (= *I. Didyma*, 123).
11 *IG*, XII, 2, 513.
12 Sachs and Wiseman, 'Babylonian King List', 205–6.
13 Clay, *Babylonian Records*, I, no. 5.
14 Burstein, 15 (= Austin, 139 = *OGIS*, 219).
15 Burstein, 25 (= *I. Didyma* 123).
16 Cary, *Hist. Greek World*, Appd. 5, 387–9; Will, *Hist. Pol.*, I, 139–42 and 146–50.
17 Str. XVI, 2, 4.
18 See, for a detailed discussion, Grainger, *Cities*, 6. Newell's suggestion of a rebellion by Apamea (*Western Seleucid Mints*, 157–8) is too narrowly based on coin evidence to be accepted.
19 Memnon, 227a, 4–6.
20 App. *Syr*, 63.
21 Memnon, 227a, 7–9.
22 Memnon, 227a, 9–14.
23 Memnon, 226b, 14–37; J. XVII, 2.
24 Hauben, *Callicrates*, and 'Philokles'.
25 Burstein, 25 (= *I. Didyma*, 123).
26 This, and all the preceding paragraph, is required by the fact that Antiochos has a fleet later, when he fought Antigonos and the Northern League, but there is no sign of one earlier. Seleukos will have had the use of ships (formerly Lysimachos'?) when he crossed the Hellespont, but surely Keraunos took them away to Kassandreia, for he would not want to leave Antiochos any means of reaching Macedonia. Hence the need to postulate a new fleet brought round from Syria for Antiochos.
27 J. XXIV, 1.
28 Memnon, 227a, 28–34.
29 Memnon, 227a, 19–29.
30 J. XXIV, 1.
31 Cary, *Hist. Greek World*, 126.
32 J. XXIV, 1.
33 Tarn, *Antigonos Gonatas*, 137–8.
34 J. XXIV, 2–3.
35 J. XXIV, 3 and 5; Paus. X, 19, 4.
36 J. XXIV, 5–6.
37 Pol. VI, 9, 2.
38 J. XXV, 1.
39 Memnon, 227b, 3–8.
40 Memnon, 227a, 28–38.
41 *OGIS*, 748.
42 Memnon, 227b, 9–12.
43 Livy, XXXVIII, 16, 1–5.
44 ibid., 6.
45 Memnon, 227b, 12–27.

46 Livy, XXXVIII, 16, 6–7.
47 ibid., 8–9: Memnon, 227b, 36–40.
48 Livy, XXXVIII, 16, 9–10.
49 *OGIS*, 748.
50 Str. XIII, 27.
51 Keil and Premerstein, II, 19.
52 McShane, *Attalids*, 36–8.
53 Ditt, *Syll* (3), 410.
54 Magie, *Roman Rule*, II, 730, note 11.
55 *Palatine Anthology*, VII, 492.
56 P. *Parallela Minora*, 15.
57 *OGIS*, 765.
58 Paus. X, 32, 4.
59 Paus. X, 30, 9.
60 *OGIS*, 765 with *OGIS*, 11.
61 J. XXV, 1–2; Trogus, *Prologue*, XXV; Ditt. *Syll* (3), 207.
62 Paus. I, 7, 1; J. XVII, 2 and XXIV, 2–3.
63 Paus. I, 7, 2; Kallimachos, *Hymn*, IV, 174.
64 *Vita Aratoi*; Diogenes Laertius VII, 1, 8.
65 Austin, 141.
66 Paus. I, 7, 1–2; Pol. II, 28, 1 and 2.
67 Pol. IV, 15.
68 Stephanus s.v. 'Ankyra'.
69 Paus. I, 7, 1.
70 Austin, 141.
71 Lucian, *Zeuxis*, 9 and *Pro Lapsu inter Salut.*, 8; Suda, s.v. Simonides; Wörrle 'Antiochos I', advocates a date for the battle just before the production of the inscription Austin, 141, dated to January 266. The argument is not conclusive, and 275 still fits the general international situation better. The 'Galatian War' of the inscription could well be an otherwise unknown war, marked by another victory, but the sense of the inscription does not require this. The peasants who commissioned the stone may simply have taken a long time to order it. If they were ravaged by the Galatians as they say, they may not have had the resources for several years.
72 Griffith, *Mercenaries*, 252–3 and see index s.v. 'Gauls'.
73 Memnon, 228a, 1–4; Str. XII, V, 1–2.
74 Lorton, 'Supposed Expedition'.

12 Saviour

1 Trogus, *Prologue*, XXVI; John of Antioch, 55 (= *FHG* IV, p. 558); Austin, 142.
2 Austin, 143.
3 Str. XIII, 4, 2.
4 Austin, 141.
5 E.g., Austin, 235, 236; Burstein, 97.

6 *CIG*, 4458, but not Austin, 139.
7 Pol. VII, 39.
8 See note 19 of chapter 8.
9 Naster, 'Fire-Alter or Fire-Tower?', 128–9.
10 Livy, XXXVIII, 16, 13–14.

BIBLIOGRAPHY

Adams W.L., 'Antipater and Cassander: Generalship on Restricted Resources in the Fourth Century', *The Ancient World*, 10, 1984, 79–88.
Anson E.M., 'Alexander's Hypaspists and the Argyraspids', *Historia* 30, 1981.
—— 'Diodorus and the Date of Triparadius', *AJP* 107, 1986, 208–17.
Atkinson K.C.T.,'The Seleucids and the Greek Cities of Western Asia Minor', *Antichthon* 2, 1968, 32–57.
Aucello E., 'La Politica dei Diadochi e l'Ultimatum del 314 av. Cr.', *Rivista di Filologia Classica* 85, 1957, 382–404.
Aymard A., 'Du Nouveau sur la Chronologie des Seleucides', *Revue des Etudes Anciens* 51, 1955, 102–12.
Badian E., 'The Administration of the Empire', *Greece and Rome* N.S. 12, 1965, 166–83.
—— 'A King's Notebooks', *Harvard Studies in Classical Philology* 72, 1968, 183–204.
Bagnall R.S., *The Administration of the Ptolemaic Possessions outside Egypt*, Leiden 1976.
Bar-Kochva B., *The Seleucid Army*, Cambridge 1976.
Bellinger A.R., 'Seleucid Dura, the Evidence of the Coins', *Berytus* 9, 1948, 51–67.
Bernard P., *Fouilles d'Ai Khanoum*, Paris 1973.
Berve H., *Das Alexanderreich aus prosopographischer Grundlage*, Munich 1926.
Bevan E.R., 'Note on the Command held by Seleukos 323–321 B.C.', *CR* 14, 1900, 396–8.
—— *The House of Seleucus*, 2 vols, London 1902.
—— *A History of Egypt under the Ptolemaic Dynasty*, London 1927.
Bi(c)kerman E.J., *Institutions des Séleucides*, Paris 1938.
—— 'Notes on Seleucid and Parthian Chronology', *Berytus* 8, 1944, 73–83.
—— 'The Seleucids and the Achaemenids', *Atti del Convegno sul Tema: La Persia e il Mondo Greco-Romano*, Accademia Nazionale dei Lincei, Rome 1966, 87–117.
—— *Chronology of the Ancient World*, London 1968.

Bosworth A.B., 'The Government of Syria under Alexander the Great', *CQ* N.S. 24, 1974, pp. 46–64.
—— 'The Death of Alexander the Great: Rumour and Propaganda', *CQ* N.S. 21, 1974, 112–36.
—— 'Alexander and the Iranians', *JHS* 100, 1980, 1–21.
—— 'The Indian Satrapies under Alexander the Great', *Antichthon* 17, 1983, 37–46.
—— 'Alexander the Great and the Decline of Macedon', *JHS* 106, 1986, 1–12.
—— *Conquest and Empire*, Cambridge 1988.
Bouché-Leclercq A., *Histoire des Lagides*, 4 vols, Paris, 1903–7.
—— *Histoire des Séleucides*, 2 vols, Paris 1914.
Briant P., *Antigone le Borgne*, Paris 1973.
—— 'Colonisation hellénistique et populations indigènes I, La Phase d'installation', *Klio* 60, 1978, 57–92; 'II, Renforts grecs dans les cités Hellénistiques d'Orient', *Klio* 64, 1982, 83–98.
Broderson K., 'Der Liebeskranke Königssohn und die Seleukidische Herrschaftsauffassung', *Athenaeum* N.S. 63, 1985, 459–69.
Cary M., *A History of the Greek World, 323–146 B.C.*, 2nd edn, London 1951.
Cawkwell G., *Philip of Macedon*, London 1978.
Chase G.H., 'Three Hellenistic Coins', *Bulletin of the Museum of Fine Arts, Boston* 46, 1948, 39–42.
Clay A.T., *Babylonian Records in the Library of J. Pierpont Morgan*, New York, 1913.
Cloché P., *La Dislocation d'un Empire*, Paris 1959.
Cohen G.M., 'The Diadochoi and the New Monarchies', *Athenaeum* N.S. 52, 1974, 177–9.
—— *The Seleucid Colonies: Studies in Founding, Administration and Organisation* (*Historia* Einzelschriften 30), Wiesbaden 1978.
Cook J.M., *The Troad*, Oxford 1973.
Corradi G., *Studi Ellenistici*, Turin 1929.
Dandamayev M., 'Achaemenid Babylonia', *Ancient Mesopotamia*, Moscow 1969, 296–311.
Davis N. and Kraay C.M., *The Hellenistic Kingdoms: Portrait Coins and History*, London 1973.
Delorme J., *Le Monde Hellénistique*, Paris 1975.
Devine A.M., 'Diodorus' Account of the Battle of Paraitacene (317 BC)', *The Ancient World* 12, 1985, 75–86.
Dillemann L., *Haute Mésopotamie Orientale et Pays Adjacents*, Paris 1962.
Droysen J.G., *Geschichte des Hellenismus* 3 vols, (new edn), Tubingen 1952–3.
Eddy S.K., *The King is Dead*, Lincoln, Nebraska 1961.
Edson C., 'Imperium Macedonicum: the Seleucid Empire and the Literary Evidence', *CP* 53, 1958, 153–70.
Ehrenberg V., *Alexander and the Greeks*, tr. R.F. von Velsen, Oxford 1938.
Ellis J.R., *Philip II and Macedonian Imperialism*, London 1976.

BIBLIOGRAPHY

Engel R., *Untersuchungen zum Machtaufstieg des Antigonos I Monophthalamos*, Kallmunz über Regensburg, 1976(?).
Engels D.W., *Alexander the Great and the Logistics of the Macedonian Army*, Berkeley and Los Angeles 1978.
Errington R.M., 'From Babylon to Triparadeisos: 323–320 B.C.', *JHS* 90, 1970, 49–77.
—— 'Alexander in the Hellenistic World', in *Alexandre le Grand, Image et Réalité*, Entretiens Hardt 22, Geneva 1976, 137–79.
—— 'Diodorus Siculus and the Chronology of the Early Diadochoi, 320–311 B.C.', *Hermes* 105, 1977, 478–504.
—— 'The Nature of the Macedonian State under the Monarchy', *Chiron* 8, 1978, 77–133.
Fard K., 'Kangavar', *Iran* 11, 1973, 196–7.
Fontana M.J., *La Lotte per il successione di Alessandro Magno dal 323 al 315*, Palermo 1960.
Fonterose J.E., *Didyma, Apollo's Oracle, Cult and Companions*, Berkeley, California 1988.
Fortina M., *Cassandro re di Macedonia*, Turin 1965.
Fox R.L., *Alexander of Macedon*, Harmondsworth 1974.
Francfort H.P., *Les Fortifications en Asie Centrale de l'Age du Bronze à l'epoque kouchane*, Paris 1979.
Fraser P.M., *Ptolemaic Alexandria*, Oxford 1972.
—— 'The Son of Aristonax at Kandahar', *Afghan Studies* 2, 1979, 9–22.
Frézouls E., 'Sur les Divisions de la Séleucide à propos de Strabon XVI, 2', *Mélanges de l'Université St Joseph* 37, 1960, 223–34.
—— 'La Toponymie de l'Orient Syrien et l'Apport des Elements Macedoniens', *La Toponymie Antique: Actes du Colloque de Strasbourg*, 12–14 Juin 1975, 219–48.
Frumkin G., *Archaeology in Soviet Central Asia* (Handbuch der Orientalistik, Abt 7, Band 3, Abschnitt 1), Leiden 1970.
Fuller J.F.C., *The Generalship of Alexander the Great*, London 1958.
Funck B., *Uruk zur Seleukidenreich*, Berlin 1984.
—— 'Die Babylonische Chronik Smith (BM 34 660 and BM 36 313) als Quelle des Diadochenkampfes (321–306 v. Chr)', *In Memoriam E. Unger: Beiträge zu Geschichte Kultur und Religion des Alten Orients*, ed. M. Lurker, Baden-Baden, 1971, 217–40.
—— 'Zur Innenpolitik des Seleukos Nikator', *Acta Antiqua* 22, 1974, 505–20.
Furlani G. and Momigliano A., 'La cronaca babilonese sui Diadochi', *Rivista di Filologia e d'Istruzione Classica* N.S. 10, 1932, 462–84.
Gattinoni F.L., 'La pace del 311 A.C.', *Contributi dell'Istituto di Storia Antica* 9, 1985, 108–18.
Ghirshman R., *Iran from the Earliest Times to the Islamic Conquest*, Harmondsworth 1954.
Gorbunova N.G., *The Culture of Ancient Ferghana, VI century B.C.–VI century A.D.*, tr. A.P. Andryushkin, (BAR International Series 281), Oxford 1986.
Grainger J.D., *The Seleucid Cities of Syria*, Oxford (1990).

Green P., *Alexander the Great*, London 1970.
Griffith G.T., *The Mercenaries of the Hellenistic World*, Cambridge 1935.
Grimal P. et al., *Hellenism and the Rise of Rome*, London 1968.
Gruen E.S., 'The Coronation of the Diadochoi', *The Craft of the Ancient Historian, Essays in Honor of G.C. Starr*, ed. J.W. Eadie and J. Ober, Lanham, Maryland 1985, 253–71.
Hadas M., *Hellenistic Culture, Fusion and Diffusion*, New York 1959.
Hadley R.A., 'Hieronymus of Cardia and Early Seleucid Mythology', *Historia* 18, 1969, 142–52.
—— 'Royal Propaganda of Seleucus I and Lysimachus', *JHS* 94, 1974, 50–65.
—— 'The Foundation Date of Seleuceia-on-the-Tigris', *Historia* 27, 1978, 228ff.
Hambly G. et al., *Central Asia*, London 1969.
Hamilton J.R., *Alexander the Great*, London 1973.
Hammond N.G.L., *Alexander the Great*, London 1980.
—— *Three Historians of Alexander the Great*, Cambridge 1983.
—— and Griffith, G.T. *A History of Macedonia*, II, Oxford 1979.
Hansen E.V., *The Attalids of Pergamum*, 2nd edn, Ithaca 1971.
Hart G.D., 'The Diagnosis of Disease from Ancient Coins', *Archaeology* 26, part 2, 1973, 123–7.
Hauben H., *Callicrates of Samos*, Louvain 1970.
—— 'On the Chronology of the Years 313–311 B.C.', *AJP* 94, 1973, 256–67.
—— 'A Royal Toast in 302 B.C.', *Ancient Society* 5, 1974, 105–17.
—— 'The First War of the Successors (321 B.C.): Chronological and Historical Problems', *Ancient Society* 8, 1977, 85–120.
—— 'Rhodes, Alexander and the Diadochi from 333/332 to 304 B.C.', *Historia* 26, 1977, 308–39.
—— 'Philokles, King of the Sidonians and General of the Ptolemies', *Studia Phoenicia V*, ed. E. Lipinski, Leuven 1987, 413–28.
Head B.V., *Historia Numorum*, 2nd edn, Oxford 1911.
Heckel W., 'The Career of Antigenes', *Symbolae Osloenses* 57, 1982, 57–67.
—— *The Last Days and Testament of Alexander the Great: A Prosopographical Study* (*Historia* Einzelschriften 56), Stuttgart 1988.
Heinen H., *Untersuchungen zur Geschichte des 3 Jahrhunderts v. Chr.*, Wiesbaden 1972.
Helms S.W., 'Excavations at ... Kandahar', *Afghan Studies* 3 and 4, 1982, 1–25.
Hill G., *A History of Cyprus*, Cambridge 1940.
Holt F.L., *Alexander the Great and Bactria*, Leiden 1988.
Hopkins C., *Topography and Architecture of Seleuceia on the Tigris*, Ann Arbor, Michigan 1972.
Hornblower J., *Hieronymus of Cardia*, Oxford 1985.
Houghton A., 'Notes on the Early Seleucid Victory Coinage of "Persepolis" ', *Schweitzer Numismatische Rundschau* 59, 1980, 5–14.
—— 'Some Far Northeastern Seleucid Mints', *ANSMN* 29, 1981, 1–9.

BIBLIOGRAPHY

Joannes F., 'Les Successeurs d'Alexandre le Grand en Babylonie', *Anatolica* 7, 1979–80, 99–115.
Jones A.H.M., *The Greek City from Alexander to Justinian*, Oxford 1940.
—— *The Cities of the Eastern Roman Provinces*, 2nd edn, Oxford 1971.
Kahrstedt U., *Syrische Territorien in Hellenistischer Zeit*, Gottingen 1926.
Keil B., 'Korou Pedion', *Revue de Philologie* 26, 1902, 257ff.
Keil J. and Premerstein, von A., *Bericht über eine zweite Reise in Lydien*, Vienna 1911.
Kertesz I., 'Ptolemy I and the Battle of Gaza', *Studia Aegyptica* 1, 1974, 231–41.
Krom N.J., 'Seleukos und Candragupta', *Hermes* 44, 1909, 154 sqq.
Kuhrt A. and Sherwin-White S.M., *Hellenism in the East*, London 1988.
Kuschke A. et al., *Archäologischer Survey in der Nördliche Biqa'*, Wiesbaden 1976.
Le Rider G., *Suse sur les Séleucides et les Parthes*, Paris 1965.
Levêque P., *Le Monde Hellénistique*, Paris 1969.
Levick B., *Roman Colonies in Southern Asia Minor*, Oxford 1967.
Lock R.A., 'The Origins of the Argyraspids', *Historia* 26, 1977, 373–8.
Lorton D., 'The Supposed Expedition of Ptolemy II to Persia', *Journal of Egyptian Archaeology* 57, 1971, 160–4.
McNicoll A., 'Some Developments in Hellenistic Siege Warfare with Special Reference to Asia Minor', *Proceedings of the 10th International Congress of Classical Archaeologists*, Ankara 1978, 405–20.
McShane R., *The Foreign Policy of the Attalids of Pergamum*, Urbana, Illinois 1964.
Magie D., *Roman Rule in Asia Minor*, Princeton, N.J., 1950.
Mahaffy J.P., *Alexander's Empire*, London 1887.
Manni E., *Demetrio Poliorcete*, Rome 1951.
Marasco G., 'La Fondazione dell'Impero di Seleuco I: Espansione Territoriale e Indirizzi Politici', *Rivista Storica Italiana* 96, 1988, 301–37.
Marinoni E., 'La Capitale del Regno di Seleuco I', *Rendiconti dell'Istituto Lombardo* 106, 1972, 579–631.
Mastrocinque A., *La Caria e l'Ionia Meridionale in Epoca Ellenistica*, Rome 1979.
—— 'Storia e Monetazione di Mileto all'Epoca dei Diadochi', *Annali Istituto Italiano de Numismatica* 27–8, 1980–1, 61–7.
—— 'Osservazione sui Rapporti tra i Diadochi e le Citta d'Asia Minore', *Xenia: Scritti in Onore di Piero Treves*, Rome 1985, 121–8.
Matheson S.A., *Persia, an Archaeological Guide*, London 1976.
Mehl A., *Seleukos Nikator und sein Reich*, Louvain 1986.
Merker I.L., 'The Ptolemaic Officials and the League of the Islanders', *Historia* 19, 1970, 141–60.
—— 'Demetrios Poliorketes and Tyre', *Ancient Society* 5, 1974, 119–26.
Merritt B.D., 'Inscriptions of Colophon', *AJP* 56, 1935, 377 sqq.

Meyer E., 'Die Makedonischen Militärcolonien', *Hermes* 33, 1898, 643–7.
Moraux P., 'L'établissement des Galates en Asie Mineure', *Istanbuler Mitteillungen* 7, 1957, 56–75.
Morkholm O., 'Cyrene and Ptolemy I', *Chiron* 10, 1980, 145–59.
Muller O., *Antigonos Monophthalamos und 'Das Jahr des Könige'. Untersuchungen zur Begründung der Hellenistischen Monarchien, 306–304 v. Chr.*, Bonn 1973.
Musti D., 'Aspetti dell'organizzazione seleucidica in Asia Minore nel IIIo sec. a.C.', *La Parola del Passato* 20, 1965, 153–60.
—— 'Lo Stato dei Seleucidi', *Studi Classici e Orientali* 15, 1968, 61–197.
Narain A.K., *The Indo-Greeks*, Oxford, 1957.
—— 'Alexander and India', *Greece and Rome* N.S. 12, 1965, 155–65.
Naster P., 'Note d'Épigraphie Monetaire de Perside: Fratakara, Frataraka ou Fratadara?', *Iranica Antiqua* 8, 1968, 74–80.
—— 'Fire-Alter or Fire-Tower on the Coins of Persis?', *Orientalia Lovanensia* 1, 1970, 125–9.
Newell E.T., *The Coinage of the Eastern Seleucid Mints*, New York 1938.
—— *The Coinage of the Western Seleucid Mints*, New York 1941.
Olmstead A.T., 'Cuneiform Texts and Hellenistic Chronology', *CP* 32, 1937, 1–14.
Olshausen E., *Prosopographie der Hellenistischen Königsgesandten*, vol. 1, Louvain 1974.
Orth W., *Königlicher Machtansprung und städtische Freiheit*, Munich 1977.
Otto W., *Beiträge zur Seleukidengeschichte des 3 Jh. v. Chr.*, Munich 1928.
Parke H.W., *The Oracles of Apollo in Asia Minor*, Beckenham, Kent, 1985.
Parker R.A. and Dubberstein W.H., *Babylonian Chronology 626 B.C.– A.D. 75*, Providence, R.I., 1956.
Pearson L., *The Lost Historians of Alexander the Great*, Philadelphia 1960.
Powell J.U., *Collectanea Alexandria*, London 1925.
Préaux C., 'Les Villes Hellénistique Principalement en Orient, leurs Institutions Administratives et Judiciaires', *Receuils de la Société Jean Bodin VI, La Ville*, Bruxelles 1954, 69–134.
—— *Le Monde Hellénistique*, Paris 1978.
Rapson E.J. (ed.), *Ancient India*, vol. 1 of *Cambridge History of India*, Cambridge 1922.
Rey-Coquais J.P., *Arados et sa Perée*, Paris 1974.
Richter G.M., *The Portraits of the Greeks*, 3 vols, London 1965.
Robert L., 'Monnaie de Troade', *Études de Numismatique Grecque*, Paris 1951.
—— 'Inscription Hellénistique d'Iran', *Hellenica* XI–XII, Paris 1960, 85–91.
—— *Villes d'Asie Mineure*, 2nd edn, Paris 1962.

BIBLIOGRAPHY

―― 'Pline VI, 49, Démodamas de Milet et la Reine Apame', *Bulletin de Correspondence Hellénique* 108, 1984, 467–72.
―― and Robert J., *La Carie*, 2 vols, Paris 1954.
Rodgers W.L., *Greek and Roman Naval Warfare*, Annapolis, Maryland 1937.
Ronzevalle S., 'Les Monnaies de la Dynastie de Abd-Hadad et les Cultes de Hierapolis-Bambyke', *Mélanges de l'Université Saint-Josephe* 23, 1942, 1–82.
Rostovtzeff M.I., 'Seleucid Babylonia', *Yale Classical Studies* 3, 1932, 1–144.
―― 'Some Remarks on the Monetary and Commercial Policy of the Seleucids and Attalids', *Anatolian Studies presented to W.H. Buckler*, Manchester 1937, 277–98.
―― 'The Foundation of Dura-Europus', *Annales de l'Institut Kondakov* 10, 1938, 99–106.
―― *Social and Economic History of the Hellenistic World*, Oxford 1941.
Roueché C. and Sherwin-White S.M., 'Some Aspects of the Seleucid Empire: the Greek Inscriptions from Failaka in the Arabian Gulf', *Chiron* 15, 1985, 1–39.
Roussel P., 'Decret des Péliganes de Laodicée-sur-Mer', *Syria* 23, 1942–3, 21–32.
Sachs A.J. and Wiseman D.J., 'A Babylonian King List of the Hellenistic Period', *Iraq* 16, 1954, 202–11.
Samuel A.E., 'Alexander's Royal Journals', *Historia* 14, 1965, 1–12.
Sarkisian O.K., 'City Land in Seleucid Babylonia', *Ancient Mesopotamia*, Moscow 1969, 312–31.
Scharfe H., 'The Maurya Dynasty and the Seleucids', *Zeitschrift fur Vergleichende Sprachforshung* 85, 1971, 211–25.
Schmitt H.H., *Die Staatsverträge des Altertums*, vol. III, Munich 1969.
Schober L., *Untersuchungen zur Geschichte Babyloniens und der Oberen Satrapien von 323–303 v. Chr.*, Frankfort-am-Main, 1981.
Schulten A., 'Die Makedonischen Militärcolonien', *Hermes* 32, 1897, 523–37.
Sedlar J.W., *India and the Greek World*, Totowa, N.J., 1980.
Seibert J., *Historische Beiträge zu den Dynastischen Verbindungen in Hellenistischer Zeit* (*Historia* Einzelschriften 10), Wiesbaden 1967.
―― *Untersuchungen zur Geschichte Ptolemaios I*, Munich 1969.
―― 'Ptolemaios I und Milet', *Chiron* I, 1971, 159–66.
―― *Das Zeitalter der Diadochen*, Darmstadt 1983.
Seyrig H., 'Arados et sa Perée sous les Rois Seleucides', *Syria* 28, 1951, 206–17.
―― 'Seleucos I et la Fondation de la Monarchie Syrienne', *Syria* 47, 1970, 290–311.
―― 'Le Monnayage de Hierapolis de Syrie à l'Epoque d'Alexandre', *Revue Numismatique* 11, 1971, 11–21.
Sherwin-White S.M., 'A Greek Ostrakon from Babylon of the Early Third Century B.C.', *Zeitschrift fur Papyrologie und Epigrafik* 47, 1982, 51–70.

Shipley G., *A History of Samos*, Oxford 1987.
Simpson R.H., 'The Historical Circumstances of the Peace of 311', *JHS* 72, 1952, 26–31.
—— 'Antigonus the One-Eyed and the Greeks', *Historia* 8, 1959, 385–409.
Skeat T.C., *The Reigns of the Ptolemies* 2nd edn, Munich 1969.
Skurzak L., 'Le traite Syro-Indien de Paix en 305, selon Strabon et Appien d'Alexandrie', *Eos* 54, 1964, 225ff.
Smelik K.A.D., 'The "Omina Mortis" in the Histories of Alexander the Great', *Talanta* 10–11, 1978–9, 92–111.
Smith L.C., 'The Chronology of Books XVIII–XX of Diodorus Siculus', *AJP* 82, 1961, 283–90.
Smith S., 'The Chronology of Philip Arrhidaeus, Antigonus and Alexander IV', *Revue d'Assyriologie* 22, 1925, 179–97.
Smith V.A., *The Oxford History of India*, 3rd edn by P. Spear, Oxford 1958.
Spyridakis S., *Ptolemaic Itanos and Hellenistic Crete*, Berkeley, California 1970.
Stronach D., *Pasargadae*, Oxford 1971.
Tarn W.W., *Antigonos Gonatas*, Oxford 1913.
—— 'The First Syrian War', *JHS* 46, 1926, 155–62.
—— 'The Proposed New Date for Ipsus', *CR* 40, 1926, 13–15.
—— 'Ptolemy II and Arabia', *Journal of Egyptian Archaeology* 15, 1929, 9–25.
—— *Hellenistic Military and Naval Developments*, Cambridge 1930.
—— 'Two Notes on Seleucid History', *JHS* 60, 1940, 84–94.
—— *Alexander the Great*, 2 vols, Cambridge 1948.
—— *The Greeks in Bactria and India*, 2nd edn, Cambridge 1951.
—— and Griffith, G.T. *Hellenistic Civilisation*, 3rd edn, London 1952.
Thapar, R. *Asoka and the Decline of the Mauryas*, Oxford 1961.
—— *A History of India*, vol. 1, Harmondsworth 1966.
Thompson W.E., 'PSI 1284: Eumenes of Cardia vs. the Phalanx', *Chronique d'Egypte* 59, 1984, 113–20.
Wacholder B.Z., 'The Beginning of the Seleucid Era and the Chronology of the Didachi', in *Nourished with Peace, Studies in Hellenistic Judaism in Memory of Samuel Sandonel*, Chico, California 1984, 183–211.
Waggoner N.M., 'The Early Alexander Coinage at Seleuceia on the Tigris', *ANSMN* 15, 1969, 21–30.
Wagner J., *Seleukeia am Euphrat/Zeugma*, Wiesbaden 1974.
Walbank F.W., *The Hellenistic World*, London 1981.
Wehrli C., *Antigone et Demetrios*, Geneva 1969.
Welles C.B., 'Hellenistic Tarsus', *Mélanges de l'Université Saint-Josephe* 38, 1962, 3–34.
—— *Alexander and the Hellenistic World*, Toronto 1970.
Westlake H.D., 'Eumenes of Cardia', *Greek Historians and Greek History*, Manchester 1969, 313–30.
Wilcken U., *Alexander the Great*, trans. G.C. Richards, introduction by E.N. Borza, London 1967.

BIBLIOGRAPHY

Will E., *Histoire Politique du Monde Hellénistique*, vol. 1, Nancy 1979.
Wolski J., 'L'effrondrement de la domination des Séleucides en Iran en IIIe siècle av. J.C.', *Bulletin de l'Académie Polonaise*, Cracow 1947, 22–31.
—— 'Les Iraniens et le royaume greco-bactrien', *Klio* 38, 1960, 110–21.
—— 'Le Problème de la Fondation de l'État Greco-Baktrien', *Iranica Antiqua* 17, 1982, 131–46.
Wörrle M., 'Antiochos I, Achaios der Altëre und die Galater', *Chiron* 5, 1975, 59–87.

(i) **Certain**

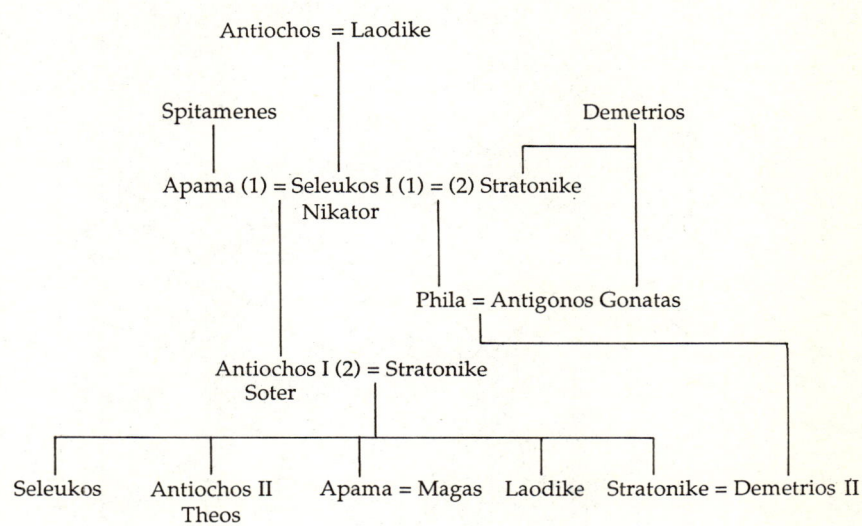

(ii) **Conjectural** (as Berve)

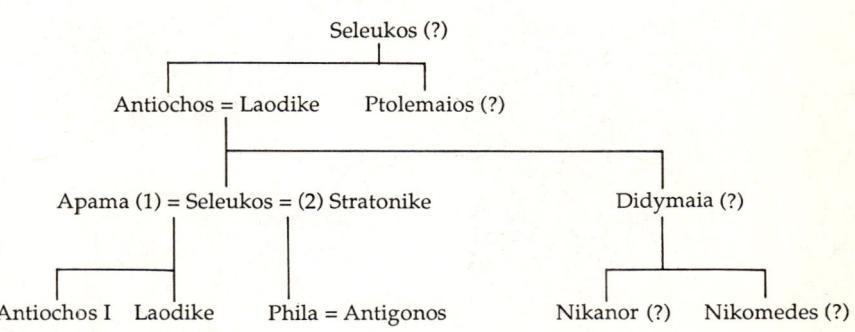

Genealogy of Seleukos and Antiochos

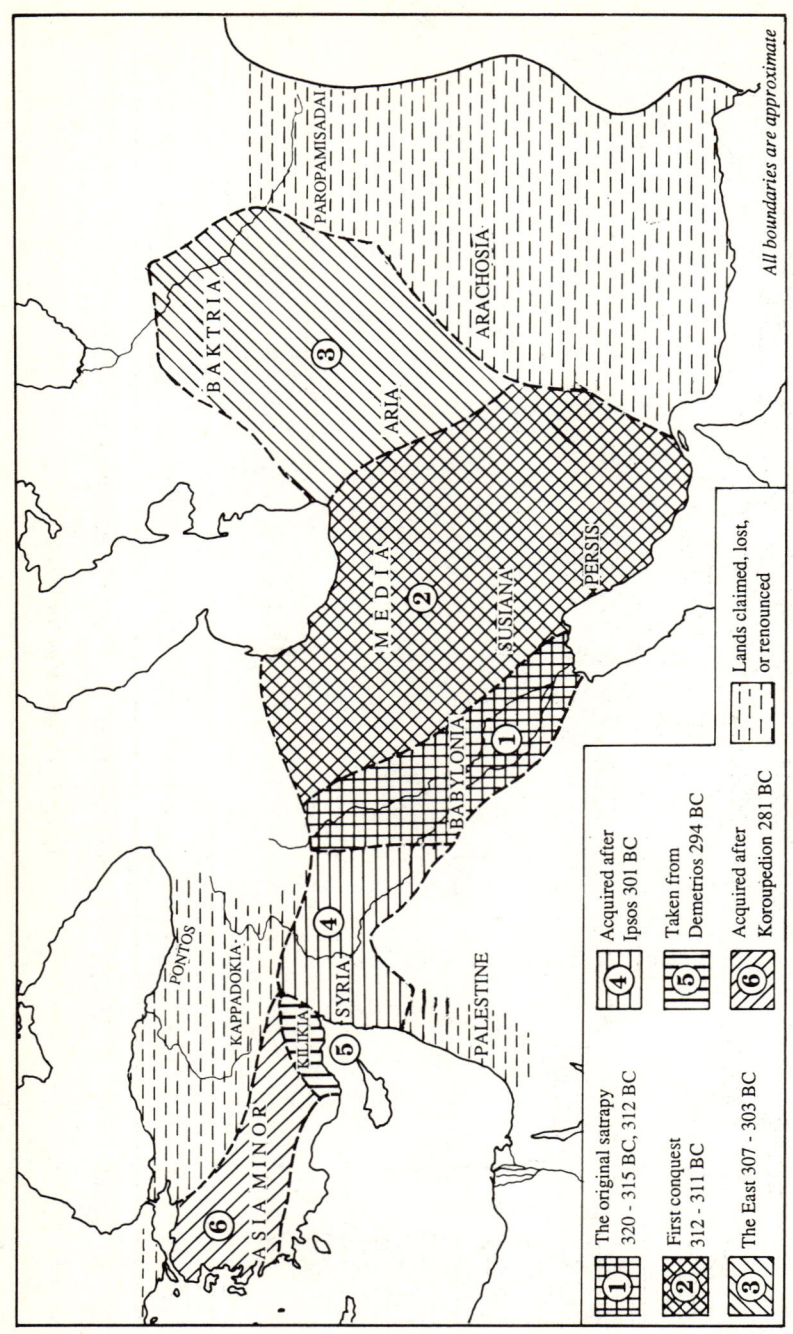

Map 1 The Growth of Seleukos' Kingdom

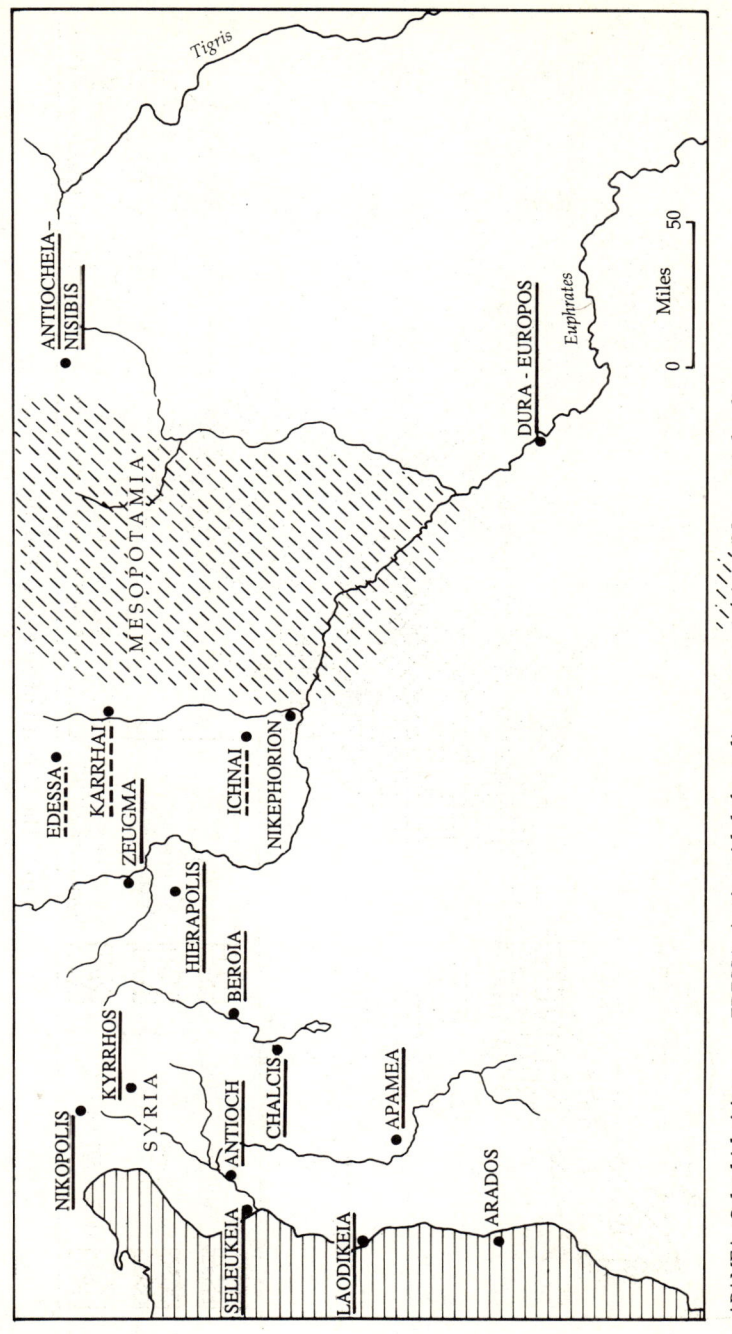

APAMEA Seleukid cities   EDESSA Antigonid defence line   //// 'No-man's land'

Map 2 Syria and Mesopotamia

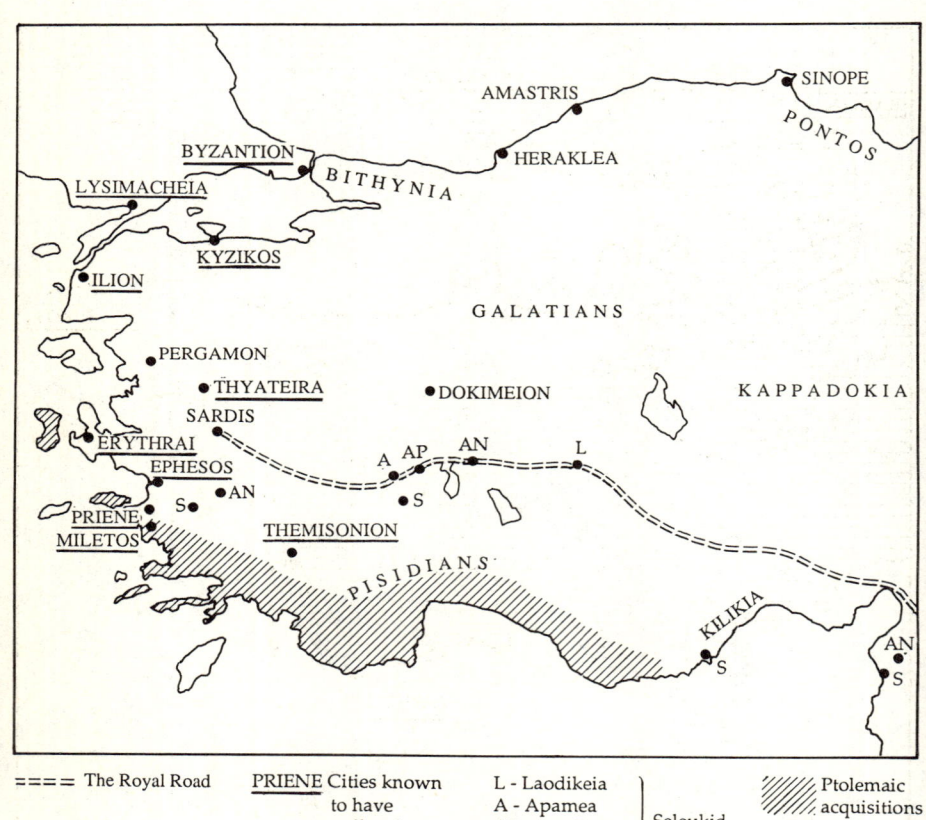

Map 3 Asia Minor c. 275 BC

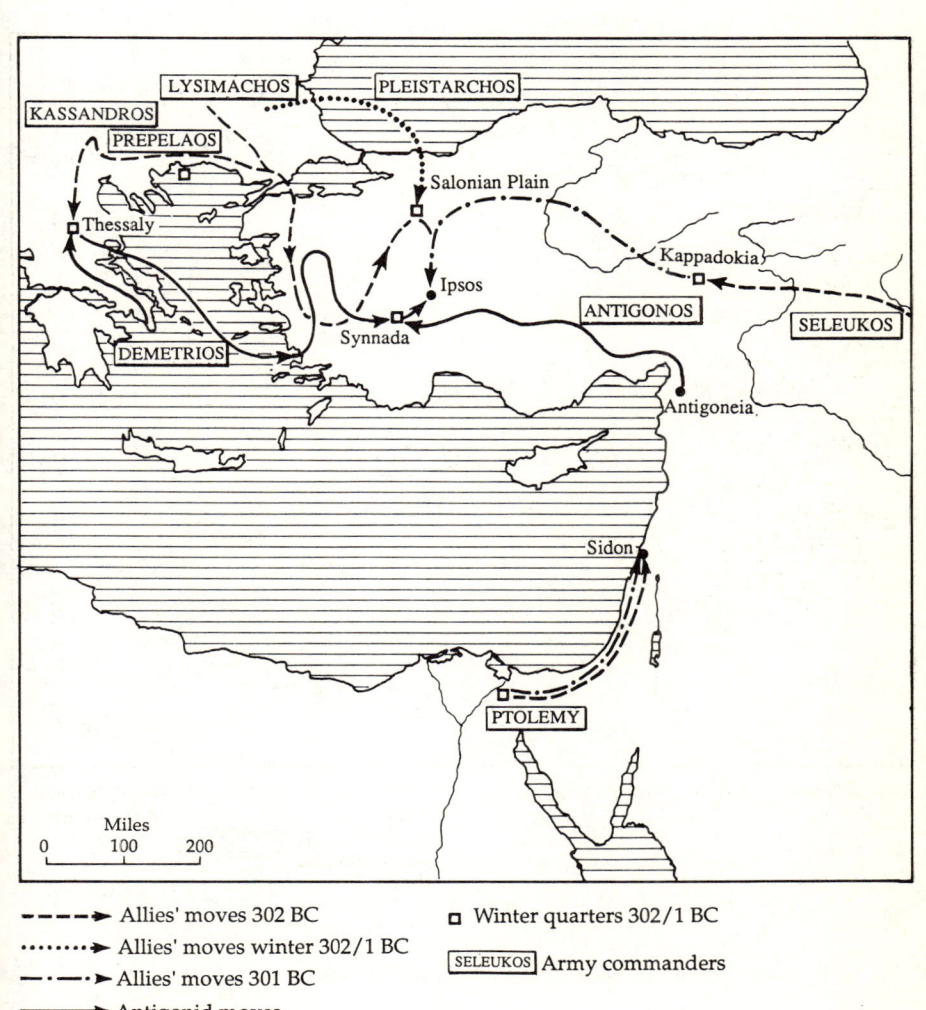

Map 4 The Campaigns of Ipsos

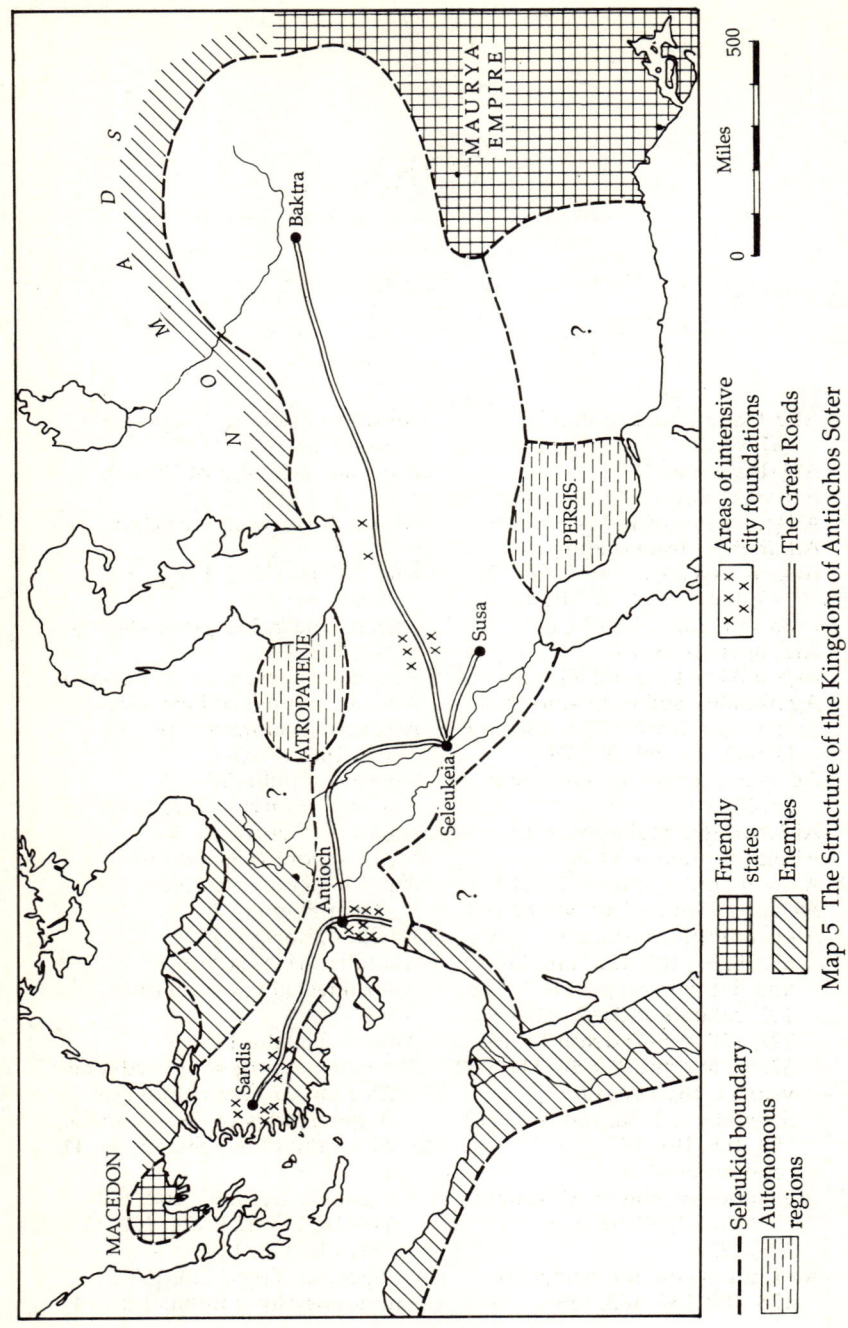

Map 5 The Structure of the Kingdom of Antiochos Soter

INDEX

Abd-Hadad, lord of Bambyke 147
Abydos, Troas 162
Acharea, shrine 185
Adea, see Eurydike
Adiabene, Mesopotamia 135
Aegean Sea 66, 67, 68–9, 86, 121, 143, 144, 196–7, 201; Ptolemies and 91, 187, 190, 195, 201
Afghanistan 88, 108
Agathokles, king of Sicily 112
Agathokles, son of Lysimachos 159, 182; death 177–9, 180; and Demetrios 169–70, 176
Agesilaos, envoy of Antigonos 56, 63
Ai-Khanum, Afghanistan 151
Aitolia, Aitolians 59, 63
Akhaimenid empire 192–3, 217
Akhaios, lord in Asia Minor 163
Alexander III, the Great 1, 7, 19, 69, 79, 97, 103, 137, 146, 216; and Babylonian priests 31, 32, 101; catafalque 21–2; cities of 127, 128, 155–7; death 14–15, 32, 62; and India 9–10, 111; last year 11–16; model for Seleukos 1, 2, 80, 100, 104, 110, 153, 166, 181, 192, 217; reputation 61–2
Alexander IV, son of Alexander III 34, 50–1, 60, 62–3, 93, 102, 103, 127
Alexander, son of Lysimachos 178, 180, 182, 183, 189

Alexander, son of Polyperchon 59–60, 63
Alexandria-by-Egypt 32, 102, 127, 177
Alexandria-Eschate, Baktria 155–7, 214
Alexandria (Kandahar), Arachosia 151
Alexandria-in-Margiane (Merv) 149, 155–7
Alexandria Troas, see Antigoneia
Alketas, brother of Perdikkas 21
Amanus, mountains 118, 140, 143, 160, 171–2
Amaseia, Pontos 184
Amastris, Bithynia 202, 203
Amathos, Cyprus 57, 64
Amisos, Pontos 56, 58, 161
Amphimachos, satrap of Mesopotamia 37
Amyzon, Karia 187
Anatolia, see Asia Minor
Androkles, king of Amathos 57, 64
Ankyra, Galatia 185
Antigenes, assassin of Perdikkas 22–3, 36, 37; commander of Argyraspides 28, 39; death 43, 44; satrap of Susiana 28, 36, 41, 43
Antigoneia, Syria 95, 100, 102, 115–16, 117, 123, 124, 126, 127, 129, 131, 141, 190
Antigoneia, Troas 123, 163
Antigonos Monophthalamos 14,

INDEX

15, 18, 24, 80, 108, 192, 218–19; ambition 53–5, 87, 104, 114; and Asia Minor 15, 40, 56, 115, 196–7; and Babylon 40, 46–51, 88; cities founded by 95, 98–100, 123, 127; and Cyprus 57, 69–70, 112; and Eumenes 27, 30–1, 34, 35–6, 40–5, 89; deposes Seleukos at Babylon 48–51; eastern settlement 46–7, 81, 104, 149; and Kassandros 55–6, 59, 62, 69, 70, 114–16; king 102, 112–13; in Media 42–4, 51; peace negotiations 67–8, 70, 85–7, 93; and Peithon 40, 44–5; power 88; proclamation at Tyre 59–60; propaganda 60–3, 218–19; quarrel with Perdikkas 21; satrap of Phrygia 21, 27, 49; and Seleukos 77–8, 82–5, 86, 90–4, 97, 103, 134, 216; at Triparadisos 26–7; and western satraps/kings 55–86, 115–21; wealth 56

Antigonos Gonatas, son of Demetrios 173–4, 177, 181, 182, 196, 200; and Antiochos I 203, 207–8; and Macedon 200, 203, 206, 207–8; and Northern League 202

Antilebanon, mountains 158

Antioch, Susiana 150

Antioch, Syria 127–8, 129, 130–1

'Antiochia Arabis' 96

Antiochia-in-Margiane, *see* Alexandria-in-Margiane

Antioch-in-Persis 214

Antioch-in-Scythia, *see* Alexandria-Eschate

Antiochia-Tarmita, Baktria 155–6

Antiochos, father of Seleukos 2

Antiochos I Soter, son of Seleukos 2, 12, 52, 106, 122, 139, 140, 164, 170, 173, 177, 179, 182, 209, 216; achievements 211–12; and Antigonos Gonatas 203, 207–8, 210; and Asia Minor 193, 195, 196–7, 208–10; and Bithynia 196, 199–200; empire of 214–15; and Eumenes of Pergamon 211; executes son 211; founds cities 155–6, 214; and India 213; and Macedon 196, 200, 203, 207–8; marriage 152–3, 155, 173; and Miletos 185; and Northern League 202; and Ptolemy II 196–7, 201, 207, 208–10; and Ptolemy Keraunos 201; ruler of the east 97, 135–6, 152–3, 155–7; and succession 193, 195–6; and Syria 196–9

Antiochos II, Seleukid king 186, 211

Antiochos III, Seleukid king 107, 129, 216

Antiochos VII, Seleukid king 216

Antipatros, Macedonian regent 15, 17, 18, 21–2, 24, 42, 59, 63; death 34; at Triparadisos 25–8, 37, 49

Antipatros, satrap of Hellespontine Phrygia 204

Antony, Mark, Roman triumvir 110

Apama, daughter of Antiochos I, wife of Magas 208

Apama, daughter of Spitamenes wife of Seleukos 11–12, 52, 106, 128, 139, 140, 145, 152, 165, 166

Apamea-Kelainai, Phrygia, 186, 205

Apamea, Syria 124, 127–8, 158–9, 173

Apamea (Zeugma), Syria 128

Aphrodisios, envoy of Seleukos 184, 188

Apollo, and Seleukos 2–4, 163–4; oracle of, at Didyma 3, 106, 140, 163, 166, 183, 188, 190, 205, 216

Apollodoros, tyrant of Kassandreia 203

Apollonia, Phrygia 186

Arabia 89, 96

Arachosia 34, 42, 46, 108, 112,

INDEX

213
Arados, Syria 125–6, 127, 132, 141, 146–7, 198
Archelaos, commander in Babylon 85, 88, 90
Archon, satrap of Babylon 18, 29–31, 33
Areus, king of Sparta 202
'Argos' 190
Argyraspides, Macedonian regiment 22, 28, 34, 36–9, 44, 46–7
Aria 34, 47, 77; Evagoras satrap 47, 79, 84, 104; Seleukos and 80–1, 83, 88, 104, 108
Ariarathes of Kappadokia 20, 21
Ariarathids 212
Aristonous, Macedonian general 17
Aristoteles, commander 69
Armenia 170
Arnaia, Lykia 187
Arrhidaios, Macedonian soldier 21–2, 27; *epimeletes* 24–6
Arsacids 107
Arsinoe, Pamphylia 187
Arsinoe, daughter of Ptolemy I 185, 187, 195; and Lysimachos 132, 178–9, 180; in Macedon 183, 189, 202; and Ptolemy II 206–8; and Ptolemy Keraunos 193, 200
Artemidoros of Miletos, envoy of Antigonos 57–9, 62, 63
Asandros, satrap of Karia 27, 58–9, 63, 69
Asia Minor 15, 40, 56, 115, 194–5; Antigonos in 55, 68, 95, 124; Antiochos and 193, 195, 196–7, 208–10; 213–14; Galatians in 204–7, 209–10, 213–14; Lysimachos and 121, 158, 160–2, 165, 170, 178–9, 180–1, 215; Ptolemy I and 86, 91, 93, 187; satrapies of, at Triparadisos 27, 28; Seleukos and 159, 163–6, 183–8, 189, 216
Aspisas, satrap of Susiana 48
Atargatis, goddess 147, 166

Athens 5, 6, 34, 100, 114, 123, 143, 196
Atropatene 137, 150
Atropates, satrap of Media 137, 149
Attalos, brother-in-law of Perdikkas 25, 61, 218–19
Attika 168, 169
Autophradates, governor of Persis 213

Babylon 10, 13–14, 17, 19, 37, 97, 214; and Antigonos 40, 48–51, 88; Archelaos, commander 5, 88, 90; Archon satrap 18, 29–31, 33; conference 14–20, 22, 60–3; decline 146, 190; Demetrios attacks 82–5; Dokimos satrap 29–30; and Eumenes 38–40; Peithon satrap 54–5; priesthood 31–2, 49, 83, 100–2, 146; Seleukos and 28, 30–4, 48–52, 54, 55, 72–5, 77, 100–2, 112–13, 117
Babylonia 11, 13, 37, 80, 86, 116, 150, 153, 196; character 28–9, 145; chronicle 30, 32, 38, 50, 88–9, 90, 92; colonists in 31, 146; economy 31–2, 211; Eumenes and 35; Seleukos and 74, 79–80, 104, 135, 137, 145, 157, 192; taxation 208; war in 82–5, 88–9, 92, 94
Bagadat, governor of Persis 213
Baktra, Baktria 151
Baktria 7, 12, 15, 35, 127, 148, 150, 196, 209, 213, 214; coins 216; kingdom 216; possible invasion 155–7; rebellion 20, 22; Seleukos and 81, 105–7, 109, 112, 116, 135, 137, 150–2, 154, 171; Stasanor satrap 34, 47, 81, 103, 127, 135
Balikh, river 98
Bambyke, *see* Hierapolis
Bargylus, mountains 158
Berenike, wife of Ptolemy I 170, 175
Beroia, Syria 128–9, 137

INDEX

Bindusara Maurya, Indian emperor 213
Biqaa valley 74, 158
Bithynia 181, 193, 213; and Antiochos I 196, 199–200; civil war 193, 200, 204
Black Sea 119, 161
Blitor, satrap of Mesopotamia 51
Boiotia 86
Borsippa, Babylonia 92
Bosporos, strait 56, 203, 204
Buddhism 216
Byblos, Phoenicia 57
Byzantion, Thrace 184, 203, 204

Calchedon, Bithynia 184
Caspian Sea 153
Central Asia 88, 105, 116, 148, 151–2
Chalkidene, Syria 135
Chalkidike, Macedonia 6
Chalkis, Syria 124, 126, 128–9
Chandragupta Maurya, Indian emperor 107–12, 116, 145, 152, 154
Charakene, Babylonia 135
Charax, Babylonia 150
Cheiles, satrap of Persis 148, 213
chiliarchy 18–20
Chios 187, 195, 201
colonists, in Babylonia 31; in Central Asia 105–6; in Media 149
Concobar (Kangaver), Media 149
Corinth 93, 116, 122, 169, 200; League of 7
Crete 186
Cutha, Babylonia 33
Cyprus 34, 47, 77; and Antigonos 57, 69–70, 112; and Demetrios 132, 140, 141–2; and Ptolemy I 57, 58–9, 63, 69–70, 91, 93, 97, 102, 143–4, 167; Seleukos in 58–9, 63–6

Damascus, Syria 22, 29, 83, 209, 210
Damietta, Egypt 22
Dareios the Great, Persian emperor 164
Dasht-i-Lut, Iran 117
Delphi 101
Demetrios Poliorketes, son of Antigonos 91, 151, 163, 192; and Babylon 82–5; and Cyprus 132, 140, 141–2; defeat at Gaza 71–2; and Kilikia 133, 140, 141–2, 169–71, 172; king 112; and Macedon 160, 165, 167–8; prisoner 173–7; and Syria 82, 85, 141–2, 157–8; victory at Salamis 95; war in Greece 92, 100, 114, 143–4; war with Lysimachos 122, 124, 126, 132, 143–4, 160, 169–71, 174–5; war with Seleukos 76–7, 82–5, 89, 90, 97, 170–2
Demetrios I, Seleukid king 216
Demodamas, Seleukid general 154, 164
Demophon, seer 61, 218–19
Didyma, see Apollo
Didymeia, purported sister of Seleukos 3–4
Diodoros, Seleukid general 214
Diodotos, satrap of Baktria 135
Dion, governor of Damascus 209
Dioskorides, nephew of Antigonos 66–7, 69
Diphilos, commander 74–5
Dokimeion, Phrygia 162
Dokimos, general and satrap 29–31, 33, 115, 162–3
Dura-Europos, Mesopotamia 95–6, 97–8

Edessa, Mesopotamia 96, 98, 117, 126
Egypt 25, 62, 68–9, 70, 85, 112, 119, 122, 147, 157–8, 167, 168, 175–6, 192, 193, 196
Ekbatana, Media 41, 44, 48, 117, 118, 148, 149
Ekregma, Egypt 67–8, 69
Elburz, mountains 117, 148
Eleutheros, river 121, 122, 157, 158
Ephesos, Ionia 115, 139–40, 162,

INDEX

163, 165, 181, 183, 185, 201, 205
Epiros 193
Erasistratos, doctor 153, 154
Erigyios, Macedonian commander 7
Erythrai, Ionia 58–9, 62, 64, 66, 124, 164, 165, 181, 185, 205
Esagila, temple at Babylon 32, 33–4, 37, 100–1
Euboia 69
Eudamos, brother of Peithon, satrap of Parthia 30, 34
Eudamos, satrap of India 34, 44
Eumenes, general 17–18, 20, 50, 79, 80, 111, 134; and Antigonos 27, 30–1, 34, 35–6, 40–5, 89; and Antipatros 22, 24; armed forces of 36, 37; in Babylonia 35, 38–40; death 44–5; satrap of Kappadokia 18, 20, 21; in Syria 34, 35
Eumenes, lord of Pergamon 211
Euphrates, river 35, 55, 74, 83, 95, 97, 98, 117–18, 128, 147, 150, 197
Europos, Macedon, birthplace of Seleukos 4–5
Eurydike (Adea), daughter of Philip II, wife of Philip III 21, 25–6, 50
Euthydemos of Magnesia, king of Baktria 216
Evagoras, satrap of Aria 47, 79, 84, 104
Evitos, satrap of Aria 47

frontier policy of Seleukos 95–8, 158–9

Gabiene, Iran, battle 43, 44, 53, 71, 111
Galatia 212
Galatians 185, 204, 211, 213, 215; and Asia Minor 204–7, 209–10, 213–14; and Macedon 202–3, 214
Gallipoli peninsula 188–9, 204, 212
Ganges, river 88, 107, 110

Gaugamela, Mesopotamia, battle 111, 126, 146, 219
Gaza, Palestine 67, 88, 89, 122, 141; battle 70–2, 77, 86, 87, 111, 164, 169, 171
Gedrosia 10–11, 108, 213
Gordion, Phrygia 161, 185
Gordyene 135
Greece 15, 34, 50–1, 86, 114, 121, 123, 132, 143, 169, 173–4, 192, 200
Guti, *see* Kossaeans

Halikarnassos, Karia 91, 187
Harpalos, treasurer of Alexander 16, 54
Hekatompylos, Media 117
Hellenic League 114, 116
Hellespont, strait 56, 66, 88, 92, 93, 161, 162, 188, 190, 194–5, 196, 200, 201, 204
Hellespontine Phrygia 27, 55, 91, 204
Hephaistion, chiliarch of Alexander 7, 9, 11, 15, 18–19
Heraklea-on-Pontos 119, 161, 199, 200; and Bithynia 202, 203; and Northern League 193–6, 200; and Seleukos 183, 184, 188, 189
Herakles, son of Alexander 16
Hermes, river 185
Hermogenes, Seleukid general 199, 200, 202
Hierapolis (Bambyke), Syria 146–7, 166
Hindu Kush 108, 111
Hippostratos, infantry commander 47
Hippostratos of Miletos, envoy of Seleukos I 162
Hydaspes, battle 9, 11, 111
Hypaspists, Royal, Seleukos' regiment 7, 9–11
Hyperberelaos of Thyateira 205

Iasos, Karia 187
Ichnai, Mesopotamia 97–100, 117
Ilion, Troas 162, 164, 185, 196,

INDEX

198, 205
India 7, 9–10, 15, 34, 89, 156, 157; Antiochos I and 213; Seleukos and 107–12, 152, 154, 171
Indus, river, Alexander's campaign 10–11, 107; Seleukos' campaign 108–9
Ionia 115, 119, 121, 163, 169, 178; League 161; Lysimachos and 161, 162, 179
Ipsos, Phrygia, battle 103, 111, 119–21, 122, 125, 132, 133, 143, 152, 160, 171
Iran, Iranians 78, 81, 104, 107, 116, 117, 145, 146, 148–54, 212–14
Iris, river 161
Isaurians 186
Istakhr, Persis 149, 213
Itanos, Crete 187

Jaxartes, river 148, 150, 154, 155

Kabul, river 108
Kallikrates of Samos, Ptolemaic admiral 201
Kallimachos, poet 207
Kallisthenes, historian 61
Kappadokia 21, 55, 86, 118, 119, 161, 212, 214; Ariarathes and 20, 21; Eumenes satrap 18, 20, 21; Seleukos and 150, 184; war in 30–1, 56 Kara Su (river) 172
Kardia, Thrace 102, 190; *see also* Lysimacheia
Karia 58, 63–4, 65, 66, 69, 70, 87, 163, 168, 187; Asandros satrap 27, 58
Karmania 35, 47, 213
Karrhai, Mesopotamia 74, 95, 98, 117
Kasios, Karia 69
Kasios, Mount, Syria 127
Kassandreia, Macedon 100, 102, 127, 183, 189, 193, 200, 201, 203
Kassandros, son of Antipatros 27, 28, 42, 60, 80, 88, 91–2, 101, 104, 122, 132–9, 165, 192; and Antigonos 55–6, 59, 62, 69, 70, 114–16; cities founded by 100, 127; king 112; makes peace with Antigonos 85–7; ruler of Macedon 50–1, 142; and Seleukos 52–5
Kataonia 171
Kaunos, Karia 69, 187
Kautilya, minister of Chandragupta 107–8, 110–11
Kelainai, Phrygia 95, 124, 162; *see also* Apamea
Kephalon, commander 42
Kerynia, Cyprus 57, 64, 70
Kieros, Bithynia 202
Kilikia 17, 22, 24, 70, 73, 91, 94, 118; Antigonos and 51, 54, 55, 56, 57; Demetrios and 133, 140, 141–2, 169–71, 172; Eumenes in 34, 36; Philoxenos satrap 27; Pleistarchos and 121, 132–3; Seleukos and 143–4, 159, 216
Kilikian Gates 183
Killes, Ptolemaic general 76
Kimiata, Pontic fort 184
Kition, Cyprus 57, 64–5, 66–7, 70
Kleomenes, satrap of Egypt 14, 15–16, 29, 54, 61–2, 218–19
Kleopatra, daughter of Philip II 21, 93
Klitor, satrap of Lydia 27
Keonos, Macedonian soldier 11
Kolophon, Ionia 124, 185
Kommagene 134
Koprates, river 42
Korupedion, battle 1, 183, 184, 215
Kos 69, 91
Kossaeans (Kassites) 89
Kotyaion, Phrygia 182
Krateros, general 7, 9, 15, 17, 18, 21, 22
Kyinda, Kilikian fortress 36, 54, 55, 133
Kynnane, wife of Philip II 21
Kyrene 21, 69, 77, 97, 167, 208, 210
Kyros the Younger, Persian rebel 97

INDEX

Kyrrhos, Syria 124, 128, 129, 172
Kyzikos, Mysia 194, 203, 205

Lampsakos, Troas 162
Laodike, mother of Seleukos 2–3, 8, 164
Laodikeia-ad-Mare, Syria 127, 158
Laodikeia-by-Lykos, Phrygia 186
Laodikeia-Katakekaumene, Phrygia 186
Laodikeia (Nihavand), Media 149
Laomedon, satrap of Syria 18, 29
Lapethos, Cyprus 57, 64, 70
Larissa, Syria 124, 126
Larsa, Babylonia 33
League of the Islanders 187
Lebedos, Ionia 123–4
Lemnos 69
Leonnatos, general 9, 17
Leonnorios, Galatian chief 204
Lepidus, Roman triumvir 110
Lesbos 195
Lissa, Karia 187
Loutourios, Galatian chief 204
Lydia 27, 169
Lykia 55, 91, 94, 163, 168, 187
Lynkestis 2
Lysandra, daughter of Ptolemy I, wife of Agathokles 176, 180, 182–3, 189
Lysimacheia, Thrace 102, 196, 200; foundation 93, 100, 127; Galatians sack 204; Seleukos and 188–91; *see also* Kardia
Lysimachos 10, 17, 80, 88, 104; and Antigonos 55–6, 59, 66, 70, 114–16, 118–21, 122; and Arsinoe 132, 178–9, 180; and Asia Minor 121, 158, 160–2, 165, 170, 178–9, 180–1, 215; burial 190; and cities 161–2; death 183; debacle 97, 167, 179–83; and Demetrios 122, 124, 126, 132, 143–4, 160, 169–71, 174–5; executes Agathokles 179; founds Lysimacheia 93, 100, 127; government of 177–8, 179–80, 193; and Ionia 161, 162, 179; king 112; and Macedon 168–70, 173, 174, 179, 215; makes peace with Antigonos 85–7; marriages 178; and Ptolemy I 132, 139, 174; and Ptolemy Keraunos 176–9; satrap of Thrace 53, 160; Seleukos and 180–3, 187, 216, 217

Macedon 4, 5, 86; Antigonos Gonatas and 167, 200, 203, 206, 207–8, 210; Antiochos I and 196, 200, 203, 207–8; Arsinoe and 183, 187, 193, 202; Demetrios and 160, 165, 167–8; Galatian invasion 202–3, 214; Kassandros and 50–1, 142; Lysimachos and 168–70, 173, 174, 179, 215; Ptolemy Keraunos and 193, 195, 200–3; Seleukos and 183, 188, 190
Magadha, Indian kingdom 107
Magas, son of Ptolemy I 208, 209
Magnesia-by-Sipylos, Lydia 185
Magnesia-on-the-Maeander, Ionia 183, 185, 216
Malli, Indian nation 10, 218
Mallos, Kilikia 70
Mauryas, Indian imperial family 151, 157
Media 170, 196; Antigonos in 42–4, 51; Atropates satrap 137, 149; Nikanor satrap 77, 96; Orontobates satrap 47, 54; Peithon satrap 18, 20, 28, 47; Seleukos and 80–1, 83, 84, 88, 89, 90, 118, 135, 137, 148–50, 213
Megasthenes, traveller to India 154
Meleagros, Macedonian leader 16–17
Melitene, Kataonia 118
Menelaos, brother of Ptolemy 59, 63, 67; and Cyprus 63–4, 91
Menes, satrap of Syria 15
Menidas, mercenary commander

263

61–2, 219
Mesene, Babylonia 135
Mesopotamia 35, 83, 88, 95, 117, 122, 135; Amphimachos satrap 37; Blitor satrap 51; Seleukos and 49, 51, 121, 125
Messenia 168
Methymna, Lesbos 195
Miletos, Ionia 3, 69, 124, 128, 139, 154, 163–5, 169, 181, 183, 185, 195, 197, 201, 205
Mithridates, king of Pontos 184–5, 202, 203, 214
Myndos, Karia 187
Myriandros, Syria 140
Myrmidon of Athens, mercenary commander 59, 63

Nabataeans 77, 82, 83, 89
Narbada, river 107
Nearchos, admiral 15
Neon Paphos, Cyprus 70
Nikagoras of Rhodes, envoy of Seleukos 139–40, 163
Nikaia, daughter of Antipatros, wife of Perdikkas 21; wife of Lysimachos 178
Nikanor, purported nephew of Seleukos 3–4
Nikanor, satrap of Media 77, 96; founder of Mesopotamian cities (?) 95–7; and Seleukos 77–9, 82, 84, 149
Nikatoreion, Antioch 199
Nikephorion, Mesopotamia 99
Nikokles, king of Paphos 57, 91
Nikokreon, king of Salamis 70, 91
Nikomedes, purported nephew of Seleukos 3–4
Nikomedes, son of Zipoetes 202, 203, 204
Nile, river 22, 67
Nisibis, Mesopotamia 96, 97, 117
Nora, Kappadokian castle 34
'Northern League' 184–5, 190, 194, 196, 200, 202, 203, 204, 208, 209–10, 212, 214
Nysa, Phrygia 185

Oborzes, governor of Persis 213
Octavian, Roman triumvir 110
Olympias, wife of Philip II 2–3, 21, 37, 50–1, 101
Olynthos, Macedon 6, 102
Opis, Babylonia, 'mutiny' at 13, 14
Orestis 2
Orontes, river 74, 127, 130, 158
Orontobates, satrap of Media 47, 54
Osrhoene 135
Oxus, river 155
Oxyartes, father of Roxane, satrap of Paropamisadai 34, 47, 104, 108

Pages, Royal 2, 6–7, 15, 16
Paionians 4
Palestine 55, 70, 141; Antigonos and 57, 76; Ptolemy I and 86–7, 117, 121, 122, 141, 167, 175
Pamphylia 93, 94, 186, 187, 201
Paphos, Cyprus 57, 64
Paraitakene, Iran, battle 43, 71
Parion, Mysia 162
Parmenio, general 7, 15, 61–2, 219
Parni, nomad tribe 107
Paropamisadai 34, 47, 104, 108, 112
Parthia 30, 43, 107; Seleukos and 80–1, 88, 104
Parysatis, wife of Alexander 16
Pasikrates, king of Soli 57
Patara, Lykia 187
Patrokles, Seleukid general 153–4, 172, 199; defender of Babylon 83–5, 88, 97
Paurava Raja, *see* Poros
Peithon 9, 17; and allied satraps 2, 3; ambition 30, 34–5, 44, 104; and Antigonos 40, 44–5; armed forces of 35, 37; assassin of Perdikkas 22–3, 37, 218–19; death 44–5; *epimeletes* 24–6; and Parthia 30, 34–7; satrap of Media 18, 20, 28, 47;

264

and Seleukos 35, 36, 61
Peithon son of Agenor, satrap of Babylon 54–5, 71–2
Pella, Macedon 100
Pella, Syria 124, 126, 128; *see also* Apamea, Syria
Pelusion, Egypt 67, 141
Peloponnese 57–9, 62, 67, 168, 202
Perdikkas, regent 2, 10, 16–23, 27, 29, 33, 57, 134; murder of 22–3, 61, 218; quarrel with Ptolemy 21–3, 69
Pergamon, Mysia 163, 180, 205, 209, 211
Perilaos, admiral 67
Persepolis 45, 46, 104, 148–9
Persian Gulf 83, 148, 210
Persians 11–12, 33, 126, 148, 213
Persis 77, 83, 88; Antigonos in 45–6, 51; coins 213; Eumenes in 43; Peukestas satrap 28, 34, 36, 44, 45–6, 79, 148; Seleukos and 80–1, 104, 150, 213–14
Peukestas 35, 61; deposed 45–6, 49, 53, 218; satrap of Persis 28, 34, 44, 79, 148
Phaselis 91
Phila, daughter of Antipatros, wife of Demetrios 142
Phila, daughter of Seleukos 139, 152; wife of Antigonos Gonatas 207, 208
Philetairos 163, 180–1, 183, 194–5, 205, 211, 212; and body of Seleukos 199
Philip II, king of Macedon 1, 4–7, 15, 21, 127, 177, 192
Philip III Arrhidaios, king 16–17, 19, 21, 50–1
Philip, satrap of India 34
Philip (?), satrap of Parthia 30
Philip, son of Antigonos 92
Philip, son of Kassandros 142
Philokles, king of Sidon 102, 168, 187, 201
Philotas (?), satrap of Parthia 30
Philoxenos, satrap of Kilikia 27
Phoenicia 55, 57, 66, 67, 73, 87, 125, 141, 168
Phrygia 115, 119, 159, 161, 179, 209; Antigonos satrap 21, 27, 49
Pillars of Jonah 118
Piraeos 169, 202
Pisidians 181, 185–6
Pleistarchos, brother of Kassandros, satrap of Kilikia 121, 132–3, 142
Polyarchos, commander 74
Polykleitos, Ptolemaic admiral 59, 63, 67
Polyperchon, *epimeletes* 34, 35, 37, 42, 50, 59, 63, 81
Pontos, kingdom of 212, 214; *see also* Mithridates
Poros, Indian raja 9, 34, 44, 110, 111
Praxippos, king of Lapethos 57
Prepelaos, general of Lysimachos 115, 119, 162
Priene, Ionia 162, 185, 205–6
propaganda 13–14; for Antigonos 60–3, 218–19; for Seleukos 2–3, 79–80, 164
Ptolemaios, nephew of Antigonos 56, 58–9, 63, 66, 68, 69, 91–2, 97
Ptolemaios, son of Lysimachos 208
Ptolemaios, son of Seleukos, purported uncle of Seleukos Nikator 3
Ptolemais, Egypt 127
Ptolemy I Soter 10, 17, 80, 88, 93, 104, 111, 139, 157, 192; and Antigonos 53–5, 57–9, 67–8, 76–7, 114–16, 117, 121; and Asia Minor 86, 91, 93, 187; and Berenike 170, 175; cities founded by 127; and Cyprus 57, 58–9, 63–6, 69–70, 91, 93, 97, 102, 143–4, 167; death 180; defeats Perdikkas 21–3; instability of kingdom 167; king 112; and Kyrene 21, 69, 97; and Lysimachos 132, 139, 174; makes peace with

INDEX

Antigonos 85–7, 88; and Palestine 86–7, 117, 121, 122, 141, 167, 175; and Phoenicia 143–4, 168; and Ptolemy II 175, 177; and Ptolemy Keraunos 175; and Sarapis 101, 218; satrap of Egypt 18, 24, 27, 61; and Seleukos 51–3, 58–9, 63–6, 68, 76, 80, 89, 112, 173–4, 181, 218–19; steals Alexander's catafalque 21–2, 29; and Syria 55, 70–3, 120–1, 122, 125, 158

Ptolemy II Philadelphos 168, 170, 176; and Antiochos I 196–7, 201, 207, 208, 210; and Arsinoe 206–8; and Asia Minor 186–7, 195, 197, 199; government system 212; and Greece 202; joint king 175, 177; and Magas 208–10; and Pamphylia 186, 187, 201; policy 175, 180, 206–7; and Ptolemy Keraunos 193, 201, 206; and Seleukos 181–2, 186, 187, 207, 216; sole rule 180; and Syria 215

Ptolemy Keraunos, son of Ptolemy I, and Antiochos I 201; and Arsinoe 193, 200; death 202–3, 206; and Egypt 175; and Lysimachos 176–9; and Macedon 193, 195, 200–3; and Ptolemy I 175; and Ptolemy II 193, 201, 206; and Seleukos 175, 176, 180, 182, 189–91, 193, 215

Ptolemy, son of Lysimachos 187
Pumiathon, king of Kition 57, 64–5, 70
Punjab, India 110
Pydna, Macedon, siege of 50–1
Pyrrhos, king of Epiros 160, 169, 170, 174, 177, 179, 194, 196

Qalat al-Mudiq, Syria 128

Raphia, Palestine 122, 141
Rhagai, Media 44, 117
Rhodes 58, 66, 69, 112, 114, 123, 218

Rhosos, Syria 133, 140, 142
River of Egypt 141
Rome 110, 128
Roxane, wife of Alexander III 16, 50, 60, 93

Salamis, Cyprus 70; battle 95, 112
Salonian plain, Phrygia 118–19
Samaria, Palestine 133, 141, 142
Samos 187
Sarapis, temple of 14, 61, 101, 218–19
Sardis, Lydia 21, 93, 119, 124, 162, 169, 178, 182, 183, 185, 188, 199, 200, 206, 211, 214
Seleukeia-in-Pieria, Syria 127, 133
Seleukeia-on-the-Tigris, Babylonia 100–2, 127, 146, 195–6
Seleukia-Sidera, Phrygia 186
Seleukeia-Zeugma, Syria 128–9
Seleukos Nikator, achievements 192–3, 215–17; administrator 25, 133–5; and allied satraps 36; and Antigonos 40–2, 48–51, 63–8, 76–94, 97, 103, 114–21, 134, 216; and Apollo 2–4, 163–4; appearance 139; and Aria 80–1, 83, 88, 104, 108; armed forces of 37, 103, 122–3; and Asia Minor 159, 163–6, 183–8, 189, 216; assassin of Perdikkas 22–3, 37; and Babylon 28–30, 32–4, 48–52, 54, 68, 72–5, 79–80, 100–2, 104, 112–13, 117, 135, 137, 145–6, 157, 192; and Baktria 81, 105–7, 109, 112, 116, 135, 137, 150–2, 154, 171; birth 1–2, 8; birthplace 4; burial 199; childhood 5, 6; children 12, 139, 207, 208; cities founded by 2, 95–6, 98–102, 127–31, 144, 186, 193; coins 166–7, 183; commander of Royal Hypaspists 7, 9–11, 12–13, 14; compared with Alexander 1, 2–3, 80, 104, 108,

266

110, 153, 166, 181, 192, 217; conquest of the east 79, 80–1, 103–12; court of 173–4; and Cyprus 58–9, 63–6; death 190–1, 195, 197, 215; and Demetrios 132–3, 139, 143–4, 169–74, 173–6; diplomacy 132–3, 141–2; education 6; and Eumenes 38–40; frontier policy 95–7, 158–9; in Gallipoli peninsula 188–91; government 133–8, 192–3; and Heraklea-on-Pontos 183, 184, 188, 189; hipparch of Companion Cavalry 18–20, 25; and India 107–12, 152, 154, 171; instability of kingdom 165–7; and Iran 148–54; and Kappadokia 159, 184; and Kassandros 52–5; and Kilikia 143–4, 159, 216; king 102–3, 112–13; loyalty to 97; and Lysimacheia 189–91; and Lysimachos 180–3, 187, 216, 217; and Macedon 183, 188, 190; marriages 9, 11–12, 106, 128, 132–3, 139, 140, 142, 152, 155, 163; and Media 80–1, 83, 84, 88, 89, 90, 118, 135, 137, 148–50, 213; and Mesopotamia 49, 51, 121, 125; and Nikanor 76–9; parents 2–3; and Parthia 80–1, 88, 108; and Peithon 35, 36, 61; and Persis 80–1, 104, 150, 213–14; policy towards 'native' peoples 32–4, 105–7, 126, 145–54; propaganda 1, 3, 8, 60–3, 140, 155, 164, 218–19; and Ptolemy I 51–3, 58–9, 63–6, 68, 76, 89, 112, 125, 173–4, 181, 218–19; and Ptolemy II 181–2, 186, 187, 207, 216; and Ptolemy Keraunos 175, 176, 180, 182, 189–91, 193, 215; purported relatives 3–4; Royal Page 2, 6–7; and Perkikkas 17–23; and Susiana 41–3, 48, 80, 88, 89, 90, 104, 149–50; and Syria 49, 72–3, 80, 121, 122, 125–31, 137–8, 146–8, 182, 192,

217; at Triparadisos 25–6, 28; 'Victor' 217
Seleukos II, Seleukid king 216
Seleukos, son of Antiochos I 211
Sibyrtios, satrap of Arachosia 34, 42, 46
Sicily 112
Sidon 57, 74, 76, 102, 117, 118, 121; Demetrios and 122, 124, 125, 132, 133, 140, 142, 157; Ptolemy I and 143–4, 168
Sigeion, Troas 162
Silpion, mount, Syria 130
Sinope, Pontos 161
Skepsis, Troas 162
Smyrna, Ionia 124, 162
Sogdiana 81, 135
Soli, Cyprus 34, 47, 57, 64
Sophytes, Baktrian leader 105
Sotas, son of Lykos 205
Sparta 202
Spitamenes, Baktrian, father-in-law of Seleukos 11–12
Stasandros, satrap of Aria 34, 35, 47
Stasanor, satrap of Aria 34; satrap of Baktria 34, 47, 81, 103, 104–5, 152
Stasikarenos II, king of Marion 57, 64
Stratonike, daughter of Demetrios 147, 166, 207, 208; wife of Antiochos 152–3, 155, 173; wife of Seleukos 132–3, 139, 142, 163, 217
Susa, Susiana 36, 38, 64, 150; mass wedding at 9, 11–12, 52; treasure at 36, 48, 50; Xenophilos commander at 36, 41, 48
Susiana 36, 77, 83; Antigenes satrap 28, 36, 43; Antigonos and 40–3, 47–8, 51; Aspisas satrap 48; Seleukos and 41–3, 48, 80, 88, 89, 90, 104, 149–50
Synnada, Phrygia 115, 124, 162
Syria 70, 82, 187; Antigonos and 55, 89, 115–16, 117–18; Antiochos I and 196–9, 211;

INDEX

Demetrios and 82, 85, 141–2, 157–8; Eumenes and 34, 35; invasion 208–9, 215; Ptolemy I and 55, 70–3, 120–1, 122, 125, 158; Ptolemy II and 215; Seleukos and 49, 72–3, 80, 121, 125–31, 137–8, 146–8, 182, 192, 217; settlements in 124, 129

Taurus, mountains 55, 68, 76, 78, 118, 121, 141, 158–61, 169, 170, 196, 197
Taxiles, Indian king 34
Telmessos, Lydia 187
Teos, Bithynia 123–4, 184, 202
Thapsakos, Syria 83, 98, 117
Thebes 60, 102
Themison, admiral 66, 162
Themison (?), king of Kerynia 57
Themisonion, Phrygia 162–3, 205
Thera 187
Thermopylai 114
Thespios, outspoken Persian 45, 46
Thessalonike, Macedon 102, 127, 142
Thessaly 6, 115, 116, 122, 123
Thrace 56, 126, 132, 179, 182, 204, 208; Lysimachos satrap 53, 160
Thyateira, Mysia 205
Tigris, river 38, 41, 83, 97, 118, 150; campaign and battle near 78–9, 104
Tlepolemos, satrap of Karmania 47
Tralles, Lydia 69

Trapezos, Pontos 161
Triparadisos, Syria, conference at 25–8, 37, 49, 53, 55, 61, 81, 103, 105, 218
Tripolis, Syria 57, 73, 74
Troad 204
Tymphaia 2
Tyre, Phoenicia 25, 74; Antigonos and 57, 58, 59–60, 64–6, 67, 124, 147; Demetrios and 122, 125, 132, 133, 140, 142, 157; Ptolemy I and 73, 122, 143–4, 168

Upper Nile 167
'Upper Satrapies' 136
Uruk, Babylonia 33, 50, 195
Urmiah, lake 118

Vakshuvar, Baktrian leader 105
Van, lake 118

Waterloo, battle 120

Xenophilos, commander at Susa 36, 41, 43, 48
Xenophon, Athenian adventurer 97

Zagros mountains 35, 42, 78, 90, 148
Zeugma, see Seleukeia-Zeugma
Zipoetes, lord of Bithynia 181, 193, 194, 199–200, 202
Zipoetes, son of Zipoetes, 202, 203, 204

LIBRARY OF DAVIDSON COLLEGE

Books on regular loan may be checked out for four weeks. Books must be presented at the Circulation Desk in order to be renewed.

A fine is charged after date due.

Special books are subject to special regulations at the discretion of the library staff.

4/11/92 ILL			